St.Helens Community Libraries

This book is due for return on or before the last date shown. Fines are charged on overdue books. Renewal may be made by personal application, post or telephone, quoting date, author, title and book number.

01. APR 03	17 Aug 2013		
02. JAN 04.			
	23. SEP 13.		
26. JUL 04.	2 0 JUN 2014		
04. NOV 04	1 3 NOV 2015		
11. NOV 05.	ILL - Lancs		
24 SEP 09.	DB. 10/2/18		
14. DEC 10.	SUBJECT TO		
18. JUN 11.	EARLIER RECALL		
28. NOV 11.	3403352		
24. JUN 13.			
29. JUL 13.			

Rosbottom, Ernest

Burscough

A87 22584

A short history of
the township of
Burscough
(including parts of Lathom)

or

Burscough

The story of an
agricultural village
in the County of Lancaster

by
Ernest John Rosbottom
August 1971
(with minor revisions by the author in September 1978)
Edited by Dr. Alan Crosby

"Remember the days of old, consider the years of many generations."
(Deuteronomy, chapter 32, verse 7)

"He who collects is laudably employed; for though he exerts no great talent in the work,
he facilitates the progress of others, and by making that easy of attainment, which is
already written, may give some mind, more adventurous than his own, leisure for new
thoughts and original designs."
Dr. Johnson

Carnegie Press, 1987

A short history of
the township of
Burscough
(including parts of Lathom)
or

Burscough — the story of an agricultural village

in the County of Lancaster

by
Ernest John Rosbottom
August 1971

Publisher's note

Almost all of the illustrations in this book are from the author's collection and were intended for inclusion in this book. Many are old and damaged, thus accounting for the relatively poor reproduction quality of some. Where no provenance was given by the author, it has not been possible to trace ownership or copyright; it has been assumed that, since Mr. Rosbotton clearly intended the illustrations for publication, he had secured prior permission so to do.

Burscough — The Story of an Agricultural Village

by Ernest John Rosbottom

This book has been published posthumously with the help and support of Mrs. Rosbottom, the author's mother. It was completed in 1970, with revisions and additions up to 1978. This book has been edited for publication by Dr. Alan Crosby.

Published by Carnegie Press, 125 Woodplumpton Road, Cadley, Preston PR2 2LS.

Printed by T. Snape & Co. Ltd., Boltons Court, Preston PR1 3TY.

ISBN 0 948789 12 3

THIS HISTORY IS DEDICATED TO THE MEMORY
OF MY FATHER WHO WAS MY BEST FRIEND AND
HELPER AT ALL TIMES.

Contents

BURSCOUGH — THE STORY OF AN AGRICULTURAL VILLAGE

by
Ernest John Rosbottom

Edited by Dr. Alan Crosby

Carnegie Press, 1987

Editor's Introduction

ERNEST ROSBOTTOM was born in Burscough on 28th September 1938. He was a pupil at St. John's Church of England School, and later attended Southport Technical College and Chorley College. All his life was spent in Burscough and he became deeply interested in the history of the village and the surrounding area. He built up a considerable collection of published works on the history of Lancashire but soon found out that, apart from isolated references in general books on the subject, and the rather brief accounts in the pages of, for example, the *Victoria County History,* nothing had ever been written on the history of Burscough.

The development of education in Burscough and the adjacent townships was a theme in which he was particularly interested and he had started work on researching and writing a thesis dealing with the schools and education of the area and the local effects of the 1870 Education Act. His researches produced large amounts of additional material relating to all aspects of Burscough's past and present, and he therefore began to compile a full historical account, *The History of Burscough,* in order to fill the existing gap in the published record and to draw together the various strands of his research. His work was encouraged by others who were aware of his interest and were anxious to see his material turned into a published book; the main driving force, however, was his own boundless energy and enthusiasm for the subject.

He knew full well that Burscough was an 'ordinary' place, one without a spectacular or dramatic history, a village scarcely known outside the immediate district; but, as this book proves, the diligent and assiduous historical researcher can find a great deal of real interest in the Burscoughs of England and a substantial volume can be written on the life of an 'ordinary' place and its people.

The work took many years: Ernest Rosbottom visited Record Offices, libraries, newspaper offices and private houses to locate original documentary material, little known and obscure printed sources and people who had known old Burscough and could tell him tales and details dating back into the early years of the last century. He walked all the roads and lanes and paths of the township, studied all the surviving old houses and cottages, investigated the factories and mills, canal banks and railway sidings, until there was not an inch of the village which he did not know well. On many of his expeditions he was accompanied by his mother or father who shared his enthusiasm and helped and encouraged him in this work. The original dedication of this book is a tribute to the memory of his father.

The material, once it had been written up and typed, amounted to some 350 pages, together with numerous maps, drawings and photographs, and additional notes and miscellanea. The author tried without success to find a publisher, and when he died, all too early, on 20th December 1985, the work was still unpublished. The book was the product of a lifetime of research and painstaking endeavour and it is indeed sad that Ernest Rosbottom did not live to see its publication. In my own work of editing his typescript in preparation for this book, I have constantly been impressed by his care and attention to detail, his vast range of knowledge and his deep and abiding love of his home village and its surroundings. I feel sure that he would have been pleased with this result.

About the book

The book covers many aspects of the history of Burscough but inevitably concentrates on the past two centuries, during which a small town has grown up around the small agricultural community which had existed for several hundred years. It begins with a brief survey of the early history, a period which is very inadequately documented and for which archaeological evidence is almost entirely lacking. The only exception is Burscough Priory, the one building in the township which was of more than purely local significance. There follows an account of the old halls and manor houses, several of which have now been demolished or drastically altered, but which were visited by or known to Ernest Rosbottom before these changes.

There are chapters on churches and religious history and on schools and education, both subjects which were of great importance in the growing community and which were of particular concern and interest to the author. His special study of education in Burscough was incorporated within the book and forms a major theme. The fourth chapter describes the growth of the village, its geography, the local government pattern, services and the physical evolution and development over 200 years and is written from a careful study of documentary sources and a deep knowledge of the shape and character of Burscough. This growth was made possible by — indeed, was partly started by — the improvements in the transport and communications of the area which are described in Chapter 5. The development of Burscough during the 18th and 19th centuries was accompanied by the transformation of local agricultural patterns with the rise of market gardening and the draining of the mosses and these changes are considered in Chapter 6. That section also covers industries and their growth, for Burscough had become, by the beginning of the present century, a community much more dependent upon industry than upon its historic mainstay, agriculture. Finally another facet of life in Burscough, leisure and recreation, is described in the chapter on entertainments and amusements.

The book was written in its first form during the early 1970s and was revised and extended in about 1978. After that time only minor alterations were made by the author to update facts. My task as editor has been to reduce the length, to make the work more suitable for publication and this has been achieved almost entirely by taking out material which relates to other places, such as Ormskirk, and by omitting the sections of more general introductory history on such topics as education, legislation, the early history of Lancashire, and the genealogy of local gentry and noble families, all of which are readily available from existing published sources. The removal of this material has not altered the shape or character of the work. My overriding aim has been to preserve, wherever possible, the original work, and where more detailed editing has been necessary — for example, to eliminate duplication — I have tried to avoid rewriting and, instead, to keep Ernest Rosbottom's own words and text intact. There has been no attempt to bring the work up to date by continuing the story up to 1987, as this would have substantially changed the sections dealing with industry, housing and entertainment, and so moved away from the original. I have, however, made minor changes in a few places in accordance with later notes made by the author and have taken out some small items which were specifically of interest at the time of writing, but clearly quickly outdated.

The five volumes of the original work, including appendices, notes and illustrative material, have been depositied with the Local Studies Section of Ormskirk District Library and may be consulted there. The author was not satisfied with the work as it stood because, as a true historian, he knew that the research could never be trusted and time does not stand still: history is happening continuously and every day which passes becomes history. But he realised that at some stage the material has to be put down on paper and this is the result. He wrote:

'no student of local history need feel that there is no more to be accomplished. No historical work can claim to be fully exhaustive or to have achieved finality. Much has perforce to be omitted if a work is to be reasonably well balanced and readable. Gaps also exist in present knowledge which future discovery may help to fill. Errors which almost inevitably arise through the necessarily incomplete nature of historical material may be exposed when fuller knowledge becomes available. Therefore I can only say that there is still an enormous amount unsaid'

As editor of his book I can only say that, without Ernest Rosbottom and his lifetime of research and writing, all the history of Burscough would have remained unsaid for many more years. The village and those who are even slightly interested in its history owe his memory an enormous debt of gratitude.

Alan Crosby,
June, 1987.

Beginnings

BURSCOUGH is a sizeable village in south-west Lancashire, about three miles north east of Ormskirk. Since the medieval period it has been surrounded by highly productive farmland: local farms for many years supplied the Ormskirk, Liverpool and Preston markets and continue to do so, although during the Second World War the building of an airfield robbed the area of much good arable land and this has not been returned to agricultural uses. Recently, too, the expansion of the residential area has begun to encroach upon the adjacent arable farmland, further reducing its area.

Burscough township, and the old township or manor of Martin which has for centuries been integral with it, are situated where a low ridge, some 50 feet above sea level at its maximum, adjoins the great tracts of lowlying and still in some places marshy land which until the early 19th century formed the largest lake of south Lancashire, Martin Mere. The network of ditches, drains and dykes criss-crossing the area below the 50 foot contour emphasises this: before drainage operations began in the late 17th century this was a district of open water or permanent and very wet marshland. The Mere took over 150 years to drain, from 1692 to 1849 - in the latter year pumps were removing 17,000 gallons of water per minute simply to keep the land clear. Today the site of Martin Hall lies among fertile fields, but there was a time when a light in an upstairs window guided boats across the water and its isolated position provided a safe hiding place for Roman Catholic priests and rebels alike, among them Robert Scarisbrick in the 1715 Jacobite rebellion.

Because of the wet and inhospitable character of the lowlands, the village — now almost a small town — has developed along the ridge around the 50-foot contour, well above the marshy ground. The ridge was followed by the main road from Liverpool to Preston and its predecessors, trackways dating back to prehistoric times, and the village has therefore assumed a linear form, stretched out along the main road. Apart from a few isolated dwellings there was little else on the lower ground until the draining of the Mere and the development of flourishing agriculture on the reclaimed land led to the building of farms on the drained area: some of these are indicated on Yates' map of 1786.

To the south east of the village the land rises again, sloping gently towards the hills behind Skelmersdale and Upholland and reaching some 200 feet above sea level. Over much of the township the land was devoted to arable farming, with potatoes, wheat, barley and oats being grown, together with many small market gardens and nurseries. The soil consists of peat on the drained areas, with a mixture of peat, sands and clays elsewhere, producing a fertile dark vegetable loam.

The greater part of Burscough and the surrounding districts is covered with boulder clay, associated with the Shirdley Hill sands, which in origin are thought to be glacial moraines. The underlying solid geology consists of the mottled Bunter sandstones and the Keuper Sandstones at depth beneath the thick drift deposits. In some places, however, the underlying solid sandstones are exposed or are near the surface, and here have been exploited in the past as building stones. In 1858 investigations and boreholes, conducted during a search for water supplies, showed some 266 feet of clays and other later deposits, a thickness which at the time was held to have no parallel in England. Ample supplies of water were found at a depth of over 300 feet, but the source was never exploited on a commercial basis. Later borings by the Lancashire and Yorkshire Railway Company in the 1880s were also abortive. There is a large erratic block of Galloway microgranite near Burscough Junction railway station, brought down by glaciation from Scotland some 10,000 years ago and for centuries a local curiosity and landmark. The abundance of clay in the area has been responsible for a major brick and tile manufacturing industry from an early date.

Of the origins of the village very little is known. The earliest references to the name *Burscough* occur comparatively late, at the end of the 12th century (eg *Burgastud* 1190; *Buresco* 1235; *Bureschou* 1241; *Burscogh* 1327) but there is no reason to suppose that the earliest written references give any indication of the age of the settlement. The likelihood is that it had been in existence for hundreds of years before the late 12th century. The name suggests a Norse origin, which would be in keeping with what little is known of the early settlement history of the area. The name *Martin* (or *Marton)*, which means settlement by a lake, is however Anglo-Saxon and might imply a mixed community of Saxons and Norse settlers in the district. Further information about local place names is given in the appendix at the end of this chapter.

Relics found in the district show its prehistoric connections. In April 1899 ploughmen unearthed an ancient British canoe on the northern shore of Martin Mere near Crossens. The canoe had been formed out of a great tree and measured seventeen feet in length and four feet two inches in width. This and about fifteen other canoes, hollowed out by fire and axes, have been found in this district during the last two hundred years. It may be safely conjectured that long before the arrival of the Romans upon our shores, the mere of Martin had a population resident round about it and that its fish afforded employment and food.

The supposition of the Mere having been plied by the ancients is fully supported by the numerous relics of canoes that have been found. Little or nothing has been handed down to us by historians of past ages as to the extent or use of this lake in the days of the 'aborigines', nor even in the times of the Roman occupation. In the time of the Seganti we are told by Ptolemy about 150 A.D. that they looked upon the River Ribble as a goddess and having influence over their lives and destinies. Ptolemy referred to the Ribble as Belisama and, if one compares the present coastline with Ptolemy's coastline it can be seen that the former shows three estuaries and the latter two estuaries only. Much controversy was aroused by this and for three centuries was hotly debated. However, due to the subsidence and subsequent erosion of the coastline, it has been accepted that the River Ribble was Belisama and not the River Mersey.

In old documents the Mere is described as a 'little inland ocean'. The River Douglas flowing through the western half of South Lancashire touched upon the borders of the Mere but the waters of the latter flowed into the channel of the Ribble. The Mere covered 3,132 statute acres of land, and was situated

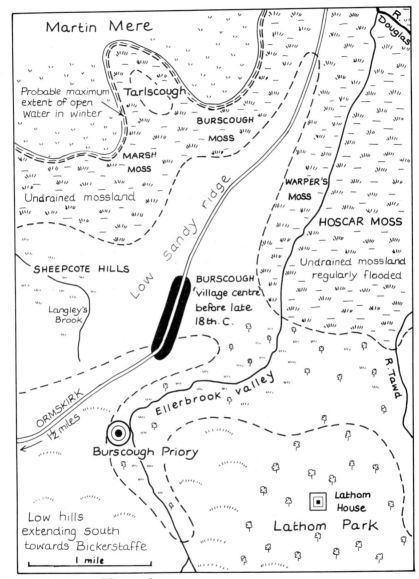

The early landscape of Burscough

The ancient routeway which is now the traffic-laden A59 followed the summit of a long low ridge which projects northwards from Ormskirk towards Rufford and Croston. Before it began to grow in the late 18th century, Burscough village consisted of a long scattered line of cottages and small farms straggling along this main route, with isolated houses and smallholdings dotted across the sandy slopes to the east and west. Beyond, in both directions, were great tracts of undrained mosslands, frequently flooded and always waterlogged. At times of highest water, Martin Mere came to about one mile from the village, although in drier periods it shrank to reveal marshy stagnant flats and seasonal grazing land. To the south, the valley of the Ellerbrook, in which stood Burscough Priory, separated the village from the low undulating hills on which Lathom House and its great park were situated.

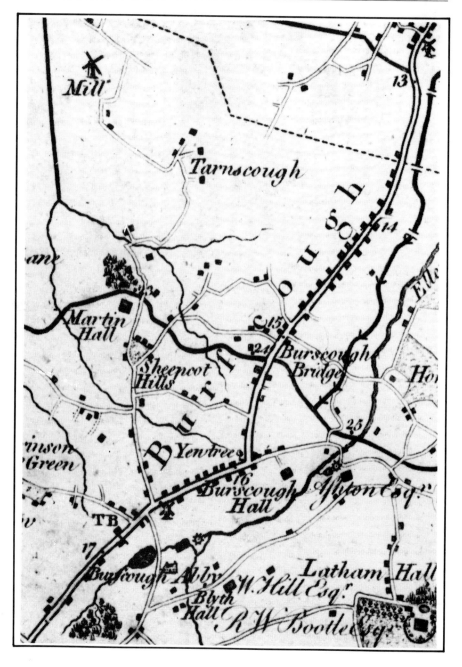

A section of Yates' map of Lancashire, 1786, showing the Burscough area.

in the manors of North Meols, Rufford, Scarisbrick, Tarleton and Burscough. About four hundred and forty years ago, when the lake retained its ancient state, Leland, antiquary to Henry VIII, made a tour through the King's dominions in search of antiquarian lore and in describing his journey through Lancashire he speaks of this watery tract as 'the greatest mere of Lancastrehire, iiii miles in length and iii in breadth'. Camden, who wrote forty years subsequent to Leland, says, 'Near the mouth of the Douglas is an extensive mere called Merton, which discharges itself at a mouth of its own, and presently after meets the Ribble in its estuary'.

The draining of Martin Mere

In the year 1692 Thomas Fleetwood Esq. of Bank Hall obtained an Act to enable him to drain the Mere. Mr. Fleetwood was one of the joint owners of the lake and he obtained from his co-proprietors a lease of the whole for three lives and thirty one years. As might be expected, the task to be undertaken was not a small one. A sluice 24 feet wide, was cut from the estuary of the Ribble through a bog a mile and a half in extent in North Meols, and then continued through the lowest part of the Mere. The sluice was constructed 10 feet lower than high water mark at spring tides and, to avoid the sea rushing up the canal and overflowing the Mere, Mr. Fleetwood had a pair of flood-gates made and put at the mouth of the sluice near the sea, which were closed when the sea rose higher than the water in the sluice, and opened again by the sluice stream when the sea receded. The winter floods brought up and deposited at the gates a great quantity of mud and this formed a destructive obstacle to remove. To overcome this obstacle Mr. Fleetwood in 1714 raised the gates 1 foot and thus a powerful current was formed to carry away the deposits of mud. Mr. Fleetwood, who believed that he had effectually accomplished the great object of his life, died in 1717 and his family erected a monument to his memory in the parish church of North Meols, which bears a Latin inscription and sets forth that 'he wished his remains to be buried here, because he had drained and made into solid land the immense Martinesian Marsh, having taken off the water by a fosse to the neighbouring sea'. The inscription also states that 'he executed this work which our ancestors durst not attempt, and which posterity will scarcely believe, at a very great expense, and with a view to the public good, not his own'.

After the principal portion of Martin Mere had been drained, great quantities of oak and yew trees were found embedded in the soil at depths varying from one to six feet. Some of the trees were very large and hampered ploughing and the farmers periodically devoted themselves to uprooting the 'stock' as they called them. In the latter part of the 18th century and early part of 19th century numbers of poor people obtained a subsistence by digging out the oak trees from the soil, which they split into firewood, unless the wood was sound and good, in which case it was used in the construction of agricultural implements, the roofing of barns and in some cases was even used for making ornamental furniture.

The fond hopes of Mr. Fleetwood that he had succeeded in effecting a permanent protection against floods proved, however, in 1775, to be groundless, for in that year the floodgates and walls at the entrance of the canal were washed down by an unusually high tide; and although the gates were subsequently rebuilt at the expense of the joint proprietors, the sluices were neglected and the result was that during the winter season the Mere was covered with water and afforded pasture for only a few cattle during summer. The value of the land then sank to only a few shillings per acre. Thomas Eccleston Esq., who by marriage became possessed of the Scarisbrick estates and afterwards assumed the name of Scarisbrick, renewed the attempt to drain the lake in 1781. The plan adopted was to put down in the main sluice three different pairs of floodgates — one pair near the sea, another pair about half a mile distant to stop the sea in case of accident to the first gates, and these were called flushing gates. This plan was so successful that in 1784 several areas of the land reclaimed were sown with spring corn and from reports it is stated that it 'yielded a tolerable produce'. In the succeeding year crops of barley and oats were sold for £11 the Cheshire acre, 'the purchaser to cut and carry off the crops at his own expense', though a few years before the land had been let for not more than 4 shillings per acre.

The engineer whom Thomas Eccleston procured for the implementation of the drainage scheme and floodgates mentioned above was Mr. Gilbert of Worsley, an eminent engineer who was responsible for some of the undertakings of the Duke of Bridgewater. Mr. Eccleston received a gold medal from the Society for the Encouragement of the Arts, Manufacturers and Commerce for his services in draining and improving the mere of Martin.

In 1784 the Douglas burst its banks and again inundated the drained land of the Mere. Although the works erected for the drainage stood unimpaired, and answered the expectations of Mr. Eccleston, yet he considered it best, in the face of the liability of the embankments to fail, to adopt grazing rather than the tillage system of agriculture. The floodgates put down in 1783 remained until 1813, when the flushing gates and the sea stop gates were swept away by an unusually high tide, but the stop gates fixed half a mile beyond the sea in the sluice prevented the land from being flooded.

During the early part of the 19th century various attempts were made to drain the Mere thoroughly, but the periodical inundation of the land by the bursting of the banks and the overflowing of the Douglas, coupled with the mismanagement of the Croston drainage, had the effect of discouraging some of the great landowners, from attempting any new schemes. However, another group of landowners, including descendants of Thomas Eccleston Scarisbrick Esq., tried to complete the task but, although they drained a large area, it was not until 1850 when pumps worked by a steam engine at twenty horse-power, with a waterwheel which raised and discharged 45 tons of water a minute into the sea at Crossens, that the Mere was effectively drained. This was mainly the work of Sir T. G. Fermor-Hesketh of Rufford. It is interesting to note that the pumps began to work on Tuesday, April 9th 1850, and by the following Thursday the waters had been lowered to such an extent that the land had already increased in value.

Since 1850 there have been several occasions when flooding has taken place, not on as large a scale as in the 18th century, but nevertheless sufficient to cause thousands of pounds worth of damage to crops in this district. Even during the 1850s it is recorded that large areas of land were flooded during the winter months and very often when frozen over were used by the local people for skating.

In September 1877 the River Douglas burst its banks, flooding the low lying land between Burscough Junction and Rufford. The flood appears to have been caused by unduly heavy rains during July (over 4″) and August (over 6″) of that year which, together with the heavy rains in September (5″) and the run off from the surrounding hills, resulted in the overflowing of the water from the River Douglas. A writer at the time said 'I have never seen anything like the lake-like appearance of the greater part of Western Lancashire which has been presented during the past rainy season. For a time it seemed as if old Neptune had resolved on a return to this portion of his former domain, and as though neither engineering skill nor other human power should stay his advance, or as though Rufford should again become, what the name implies, a rough fording place'.

Slight floods occurred in 1896 and in 1927 both the Ellerbrook and the River Douglas overflowed, the old mill wheel was set in motion at the Mill Dam and several boats loaded with stone were washed out of the Lower Douglas Navigation (Rufford Line) at Tarleton into the River Douglas where they were carried out to sea and later sank near Lytham. Even as late as 1956 the Ellerbrook overflowed resulting in a loss of crops worth about £250,000. Floods also occurred in October and November 1954 damaging potato crops and, in 1957, Geld Hey Sluice at Banks burst.

The draining of the Mere inevitably produced very substantial physical changes in the appearance and landscape of the Burscough area. Old maps, although sometimes of doubtful accuracy and particularly suspect in relation to scale, show three islands in the Mere: Bowen's map of the mid-18th century, for example, indicates three islands at the corners of the roughly triangular lake. These islands are now represented by low hills in the middle of the flat lands: a good example is the long ridge now crossed by the B5246 between Mere Brow and Rufford, on which Holmeswood stands. Another is the very pronounced low hill at Tarlscough, between Burscough and the Martin Mere Wildfowl Reserve.

The Mere lands are now very fertile, as is often the case with such drained areas, and comprise some of the best farmland in Lancashire. Up to the 1850s the area was noted widely for its plentiful wildfowl and as early as the 18th century the local farmers found a profitable sideline in catching young ducks and other birds for breeding. Local epicures esteemed the 'cross breeds' between tame and wild birds as delicacy and many ducks and geese were sold to supply the tables of Liverpool and other towns in the area. In recent years this same attraction for wildfowl has been used to develop the immensely successful R.S.P.B. reserve at Martin Mere, on the minor road from Burscough to Mere Side and Holmeswood.

The draining of the Mere and the development of a flourishing and intensive agriculture on the reclaimed lands brought many changes to the Burscough area, and was in considerable measure responsible for the growth of the minor village of the 18th century into the large and spreading community of the 19th and 20th centuries.

Manorial history

The area of Burscough which included Martin Mere was referred to in the 1086 Domesday Survey as the manor of *Merretun,* and was held, together with most of the West Derby Hundred, by Roger de Poictou, one of the closest friends and companions of William the Conqueror. Burscough itself is not mentioned at all, possibly because the name was not used for a separate manor or *vill* (hamlet) until a slightly later date. This is by no means unusual and does not mean that there was no settlement here in the middle of the 11th century. It is also significant that for Lancashire as a whole the Survey is noticeably less detailed than for most of the rest of the country. Indeed, Lancashire itself was not recognised as a separate unit at this stage.

According to the Survey the manors of Lathom and Martin, and thus presumably also Burscough, were held by Ughtred in King Edward's time (that is, in 1066) and he is recorded as having held 17 manors in the Hundred of West Derby in total. It is thought by some authorities that Ughtred's successor, Robert, grandson of Siward, was the founder of the Lathom family which was responsible for the establishment of the Priory of Burscough, but the exact descents involved are suspect and uncertain.

Burscough after the Conquest held in thanage or free farm one carucate or teamland and it is also suggested that it was probably free of Danegeld at certain times, because of the low lying land being liable to flood. The term carucate has to be used with caution, because it can easily be misinterpreted, e.g. one definition is the following: as much as a team can plough in a year, another as 100 acres of land. Probably the first definition is correct, but the area of land ploughed would be variable because of the different varieties of land that could be ploughed. Therefore, it is difficult to say just how large the area of the carucate was, but approximately it would probably have ranged from 80 to 200 acres.

Records exist of all the plough teams held by Roger of Poictou's military vassals in 1086. The total of teamlands held in the West Hundred was 125½. It has been suggested by some authorities that the population can be estimated from the teamlands but, because of the difficulty of assessing the area as to quality of the land and the like, results are rather dubious. Using the system of estimation by teamlands, the population estimated for a manor in the West Hundred was an average of 46 persons per manor. It was estimated by this method that about 439 persons were engaged in agriculture in the whole of the West Hundred. This figure was then multiplied by 7, which represented the following groups: women, children, craftsmen, priests, herdsmen, cultivators and officers. $439 \times 7 = 3073$. This figure, 3073, was to represent the total population of the West Hundred of Derby in 1086, the average population of the individual manors being arrived at by dividing this number by 66 (the total number of manors in the West Hundred).

Even though it was not named in the Domesday Book, a separate and defined manor of Burscough was certainly in existence by the second half of the 12th century and was property of the de Lathom family. It was granted to them by the new Priory of Burscough, founded by the family probably in the late 1180s. The manor was one of the major endowments of the new religious house and remained in their estate throughout the medieval period and until the Dissolution, the estates being managed as a 'home farm'.

At the Dissolution, the property passed automatically to the Crown and remained as a royal possession until 1547 when it was granted to Sir William

Paget, the King's Secretary of State in the last years of the reign of Henry VIII. Paget did not hold the property for long, for in 1549 it was sold to the Earl of Derby, and so added to the already extensive Lancashire estates of the Stanley family. Thereafter Burscough, together with Lathom and the other local estates, was usually held by one or other member of the Derby line, sometimes being held by younger sons and cousins but, after 1591, always part of the estates of the earldom.

Some of the later records of the Manor Court of Burscough have been preserved: they were found in April 1901 at the *Bull and Dog* public house, which had been one of the meeting places of the Court in the 18th and early 19th centuries. The records were kept in a wooden chest six feet long and two feet deep, weighing over 5 cwt.

The Court Books do not go back beyond the year 1677 and there are a number of books missing. However, there is sufficient evidence in the existing books to indicate the usage and customs of the court. In ancient time, the Crown was the main source of justice and where the king was, there was law administered. Subsequently, with the increase in population and the division of labour, it was found more expedient to administer justice by means of courts leet and these were established to deal with crimes and public nuisances within their territory. The Court Books of Burscough always open as follows:

> 'The View of Frankpledge (another name for court leet) and Court Baron of the Right Honourable . . . Earl of Derby Lord of the Manor aforesaid in and for the said manor on . . .'

The Earl of Derby was represented by his steward and as such was judge of the court leet. He was a judge of record and could commit to gaol for felony, and fine for contempt. A jury of 12 men was chosen, and they were sworn, amongst other things, 'to keep the king's counsel' as the following entry which was always entered in the court books confirms:

> 'The Jurors to Enquire for our Soverign Lord the King and the Lord of the Manor aforesaid . . .'

A 'foreman' was also chosen and his name headed the list of jurors who all swore on oath to the above. It was customary at the court leet for everyone over the age of twelve who resided within the manor for a year and a day to swear allegiance to the King, but as the ages are not given in the court books I cannot say whether this was strictly adhered to. The majority of the lands were copyhold, but there were a number of freeholders as well, and both were listed in the court books. The Court thus constituted took account or notice of all offences against law and order and, therefore, acted as a Licensing Bench, and at the Burscough Court the following were appointed:

> Constables (usually 3); Churchwarden; Overseer of the Poor; Supervisors of the Highway (usually 2); Ley layers (usually 4, similar to rate collectors); Collectors of the Tithe (usually 3); Appraisers of Distress (usually 2); Burley Men (usually 2, they inspected drains, water-courses etc.); Overlooker of Game; Aletasters and Inspectors of Weights and Measures (usually 2); Court Bailiff; Moss Reeves (usually 2); Pinder (he looked after the pinfold and collected stray cattle within the township); Pinder of Common and waste lands (usually 2) and House Lookers or peepers (to assess window tax and the state of repair of the houses).

The court books record mainly fines which were imposed for the neglect of watercourses or for the non-repair of houses and other property. A few extracts from the court books will give a fair idea of the various offences which were dealt with. In April 1790 the following was recorded:

> 'We the Jurors do Amerse (fine) Ann Gradwell, William Hill Esq., Thomas Haskain, Daniel Forshaw, Henry Bridge, Mr. Thomas Brandreth, John Culshaw, William Culshaw and William Baxendale, in the sum of one Pound nineteen Shillings and eleven pence half-penny each, payable to the Lord of this Manor if they, and everyone of them do not well and sufficiently repair their house and outbuildings, as presented to us by Edward Monk and William Culshaw the House Lookers on or before the 29th day of September next'.

> 'We the Jurors do Amerse (fine) William Reynolds, Edward Banks, James Gobbin, James Halsall's heirs, John Tasker, Mr. Thomas Brandreth and Thomas Haskain in the sum of one Pound nineteen Shillings and eleven pence half-penny each payable to the Lord of this Manor, if they and everyone of them do not well and sufficiently scour and cleanse their respective parts of the Water Course leading from a place near Thomas Haskains House to a place called the "Ring Ditch" on Martin Mere, on or before the 29th day of September next.'

Sometimes the reports of the house lookers were attached and in this case in relation to the above are some of the repairs which were reported and found wanting:

> 'Mr. Gradwell — gable end of the Barn Damaged by an Arch held up by a prop'.

> 'William Hill Esq., — A Barn Wall held up by props'.

> 'Thomas Haskain — The out building thatch and daub'.

> 'Daniel Forshaw — House and Barn thatch and daub'.

One of the chief officers of the court was the constable who had numerous duties to perform which often concerned him with the other officers in the execution of their duties as well. Before the introduction of the County Police Force in the 1840s the keeping of law and order in the township of Burscough was practically in the hands of the constable alone. It was customary in those days to have appointed a number of male inhabitants to act as special constables, and a certain number were annually 'sworn in' to assist the constable in cases of disturbance. Any inhabitant could be asked to assist the constable and, if they refused, a fine of £1 was imposed upon them. The position of constable was unpaid and any person refusing to serve in that office after being elected by the jury of the court leet had to forfeit £1 for every day that he refused to serve. There were numerous by-laws applicable to the parish of Ormskirk during the 17th, 18th and greater part of the 19th century and to list all would serve no purpose, but the undermentioned extracts from the constable's accounts will give the reader an insight into his many and varied duties.

The earliest account of the constable of Burscough goes back to the year 1707 (earlier accounts are not extant) when a Mr. William Green held the office of constable, and the following extracts are from the accounts of 1707-8, 1718, 1758 and 1771:—

> '1707 October — The Accountants expense in attending
> at Wigan Sessions...0-1-6d'.
> '1708 January 5th — For going a privet serch.....................1-4d'.

A privy-search was an investigation or search after all ill-disposed strangers, aliens and improper settlers. This was in connection with the Settlement Laws and according to the by-laws of this area at that time, if a stranger was found in a household, the occupier of the house was fined 10 shillings.

'1708 April 12th — For attending Darby Court......................1-6d'.
'1708 April — paid William Grice for riting........................10-0d'.

William Grice was the clerk at Ormskirk and he received a salary of £2 per annum made up as follows:

From the Constable he received................................20s.-0d.
Overseers of the poor...10s.-0d.
Supervisors... 5s.-0d.
Churchwardens .... 5s.-0d.

                                          Total   £2-0s.-0d.

'1718 May 6th — To myself attending sessions at Ormskirk............6d.'
'1758 September 19th — Paid the window lookers..................2-0d.'

This window tax was the forerunner of the inhabited house duty and was only repealed after the Crystal Palace exhibition of 1851. The tax was applicable to houses with more than 7 windows and in country districts pantry windows and food storage rooms went free. However, because of this tax, numerous houses bricked up their windows and evidence exists of this at several of the older farms in this district. From the window peepers (or lookers as they were called) list of May 1773, I found 10 inhabitants with 8 to 11 windows in their houses; the rest ranged from as low as 3 to 7, but the greatest number of houses had from 6 to 7 windows.

'1771 28th May — Spent at Dealing Peter Lathom Charity............3-0d.'

The constable was usually responsible for the charities of the manor.

Amongst other things, the constable was concerned with obtaining warrants, attending the sessions for licensing alehouses, the issuing of passes and many other duties.

Pinfold or pound

At Burscough Town nearly opposite to Dutton's shop stood until recent times what was known as the 'pinfold' or 'pound', which was used by the pinder to put cattle into when they were found straying onto lands not belonging to their owners. The cattle were kept in the pound until the payment of a small fine was made by their owners. When the Turnpike Acts were passed, straying cattle were a constant problem on the roads, especially those belonging to cottagers who also were guilty of removing turfs at frequent intervals from the side of the turnpike roads. The old pinfold was subsequently used by the council for refuse, but in recent years has been removed and the site is now partly occupied by a bungalow.

It was always customary for the inhabitants to attend the court leet to answer their name, or send twopence in lieu thereof. Failing this, a fine of one shilling was imposed and, if not paid, a levy on some small portion of portable goods was made and sold for its payment.

During the 17th, 18th and part of the 19th century there was no system of sewerage as there is today and the water passages or channels of the streets were often like small rivers. Each householder, too, was expected to sweep and clean every Wednesday and Saturday not only the parapet fronting his house, but half the cart way and carry away the refuse to his own midden. A fine of 1 shilling was imposed if this was not done.

This ancient court did some of the work which is today the responsibility of local authorities but, by the middle of the 19th century, it was falling into decay as the manorial system itself began to disintegrate. The last meeting was in 1876. In 1890, however, it was revived for reasons which are not clear, and continued to meet until 1902. The revived court met mainly at the *Packet House Hotel* (now the *Admiral Lord Nelson)* or at the *Bull and Dog Inn.* In 1901 the main business appears to have been the choosing of a churchwarden for Ormskirk parish church. It had been the custom for such a choice to be made, since the Derby Lords of the Manor had had this right and had their own family chapel in the church.

The appointment of the officers was done on the same basis as I have described, but they were elected for one year instead of for life as had been the custom in the past. In 1901 John Bailey Gorst was elected warden and Mr. Samuel Brighouse was the steward.

The duties of the officers were carried out as in ancient time and from the following report it appears that old pinfold was still in use as late as 1901:

The Report of the Burscough Court Leet, 1901.

'The ale-tasters went once round the brewhouses and public houses during each year with their pint glasses, and that while they found some ales better than others, they condemned none; the pinders also took charge of stray cattle out of the pinfold; and the work of the appraisers of distress in assessing the damage done by trespassing cattle received the approval of the steward, who, though he was a solicitor (Mr. S. Brighouse), thought that the method was better than a resort to the law courts'.

Burscough Priory

Lancashire had comparatively few religious houses and most of these were founded by the Augustinian order in the late 12th and early 13th centuries. Before 1127 there were only three priories or cells, at Lancaster, Kersal and Penwortham, and a hospital for lepers at Preston. Amongst the most important of the subsequent foundations was Burscough Priory, which, with its near neighbour the Benedictine priory at Upholland, was the only substantial religious house in the whole of south-west Lancashire.

The reason for the absence of other foundations may be the existence of very extensive tracts of marshy land, although it is clear in other parts of the country that poor land and difficult conditions did not necessarily discourage monastic foundations, and sometimes were a positive incentive.

The date of the foundation of the Priory has been established as about 1189 when Robert Fitz-Henry, Lord of Lathom, granted it to the Prior of Burscough. It was endowed with the patronage of three churches, Ormskirk, Huyton and Flixton, and the monks also derived revenue from the weekly market of Ormskirk and glebe lands in the bulk of the neighbouring parishes, and also some in the neighbourhood of Leicester. The annual fair which used to be held in Ormskirk on August 28th, also benefited the Priory under grant obtained from Edward I and his brother Edmund 'Crouchback' earl of Lancaster in 1286.

The Priory was dedicated to God under the invocation of St. Nicholas and

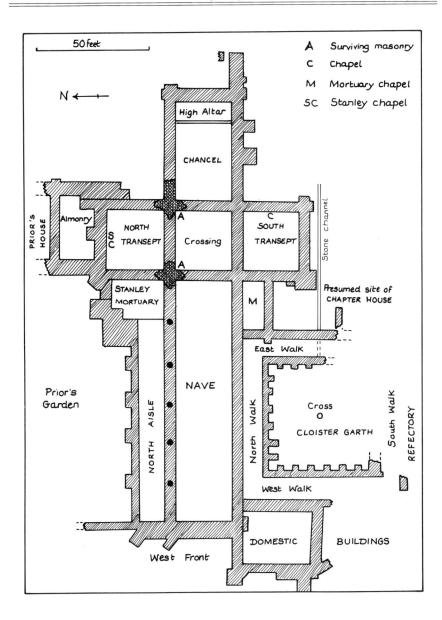

50 feet

N ←—●—→

A   Surviving masonry
C   Chapel
M   Mortuary chapel
SC Stanley chapel

High Altar

CHANCEL

Almonry

PRIOR'S HOUSE

SC

NORTH TRANSEPT

A

Crossing

A

C

SOUTH TRANSEPT

Stone channel

STANLEY MORTUARY

M

Presumed site of CHAPTER HOUSE

East Walk

Prior's Garden

NORTH AISLE

NAVE

North Walk

Cross O

CLOISTER GARTH

South Walk

REFECTORY

West Walk

DOMESTIC   BUILDINGS

West Front

Burscough Priory

During the 1880s James Bromley was able to excavate much of the Priory, and to produce a plan of the greater part of its buildings: this is a somewhat simplified version of that plan, taken from his report on the excavations (published in the Trans. Hist. Soc. Lancs. and Cheshire *1889). The entire church and most of the adjacent buildings were revealed but the domestic ranges remained unexcavated.*

the monks belonged to the Black or Canons Regular of the Augustinian Order. In the Lancashire Pipe Rolls there is further confirmation of the date for the foundation of the Priory. Among the witnesses to the foundation charter was the Prior of Norton (1178-1190) which limits the date to no later than 1190. It is also suggested that the first canons established at Burscough came from Norton, Co. Chester, which was an Augustinian House.

It is of interest to note the following *novel disseisin* in connection with the date of the foundation of the Burscough Priory, which appears in the Lancashire Assize Roll number 405 in the fourth year of the reign of King Edward I (15th Sept., 1276) before John De Reygate and William De Northburg:

> Novel disseisin — John de Merolhan *v* the Prior of Burkscou, Henry le Suur, Edmund de Assenheued, Thomas le Buker, Henry le fiz le Keu, William son of Edmund, Ralph de Bikerstath, Richard del Dam, Agnes who is wife of William Wyth, Adam le Feuere, Richard son of Stephen, Adam son of Edda, Henry son of Adam de Mounteslay, Robert de Redwryth, Henry son of Hugh, John son of Sabin, Henry Trauers and Alan le Peleter re common of pasture in 40 acres of land of moor and marsh in Lathom.

> Same *v* the Prior of Burskou, William le Charpenter, Simon le Charpenter, Adam de Birskou, John son of William, Stephen le fiz Pauwel and Richard le fiz Bertilloun re 1 acre in Dalton.

> The Prior says that one Robert de Lathom, 100 years ago gave the said common to the Prior and Convent of Burscou in pure an perpetual alms. Verdict in each case for defendant, with judgment.

The above evidence may indicate that the Priory was founded before 1190, that is in the 1170s. That it was founded before 1191 is quite certain and that it could have been established in the 1170s is a possibility because the witnesses to the Foundation Charter limit it to the following dates: Robert Archdeacon of Chester, who held office from 1149-1192, and Henry, Prior of Norton from 1178-1190.

The Robert de Lathom referred to by the Prior of Burscough died in year 1199 and he was alive in 1168-9 as witness in the Pipe Roll of 15 Henry II., 1168-9. He was married twice, his first marriage taking place before 1178 to an unknown lady and secondly he married Amabil, daughter of Simon, canon of Burscough, who survived him and subsequently sued her stepson Richard in 1199 and, by fine made 29th October 1199, she obtained Knowsley and Anglezargh for term of her life.

The charter was also confirmed by Hugh, Bishop of Coventry and Lichfield, in 1191. His immediate successors, Geoffrey de Muschamp and William Cornhill did so too. There was a more solemn confirmation of charters by Pope Gregory IX in 1228 (which allowed burials to take place in their church), and again, by Pope Boniface VIII, in 1295.

After 1189 the Priory expanded its territory for about 100 years, obtaining its land by means of grants. The early acquisitions appear to have been the most important because in the 14th century the grants are mainly concerned with territorial adjustments. The *Cartulary of Burscough Priory* is a leather bound volume measuring approximately 9¾ inches by 6¼ inches, containing 110 parchment folios gathered into 13 quires. The first part deals with the lay grants of land and other property, together with a few grants by the Priory and leasing agreements. The second part deals with ecclesiastical confirmations and grants of privileges.

The Priory's interest did not spread very far; most places of interest were within a 15 miles radius, with the exception of Ellel and Bury, and many existed within a radius of 6 to 7 miles. It appears that the territorial strength of the Priory lay in the estates immediately surrounding it in Lathom, Burscough, Martin, Scarisbrick and Hurleton.

There is some indication of what the land was used for; several of the grants of land obtained by the Priory suggest an open-field system of cultivation and there is nothing in the *Cartulary* about a two or three field system involving the use of one fallow field for pasture, thus confirming that Lancashire lay outside the Midlands three-field system. Although there were large areas of land that were moor, moss and waste in the 13th century, it is also probable that a considerable proportion was cultivated, though whether upon an out-field system or some sophisticated manner is not clear. The above is strengthened when one considers the number of mills belonging to the Priory. In the *Cartulary* a list of the mills of the Priory in the parish of Ormskirk in the year 1228 names no fewer than seven windmills and watermills in that parish alone. Many explanations may be put forward to explain the high number of these mills, but it is evident that there was much arable land under cultivation at the time. Further proof of their value is the many disputes over them mentioned in the charters of the Priory.

The few leases that have remained or have been recorded in the *Cartulary* are insufficient to give one much insight into the management of the Priory's estates. In 1229 an agreement concerning Lathom Mill allowed Richard of Lathom II to hold the mill for life at 2 shillings rent and in 1245 Huyton Mill was leased for 30 years at 3 shillings rent. These and many more leases are recorded in the *Cartulary*.

There is much more information in the *Cartulary* about the ecclesiastical property of the Priory which in a work of this nature is too detailed to be included here. However, I should like to say that in 1190 Robert de Lathom gave Flixton church to his monastery at Burscough, but about sixty or seventy years later it had passed into the hands of Meiland, Bishop of Lichfield, who about 1280 gave its advowson and impropriation to form a prebend in Lichfield Cathedral. Bishop Meiland was the son of William Longspee, Earl of Salisbury. How he obtained possession of the advowson of Flixton is not fully known, but for about five hundred years the connection between Flixton and Lichfield existed. Burscough and Chester were both in the diocese of Lichfield until the new diocese of Chester was formed in 1541.

In 1536 the Priory was dissolved, and at that time was staffed, according to the 'Brief Certificate' of the Commissioners, with one prior and four canons, twenty-two waiting servants and officers of the household, and eighteen men employed to work the monastic demesnes. This gives one the impression that the Priory was like a comfortable country house. Two of the canons after the dissolution of the Priory wished to be further advised 'in the event' and one wished to continue in religion and, if necessary, would be prepared to transfer to another house.

The valuation of the Priory in 1536 was £122-5s.-7d., and this included incomes from the three rectories of Ormskirk, Huyton and Radcliffe-on-Soar. Burscough Priory gave £7 worth of grain each year to the poor, but this was disallowed by the Commissioners. The inventory of goods indicated that they had a good supply of silver plate, cooking utensils, household goods and bedding which an ordinary peasant would have found luxurious. The total value of the above goods, including the ornaments of the church, was £192. The building with the bells and including the lead was valued at £148-10s.-0d. In 1536 Burscough Priory had 19 sets of vestments as well as three old ones, 6 copes which the Earl of Derby had given and 15 old copes, which would seem to suggest that in the past the number of canons had been greater than four. The Brief Certificate also stated that there were four chalices, four crosses (2 of them of silver) and a relic of the true Cross.

The principal reason for the suppression of the monasteries is best understood from the visitation records and reports. These visitations were to seek out and remedy lapses (slide or slip in moral conduct), and so present the faults of a house rather than its virtues. For Lancashire the records exist for Cockersand, Burscough and Holland only. There was only one accusation made by the commissioners against the monks of Burscough — one monk was incontinent.

In 1535 an Ecclesiastical Commission sat at Wigan and several gentlemen of substance were convicted of adultery and keeping concubines, amongst whom was Sir James Stanley, who was Steward of Burscough Priory. As early as 1524 Henry VIII held a visitation of the monasteries and suppressed forty which had less than seven inmates. Burscough Priory was not amongst this number, which would seem to suggest that there were more than seven canons at that time and, according to the number of vestments I have previously stated, this would appear to be correct. Some of the endowments of the suppressed monasteries went to found Cardinal College (now Christ Church College) at Oxford, and a College at Ipswich. Many of the monasteries were no longer places of learning and the monastic ideal was declining. The large profits derived from tolls and fairs held by the monasteries were also very unpopular. However, in many areas they did good work by encouraging farming, they kept schools, encouraged trade (wool) and helped the sick and poor. Lastly Henry VIII wanted money and in February 1536 the Reformation Parliament suppressed those monasteries with an income of less than £200 per year. Burscough Priory was suppressed at this time along with 375 other religious houses.

At the dissolution of the monasteries it was very difficult for an ex-monk to find employment and especially so if he was not in receipt of a pension. Many turned to teaching and others did clerical jobs; some had to work on the land or depend on temporary clerical occupations, or rely on the charity of his neighbours. In 1592 William Aspinall died in Lancashire, poor and unemployed; he had formerly been a canon at Burscough Priory.

The last Prior was Hugh Huxley, who surrendered the Priory and its lands to the Crown at a time when its community had been greatly reduced and its lands dissipated. His burial is recorded in the parish register of Ormskirk as follows:

'1558, May 2 Ser Hugh Huckesley Prior of Burscough, in this Church.'

In 1547 records disclose the fact that the Priory was granted to Sir William Paget, who was principal Secretary of State in that year, but the burial ground

The Erratic Block, near Burscough Junction railway station, taken looking north west. This stone was removed when Rivington Drive was built during the early 1970s. The new Lordsgate Township School is in the background.

The Burscough Priory Cross — only the pedestal remains.
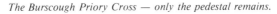

was used as a place of interment up to year 1572. Some burials took place at the Priory after its destruction; in the register of the Ormskirk parish church are recorded two burials at the Priory: Richard Johnson of Hoscar (Oct. 15th 1656) and Joseph Rigby (April 18th 1657). Besides these there were some years ago two weathered tombstones which stood between the two remaining pillars of the old Priory church, but in 1962 only one tombstone remained, on which was the following:

'17th April 175?' (the fourth figure had gone and almost the name).

The full inscription of the stone was the following:

'Ann Cooper Died ye 17th April 1752'.

The other gravestone bore the date 1715 but the name of the person buried here I could not find, and there is no indication in the Ormskirk parish registers to suggest who it might have been.

The Priory buildings

Pennant, who passed by here in 1773 wrote (in his *Tours to Alston Moor)* 'Nothing is left of this pile, but part of the centre arch of the church, and instead of the magnificent tombs of the Stanleys, which till the Reformation graced the place, a few modern gravestones peep through the grass, memorials of poor Catholics who fondly prefer this now violated spot . . .'. Virtually nothing was known of the plan or extent of the Priory, or the character of its buildings, until 1886 when excavations took place under the supervision of Mr. James Bromley, the then Earl of Derby giving permission for the work, and also defraying the cost. No doubt he was specially interested in settling doubts which existed regarding the removal of the Stanley dead and effigies. These were not found but, as a result of the excavations, it was possible for a good general idea of the layout of the Priory to be formed and a plan prepared.

Burscough Priory differed from many monasteries in that the Prior's House was separated from the monastery by the church, which possessed the unusual feature of having only one aisle. The extreme dimensions of the church were 175 feet 10 inches by 83 feet 7 inches across the transepts. The walls varied in thickness from 7¼ feet to 2¾ feet. There was a cloister on the south side of the church, the dimensions of which were 67½ feet square.

The church had battlement parapet round it with stone gargoyles here and there and the windows were for the most part stained glass and the altars were decorated with mosaics. Some Norman mouldings were found, but the architecture was mainly of the early 13th century transitional period.

There was a low level passage also and this would appear to lend some colour to the tradition that a subterranean passage connected the monastery with Lathom House, which as the crow flies is nearly two miles to the east of the Priory. The passage that Mr. Bromley excavated was found in the south-east corner of the chancel and it descended to 9 feet below the level of the chancel floor and continued for 15 feet from the entrance; at this point the passage abruptly turned right and left, but was traced no further. Local tradition still holds that there was a tunnel from the Priory to Lathom House, but this has not yet been proved. It has also been suggested that a passage could have connected Blythe Hall with the Priory because in the late 19th century in the cellar of Blythe Hall there was an entrance to an ancient passage. However, most of the information is conjectural and, given the distances involved and the awkward climate and geology, the suppositions about tunnels are at best doubtful.

A 13th-century chalice was also found, which was probably buried with the first Prior, who died after the erection of the Priory church. The first Earls of Derby were buried here, for their home, Lathom House, was situated only two miles to the east of it. However, after the Reformation and the destruction of the Priory, they were transferred to the parish church of Ormskirk.

Besides the above finds, the following items might be of interest to the reader in connection with the Priory. Mr. Roby, in his *Traditions of Lancashire,* published in 1828, under the title 'The Prior of Burscough' gives the following account:

'The Priory was dedicated to St. Nicholas and a rude effigy of the Saint was carved over the south porch of the chapel, with two or three naked children at his feet'.

Mr. Roby gave no authorities for the above description, but in 1864 Mr. Peter Draper of Ormskirk, in his book, *The House of Stanley,* stated the following:

'The head of the effigy of the saint formerly occupied a position on the wall at the front of the abbey farm house, near to the gate, but was afterwards displaced, and lay about for many years, and was often used as a "scotch" for cart wheels'.

This effigy was either lost or destroyed about the year 1860. In *A Manual of Church Decoration and Symbolism,* by the Rev. Ernest Geldart (1899), the symbolism attached to St. Nicholas is as follows:

S. Nicholas B.C 342. Three children (in tub); three golden balls (or six); three golden apples; or loaves; or purses; an anchor; a ship.

The above would, therefore, seem to confirm the descripton of the effigy over the south porch of the Priory chapel, as mentioned by Roby.

Mr. Peter Draper also mentioned a large christening font which lay under the pantry window of Abbey Farm, and was then (1860s) used as a mash vessel for pigs' food. This font was subsequently found by a daughter of Lord Skelmersdale, who had it removed to Lathom Chapel. The font is thought to be Norman (circa 1100) and is supposed to have come from the Priory. It has seven sides, which is an old arrangement, but also popular in the middle of the 15th century. The sides of the font represent the Sacraments of Baptism, Confirmation, Penance, Mass, Marriage, Extreme Unction and Ordination. From the 13th century onwards, fonts were invariably octagonal in form and were raised on a stepped platform. The Priory also had a rood screen which was made of wood and this now stands in Lathom chapel. The lovely eagle lectern which also stands in the above chapel is also said to come from the Priory. This lectern was possibly made in the 15th century and so might have been the original lectern of the chapel.

When the Priory church was knocked down, the bells from the Priory were removed to Ormskirk parish church, for the accommodation of which a tower was built, and this is probably the best explanation for the church possessing a tower and a steeple side by side. The legend, however, attributes it to the two daughters of the pirate Orme who, rather than quarrel over whether the church should have a tower or steeple, compromised by having both. There are only two other examples in England, one at Purton in Wiltshire and one at St. Andrews, Wanborough.

There has been much controversy in the past regarding the origin of the tower and steeple of Ormskirk parish church, but I think that the explanation put forward by Mr. James Bromley is probably the most authentic. During the excavations at Burscough Priory in 1886, Mr. Bromley copied from the walls of the Priory numerous masons' marks and compared these with the masons' marks on the tower at Ormskirk. Many of these marks were identical, thus indicating that there was a good probability that the tower was built from the ruins of the Priory. It is important to note that the church of the Priory was not demolished until some time after the Dissolution, but continued more or less intact until 1572. Unfortunately, before Mr. Bromley began his excavations, the parish church at Ormskirk had undergone much restoration and many of the masons' marks had been removed. Therefore, if these marks had remained, a greater comparison could have been made. It is interesting to note that those parts of the church which tradition connected with the Priory were the very portions upon which the marks were found. The Bickerstaffe Chapel contains two examples of one of the Burscough Priory mason's marks and before the restoration in 1877 had contained many more. Each mason had his own mark and it has been calculated from the evidence available that about 20 masons would have worked on the Priory.

The bells

However, there only appears to be one bell in the parish church of Ormskirk that came from Burscough Priory. This is the great tenor bell which was in use up to the year 1948, when the peal was recast and a new tenor made to replace it. The old tenor bell, which weighs 25½ cwt., is now placed on the floor below the tower.

The bell bears the following inscription:

'J. S. de B. Armig. et. e. ux. me. fecerunt in horore Trinitatis. R. B. 1497'. (J. S. of B. Esquire and his wife made me in honour of the Trinity. R. B. represents the maker of the bell, but his name is not known).

This inscription has been variously interpreted by local antiquaries. The most likely explanation as to the donor of the bell appears to be that given by Mr. James L. Thornley. He found on checking through various inquisitions (namely inquisitions of Henry VII), that a James Scarisbrick held lands in Burscough and Bretherton. This James Scarisbrick was living in 1494 and died about 1501, his wife Elizabeth surviving him. His son Gilbert's will shows the family's interest in the Priory of Burscough and Ormskirk parish church:

'I will that mine executors content and pay towards the buying of a cross to the Church of Ormskirk, 5 shillings'.

Therefore, it is possible that this James Scarisbrick was the donor of the bell.

A second date of 1576 appears half-way down the bell, indicating the date that it was remoulded. As I have said before, the Priory Church was only destroyed in 1572 and this would fit in with the recasting of the bell in 1576. No doubt when the bell was being removed from the Priory in 1572 it is quite possible that it was damaged and needed remoulding. This date also gives an indication as to when the tower was erected to house the bells. The present peal consists of eight bells, five of which probably contain metal from the Priory bells. Four bells were recast in 1714, and two more added in 1774. In 1948 all the bells were recast when the new tenor bell was added.

Leper Hospital

A Leper Hospital was run by the monks of Burscough Priory, but the precise site of it is not known. It has been suggested that it was on the site of the present Blythe Hall, but there is no written evidence or customs to confirm this. *The Victoria County History* gives the following information:

'In 1283 Henry de Lathom, Lord of Tarbock, gave a place called Ridgate*, which Richard son of Henry his ancestors had originally set apart for the use of lepers, but which the parishioners had diverted for their own use'.

The Priory certainly had a hospital for lepers because in 1285 Henry de Lacy, Earl of Lincoln, stipulated with the Prior and canons for the 'perpetual right of admittance of one of his tenants of the fee of Widnes into it'. During the excavations in 1886 the Infirmary was not found. Throughout the medieval period there were only three hospitals of note in Lancashire: St. Mary Magdalen in Preston was the oldest, being established in the late twelfth century for the care of lepers, though by the middle of the 15th century it had become disused. A similar hospital at St. Leonard's, Lancaster, in the 14th century was caring for 3 lepers and six almsmen, but by 1531 was in a state of ruin. The third hospital was St. Saviour, at Stidd, which had abandoned its charitable function as early as the 14th century.

Smaller hospitals appear to have been attached to most of the priories because at Coniston, in 1188, a small hospital for lepers was founded. This hospital, similar to the leper hospital at Burscough, was looked after by some Augustinian monks.

There is very little information on how the lepers were dealt with but by all accounts they were treated as outcasts. In April 1220, Henry III addressed a letter to Hubert de Burgh, instructing him to order the sheriff and forester of Lancaster to desist from annoying the lepers there but the order was ignored. However, a Royal writ was issued to the sheriff directing him to see that the lepers were no longer molested, and that they were to have their beasts and herds in the forest without exaction of ox or cow. They were also allowed to take wood for fuel and timber for building.

The lepers, therefore, appear to have lived apart from the rest of the community and by all accounts erected their own buildings in which to live. Therefore, the hospital at Burscough would probably have been built in a similar manner, at a short distance (not more than ½ mile) away from the Priory. Apart from Blythe Hall, which Mr. Bromley suggested as being the most likely site for the infirmary, the site of 'Martland's farm' which lies immediately north west of Blythe Hall has also been put forward.

The Vicars of Ormskirk

In the second decade of the 13th century, the advowson of Ormskirk was granted to Burscough Priory by Bishop William de Cornhill and in 1285 Bishop Roger Longespee granted the Priory his licence to present one of its canons to the vicarage. Before 1285 Ormskirk had remained a curacy.

---

*This place has not yet been identified either in Lathom or Burscough and, in some documents, it is spelt 'Ruddegate'.

The evidence of the taxation of Pope Nicholas valued Ormskirk at £13-6s.-8d. which, financially, was not very important to the Priory. In the grant of appropriation of Ormskirk the terms of Bishop William de Cornhills only provided for a competent vicarage, the vicar paying all the charges. However, the vicar had a house and 4 acres and received from Burscough Priory £10 a year. This state of affairs existed from the early part of the 14th century. These provisions were often the cause of disputes between the vicar of Ormskirk and the Priory, but why this should have been so is not easily understood. The Priory supplied vicars to Ormskirk church from 1286 to 1530.

The most valuable endowment that was granted to the Priory was the appropriation of the church at Radcliffe-on-Soar in 1381. The value of the endowment in the 13th century was £46-13s.-4d. The Priory received this endowment because of the generosity of Richard Winwick, who obtained the licence from Richard II to divert the advowson of Radcliffe from the master and scholars of Oriel College, Oxford, to Burscough Priory. The purpose of the endowment was to found a charity in Huyton church for the soul of Richard Winwick's brother, John of Winwick, who had been the treasurer of York. In 1383 the chantry was established and was supplied with two priests, their stipends being fixed at 10 marks each. Before the dissolution of the Priory the surplus revenue obtained from the rectory amounted to £20 a year.

Curious Episodes in the history of the Priory.
The murder of Brother Adam of Burscough.

Walter Gorsuch and his son Adam, of Gorsuch Hall, were charged with the murder in 1332 of another Adam who was a monk of Burscough Priory. They were acquitted in 1333. Homicide was not uncommon it seems in this family, because Robert Gorsuch was slain in Church Street, Ormskirk, by a dyer, William of the Cross in 1305. Robert Gorsuch met his death by being struck on the left side of the head with a staff or 'dodge spade'. The murderer was subsequently tried in 1305.

The indictment in 1347 of Thomas of Litherland, Prior of Burscough.

The Prior was indicted for his alleged participation in the lawless proceedings of Sir John de Dalton, who was responsible for the abduction of Margaret de la Bech from her manor of Beams in Wiltshire. Roby, in *Traditions of Lancashire,* under the title 'The Prior of Burscough', gives a full account of the incident. The facts are too detailed to enter into here, but the main points were that during the abduction of Margaret de la Bech two persons were killed: Michael de Poininges and Thomas le Clarke and many more were injured. It is curious to note that the King's own son Lionel, who was keeper of the realm in the King's absence abroad, was staying there at the time of the abduction. The Prior seems to have been fortunate in those days, because a number of Lancashire gentlemen came forward and declared that he was innocent. According to Roby, but not mentioned in the *Victoria County Histories,* a free pardon was granted by Edward III. The prior retained his position at Burscough until 1385, when he resigned, which seems to confirm that the charge was disproved.

A case of black magic.

In 1454 charges of divination, sortilege and black magic were brought against the Prior, Robert Woodward, one of the canons, Thomas Fairwise and the vicar of Ormskirk, William Bolton, who had been a former canon of the Priory. In the *Victoria County Histories* the following account is given, which is a summary of the episcopal investigation:

> 'One Robert, a necromancer, had undertaken for £10 to find hidden treasure. After swearing secrecy on the sacrament of bread they handed it over in the pyx (a little chest in which the consecrated host is kept) to Robert. Three circuli trianguli were made, in each of which one of them stood, the vicar having the body of Christ suspended at his breast and holding in his hand a rod, doubtless a diviner's rod. The story ends here, but all three denied that any invocation of demons or sacrifice to them had taken place'.

They were suspended for two years by Bishop Boulers and the vicar of Ormskirk and the Prior were deprived of their positions. The ex-monk, however, did quite well for himself for he was allowed a pension of 10 marks, with a 'competent chamber' in the Priory, and as much bread, beer and meat as was sufficient for two canons.

The seals of Burscough Priory

The seal of Burscough Priory was about the size of a five shilling piece (i.e. about 4 cm in diameter). It depicted a representation of the south front of the monastic buildings with the roof and tower of the church rising above them. The legend around the seal was as follows:

+ SIGILLVM SANCTI NICHOLAI DE BVRCASSVGHE +
seal of (the Priory of) Saint Nicholas of Burscough.

Draper, in his book *The House of Stanley* describes a different seal as follows:

> 'The area of the seal had two compartments the upper one bearing the figure of a canon in a square cap instructing a child; and the lower, that of St. Nicholas, and around the area this inscription: "SIGIL.SCI.NICHOLAI DE BVRISKOV +".'

I have seen the first seal but not the second, and have been unable to verify the existence of the latter: Draper does not quote any authorities for his description or say where the seal was to be found.

The armorials of Burscough Priory

The origins of the arms of the Priory go back well beyond the earliest records of the College of Arms and it would appear that they are based on the coat of arms of the the the de Lathom family, founders of the Priory. The arms of benefactors and founders of religious houses were often adopted by the houses themselves, with suitable and appropriate modifications, in the 11th and 12th centuries.

The armorials of Burscough Priory are as follows:—

> This shield is usually described or blazoned, 'Indented per fesse Argent and Or; in chief two crosiers between three annulets Or;' but this is not correct heraldry, and accordingly the proper colours of the de Lathom's coat of Arms have been adopted; namely blue and yellow.

The tenor bell which is supposed to have come from Burscough Priory.

All that remains of the Priory today.

The Priors of Burscough

1. Henry, probably the first Prior, not earlier than 1189.
    (He is first mentioned in Charter No. II)
    (1189-1198 1-9 Richard I.)
2. William, occurs before 1199.
3. Geoffrey, mentioned as predecessor of Benedict.
4. Benedict, occurs 1229 and 1235.
5. William, occurs 1245.
6. Nicholas, occurs in two charters, both of which can be dated between c.1260 and c.1275.
7. Warin, occurs between 1275 and 1286.
8. Richard, occurs March 1303 and February 1303/4.
9. John of Donnington, occurs September 1322 and Nov. 1338.
10. Thomas of Litherland, occurs 1347-83, resigned 1385.
11. John of Wrightington, elected 1385; died 1406 or 1407.
12. Thomas of Ellerbeck, elected 16th Feb. 1406-7; died before May 1424.
13. Hugh Rainford, election confirmed July 1439, resigned 4th October 1454.
14. Henry Olton, elected 28th Feb. 1454-5; died before 9th Oct. 1457.
15. Richard Ferryman, elected before 9th Oct. 1457, occurs down to 1478.
16. Hector Scarisbrick, occurs 1488; died 1504.
17. John Barton, election confirmed 6th December 1504; deprived 1511.
18. Robert Harvey, preferred 12th May 1511 on 'just deprivation' of Barton; died before 17th April 1535.
19. Hugh Huxley, election confirmed 17th April 1535; surrendered 1536; buried at Ormskirk 1558.

Ancient halls and their owners

Burscough Hall

After the dissolution of the Priory in 1536, the people of Burscough had no place of worship, although I believe that up to 1572, when burials were still being undertaken at the Priory, it is possible that some form of service could have been taking place there. For those who became Protestants they would have to attend the parish church at Ormskirk but for the Roman Catholics there was nothing. It is possible, however, that the Catholics held their services in the Burscough Hall, in Chapel Lane, Lathom, in the township of Burscough. This name seems to indicate some connection with Burscough or Burscough Priory, but it has none with either, and the charters of the Priory contain no reference to the place or its owners.

Burscough Hall derives its name from its owners, the family of Burscough of Lathom. This family belonged to the once numerous but now almost extinct class of smaller gentry, which bore no arms and were adherents of the great houses.

The Burscough family during the time of the canons of Burscough Priory obtained lands in the neighbourhood, taking their name from the locality. The following is recorded:

'Thus Richard son of John de Burscough sued Robert de Lathom in 1292 concerning a tenement here, but was non-suited'.

There are some deeds in the Townley M.S. relating to the Burscoughs, who had lands in Westhead and elsewhere in the 14th century. There is reference to the family in the 15th century in various records and in the 16th century the family moved to Lathom, where the main line remained for about 200 years. They were very strong in the Roman Catholic faith, which resulted in their ruin about 195 years ago.

The following extracts throw interesting light on the connections of this family:

The wardship and marriage of Johannes Norreys (of Tarleton) was granted to Richard Burscough, 1st October, Henry V (1418). *(Lancs. Inquis.* V. 1. p 125)

The same 'Ricardi de Burscogh' was one of the jurors for the proof of age of Thomas de Hesketh, 5th March, 6 Henry VI (1423) — *(Lancs Inquis.* V 2 p 21)

'Syr Rogr Burskowe, chapleyn', was one of the witnesses to the will of Thomas Scarisbrick armiger. 4. Oct., 22 Henry VIII (1530) — *(Wills and Inventories* p 187)

The same 'Rogerus Burscogh' was chantry priest. 26-7 Henry VIII (1535) serving at the altar of Our Lady of Pity, founded by Thomas Atherton 'de Bykerstaffe', in the Bickerstaffe chapel of Ormskirk church, and his pay for duty was £4-13-4d. per annum.

There was another altar in the Bickerstaffe chapel, dedicated to Mary Magdalene. It was founded by 'Petri Garrard clici' (Peter Gerrard clerk) and served in 1535 by 'Rogerus Shaa' whose pay was £2-7-9d. per annum. This Roger Shaw was chaplain to the Atherton family and became vicar of Ormskirk in 1548. *(Valor Ecclesiasticus,* p 223; *Lancs. Charities* pp 101-2).

The will of Gilbert Burscough, of Lathom, in the County of Lancaster, gentleman,

Decr. 12th, 4 and 5 Philip and Mary (1557), 'To be buret in Saynt Nicholas chauncel within the Parish Churche of Ormskyrke as nere unto the place where my father was buret as conveniently may be'. He mentions 'my brother Syr William Burscogh, Raufe Burcogh my bastard brother, my syster Elizabeth, my other II systers Margarett and Anne'. 'To the almsmen of the Chapell of Lathom every of them VI d.' (6d.) 'Elenor my wife and Rauff Burscough my said bastard brother to be executors, and my cosyn John Moore esquier and my brother Syr William Burscough clerke, to be supervisors'. Proved Jan 11 (old style — same year).

From one of the earliest entries in the burial register of Ormskirk church it is clear that the lawful brother only survived the testator by six months — '1558 May 3 Syr Willm Burscogh'.

'Syr' is the medieval equivalent for 'Reverend', though it is probable that this Syr William Burscough served some cure in the neighbourhood or was a canon of Burscough Priory at its dissolution; these are the only records to be found of him. The following, read in connection with the extracts from the will of Gilbert of Burscough, recites the endowments and definitely fixes Saint Nicolas's chantry in some part of the Scarisbrick chapel:

Will of Thomas 'Scharesbreke esquir', 4 October, 22 Henry VIII (1530) 'I beqweth my sowle to almighty God of heave; and my body to be buret in the Pych churche of Ormskyrke before the ymage of Sanet Nicholas on the sowthe syde of the sayd churche. Also I beqwethe my best q vyke catell to the curate of my Pych churche in the name of my mortuer'.

The testator goes on to bequeath land of the yearly value of 6 marks (£4) for seven years as the endowment of an honest priest to say Masses at the altar of 'Sanet Nicholas in my Pyche Churche of Ormyskirke' and to pray for the souls of himself and his parents *(Wills and Inventories* p 187).

'John Burscoghe' signs 'A list of all the soldiers and munition in the Castle of Rushen and Castle Peel in the Isle-of-Man', sent to Henry, 4th Earl of Derby, 27th Dec. 1585 — *Funeral Certificates* p 21.

The later records show that the Burscough family had left its ancient home and had become comparatively poor and, as there are no subsequent records of its members, it is probable that the family soon after became extinct.

The Burscough family left the Hall about 1585, which was subsequently tenanted by the Tarscough family until the year 1630 or thereabouts. (I have been unable to find their exact date of arrival). However, about this time, the Hall was occupied by the Longes. In 1659 Henry Longe (the famous Dr. Longe) entered the English College of Rome; he was the son of Elizeus Longe and Alice Ashton. He stated in his reply to the English College at Rome that his parents had always been Catholics, and had suffered much for their religion. He had two brothers and one sister; he was never a heretic and made his humanities studies in England. The fame of Dr. Longe of Burscough Hall has been characteristically fleeting and, like the Burscough family, has left behind very little trace of its why or wherefore.

The Longes were followed by Peter de Lathom who took possession of the Hall in 1667 and it continued to be used as a Catholic centre. During his stay here I have been told that his brother Christopher Lathom was priest here, but I have been unable to find any evidence of this. Peter Lathom of Bispham, 'founder of the Lathom Charity', leased Burscough Hall for 999 years at a rent

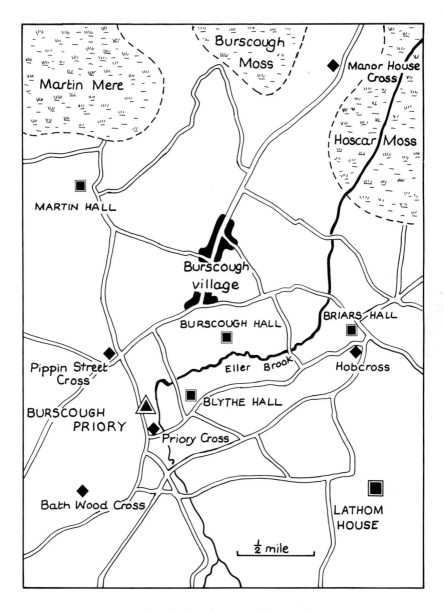

Ancient halls and crosses of Burscough.

of £10 per annum to John Heyes of Ormskirk, and this was in trust for the Roman Catholic Mission. The priest was to be supported by the farm in addition to paying the £10 annually for the poor. This state of affairs has continued to the present day and so Burscough Hall land is still called, 'Lathom Charity'. The old Burscough Hall, alongside the church, is now a farmhouse, retaining, however, the rooms where Mass was said for so many years.

The following is a quote from the *Handbook to Ormskirk,* by George Lea, who gives a description of the Hall in 1890:

'There are no armorials, stained glass, spout heads, initials, or dates about the farmhouse "Burscough Hall", to give any indication of its age or identity; though judging from other appearances its older portions probably date from the close of the 16th century to the beginning of the 17th century. The place has been added to and altered till little idea of its original plan can be formed. "The Great Chamber", on the ground floor (now the kitchen), has still its Gothic moulded and stopped oak beams; and "The Chapel" upstairs (now divided into bedrooms) has its two semi-circular cased principals; and both rooms, though badly cut up, reveal to the practical eye something of their original proportions. The third principal of this floor is undressed and differently constructed, and the modern portion under it doubtless occupies the place of one much older, as behind the partition is a small room with a fireplace and diminutive window, both now bricked up, which has been a "priests hiding-place" or a "sacristy".'

The later history of the Hall and the Catholic community which it served is recorded in the following chapter.

Martin Hall and its associations

Today, Martin forms the northern half of the township of Burscough, but originally it belonged to the demense of Martin. Before 1066 one half of Martin had been united to Hurleston and the other half probably merged with Lathom. In 1140-1149 Warine Bussel granted to the Abbot of Evesham one teamland and a half land in the town called Martin, with a half of his stock there viz. four cows, four oxen and sixty sheep. The area adjacent to Martin Hall is known as 'Sheep Cote Hills' and, as its name implies, afforded 'a shelter for animals'. About the middle of the 13th century the name 'Sheep Cote Hills' was adopted, and no doubt would be attributed to the number of sheep kept there in the 12th century. However, by 1160 the Abbey of Evesham no longer held the carucate and a half of land in Martin. Instead the monks had received two oxgangs in Longton, two-thirds of the tithes of the demesne in Warton and Freckleton and certain fishing rights. The area of Martin probably passed to Gilimichael de Martin who was living in 1163. In 1189 the township of Martin was included in the foundation charter of Burscough Priory. Thus Martin, together with the area of Tarlscough, became the property of the Priory.

The first mention of Martin Hall occurs in the Pipe Roll of the eighth year of King John (1206): 'Matthew de Marton, ½ mark; Martin Hall, held of Robert de Lathom, who held by Military Service'. This Matthew de Martin appears to have been the first tenant at the Hall. However, according to the Pipe Roll of 1210-11, the heir of Matthew de Marton offered 20 marks (instead of ½ mark) for deliverance of land in Martin, in West Derby Hundred. The reason for this fine was attributed to his father's probable 'disappearance about the time of the last Lancaster Assizes'. Therefore, this account suggests that the land had been confiscated. How the matter was settled I do not know, but subsequently Martin Hall became a moated grange of Burscough Priory.

It is also possible that the road known as Lordsgate Lane (or Lord's Lane) was constructed by the monks and lay brethren to connect with the Priory. The name Lordsgate Lane itself implies that the road was on demesne land. Martin Grange was held by the Priory until its dissolution in 1536, after which it remained in the King's hands for about 10 years, but in 1538 the Earl of Derby held a lease which he obtained from the King's Commissioners. In 1547 Martin Grange was granted to William Paget who took possession of the Hall until 1549 when he sold it to the Earl of Derby.

The first tenant under the Earl of Derby appears to have been a Mr. William Stopford who was there in 1554. During Mr. Stopford's stay there was a dispute about some land which belonged to the Gorsuches of Gorsuch Hall, and the Lord of North Meols. The dispute arose over 12 acres of land which had been either given or sold to Walter Gorsuch by Alan Lord of North Meols, towards the close of the 13th century. Subsequently the land was let to the Lords of North Meols at a nominal rent, but after many years possession they assumed ownership. However, when Thomas Gorsuch took up residence at Gorsuch Hall (Gorsuch Hall had been in the hands of the Suttons for over 100 years) he took up the family rights and let the disputed land to William Stopford of Martin Hall, for his life. On 26th June 1554, John Bold, Lord of North Meols, came with his tenants, who mowed all the grass off this land and carried it away. The matter was referred to Queen Mary's law courts where a conflict of evidence arose; however, the land was retained by the Gorsuch family, which seems to indicate that the verdict was in their favour. The land in question was originally called 'Balder's many oaks', but subsequently was named 'The Hooks'. During the latter part of the 19th century a monolith existed here, the place being attributed to the worship of Balder the Beautiful.

In 1612 Martin Hall was granted to John Breres of Martin who subsequently sold it to the Wrightington family, who then leased it back to John Breres. The heraldry of John Breres and his wife Katherine were displayed on one of the window panes which bore the date 1614.

The members of the Breres family can be traced back many generations and their name can be found in the early records of the Preston Guild. The earlist mention that I could find was in the Guild of 1397, in which the Breres appear as skinners and farriers under the list of masters of the trade companies. The Breres are subsequently found as burgesses (borough freemen) in the successive rolls of the Preston Guild as follows:

In 1542 Oliver Breres was a steward of the Guild.
In 1562 Oliver Breres was listed as an alderman.
In 1582 Thomas Breres was a steward of the Guild.
In 1602 John Breres was clerk of the Guild.
In 1622 Henry Breres was a steward of the Guild.

After 1622 the name of Breres does not appear in the records of the Preston Guild. Henry Breres was Mayor of Preston in the following years: 1611, 1618, 1627 and 1637.

During the period of the Civil Wars, John Breres' son, Alexander, appears to have supported Lady Derby initially, for he had been within the garrison of Lathom House. However, in March 1644 he took the National Covenant and at the second siege was sympathetic to Cromwell's army. It is interesting to note that Alexander Breres' name appeared on the Recusant Roll for West Derby Hundred in 1641. In 1646 Alexander Breres appears in the 'Catalogue' of the Lords, Knights and Gentlemen of Lancashire who compounded for their estates; he is recorded as a gentleman of Martin and the sum he paid was £82-4s.-5d. Subsequently in the year 1647 it was ordered that a fifth of his estate, except the demesne of Croston, should be allowed to as many of his children as should be brought up in the Protestant religion.

These were difficult times for many Catholics and, no doubt, Alexander Breres tried to protect his family and their interests as much as possible. He lived at Lathom as well as holding the estate of Martin Hall; the administration of the estates being granted in 1646 and 1671 respectively. Breres or Briars Hall in Lathom takes its name from the family.

The Breres occupied Martin Hall until 1663, because in that year it is recorded that the demesnes of 'Martin was leased to Alexander Breres by Sir Edward Wrightington'. At the beginning of 1664 the Hall appears to have been occupied by Mr. James Starkie.

In 1682 James Starkie, together with his father the Rev. James Starkie, appeared at the Preston Guild as burgesses. At this time the Rev. James Starkie was living with his son at Martin Hall and, being associated with non-conformity in this area, he was described by Bland, in his *Annals of Southport,* as a veritable 'Vicar of Bray'. Martin Hall became a farm house during the time of Mr. James Starkie's tenancy.

The Hall was occupied by the Holcroft family after Mr. Starkie early in the 18th century. Thomas Holcroft the dramatist belonged to this family. From the records of the British Museum (no 9902bb6) it is shown that the father of Thomas Holcroft the dramatist was born at Martin Mere, near Southport, in 1717. It also states that he went to school at Rudderford (Rufford) and lived for a period in the area of the Sheepcote Hills. He died at Knutsford in Cheshire in 1797. The grandfather of Thomas Holcroft the dramatist is given as Thomas but on checking the Ormskirk parish church registers, his name appears as William.

The Holcroft family have resided in Ormskirk parish since Elizabethan times and can be traced in the Burscough area back to the beginning of the 17th century. The grandfather William Holcroft was a cooper by trade, according to the writings of Thomas Holcroft (the dramatist), who also stated that 'he was possessed of good qualities, passionate and a dear lover of Sir John Barleycorn'. Thomas Holcroft the dramatist was born in London in December 1745, his father having left Martin Hall for London about the early part of that year. It appears that either one of his brothers or other relations in the area remained at the Hall, for until 1850 it was occupied by the Holcrofts.

John Holcroft occupied the farm up to about the year 1851, when the Hall was tenanted by the Leyland family. Ralph Leyland occupied the Hall from the 1850s until the 1870s, being followed by Peter and Arthur Leyland, who tenanted the Hall during the 1880s and 1890s respectively. The house descended with the Wrightington Estate till about 1900, when it was purchased by the Earl of Derby.

The farm was subsequently tenanted by Mr. William Scarisbrick in 1902 and in 1939 Mrs. Annie Scarisbrick bought Martin Hall from Lord Derby. She was followed by her son Mr. Thomas Scarisbrick and his wife. Unfortunately the Hall was demolished in 1965 and a new farm house has been erected on the same site, which is owned by and occupied by Mr. Ledson, junr. of Merridale Farm.

Martin Hall was a brick building which possessed a low, long mullioned window (which contained the coat of Arms of the Breres family) and the roof was covered with Holland flags. The tall central building was the oldest part and at the gables rose to nearly 40 feet in height. It is interesting to note that during the 15th and 16th centuries a light is supposed to have been placed in one of the windows of this building to guide boats across the Mere and, thus, acted as a lighthouse. On the north side of this building which faced Martin Mere there were windows, but on the south side there was none.

Because of its isolated position Martin Hall was used by Roman Catholic priests and by rebels as a hiding place. It has been suggested that there was one room that was used as a chapel but there is no evidence to support this. Nevertheless, Robert Scarisbrick, who was concerned in the Pretender's Rebellion of 1715, concealed himself on numerous occasions over a period of two years in the attic at Martin Hall. In 1717 he gave himself up and, after spending eight months in Newgate prison, he was acquitted at the Lancashire Assizes. Later he was also suspected of taking part in smuggling activities in this area.

Today most of the old out-buildings are still in existence but they are in need of much repair. The barn roof has been renewed, but in former times contained 'crooks of oak timbers' which supported the roof. Only a small section of the moat remains and this is also fast disappearing. The total area of land belonging to the farm at the moment is 220 acres, compared with 242 acres or more in the mid-18th century. However, the land use has changed, because today it is a cattle farm, the stock being mainly beef cattle and the greater part of the land is used as pasture. In the 18th and 19th centuries and possibly earlier the farming was 'mixed' and no doubt they would have kept pigs and poultry for their own use as well.

In the 1840s the land-use was the following:

	Acres	
Land under wheat	70	
Land under oats	32	
Land under potatoes	18	
Land under beans	1	
Land under potatoes)		These items
Land under turnips)	13	*were recorded
Land under onions)		together.
Land under potatoes and onions	8	
Land under pasture	16	The remainder of the land
Land under clover meadow	43	consisted of pits, roads, wharf,
Land under meadow	17	orchard, the Hall and
Land under arable	7	Outbuildings.
Total	225	acres

Briars Hall (Briars Lane, Lathom)

As I have mentioned before the name of the Hall was taken from the Breres family who resided in this area of Lathom in the 1640s. However, the present house was built in 1745 and from that date was known as Briars or Briers Hall. The history of the Hall is uneventful and the first family that lived there appears to have been the Ashtons. Other members of the family occupied Burscough Hall up to the year 1890 and a branch of the family lived at Fairhurst Hall for a time.

Early in the 19th century Briars Hall had become a farm and as such was tenanted by Mr. William Swift about the year 1820. The owner of the Hall during the greater part of the 19th century was a Mr. Edward Riddle. Briars Mill was also under the control of Briars Hall, and I shall have more to say about the mill when I discuss the development of industry in the Burscough area. Subsequently in 1874 the Hall was occupied by a Mr. Unwin, who resided there until 1879. He was followed by Mrs. Shawe who stayed there for about 25 years. In 1894 Mr. Walter Esplin Mason occupied the Hall and in 1899 was followed by Mr. Henry E. Steel, who left about 1902. Mr. John Ainscough (of H. & R. Ainscough Ltd.) was next to occupy the Hall and under his direction certain modifications and additions to the Hall were made in 1910.

Briars Hall was, together with Mr. James Rigby's residence in Junction Lane, one of the first to receive electricity in this area. The electricity was supplied from H. & R. Ainscough's Flour Mills where electricity had been generated since 1885. The electricity was conveyed to both houses by means of overhead wires, and was direct current. The date of the installation of the electricity was about 1910; the rest of Burscough and Lathom did not receive electricity until 1932.

Under the Ainscoughs, Briars Hall became a stud farm for shire horses and they also had another stud farm at Risley near Warrington. In 1922 at the Worsley Agricultural Show, Messrs. H. & R. Ainscough of Burscough won the shire male championship with their four year-old stallion, Burscough Premier. Burscough Boadicea won the second prize in the mare or gelding class and Burscough Beautiful won the second prize yearling fillies. In 1927 at the Rufford Show, Burscough Ironcladia won the Fermor-Hesketh Challenge Cup. The Burscough Ironcladia by Burscough Premier was a massive brown three year-old filly. These and many more horses too numerous to mention were the pride and joy of those who looked after them; they were magnificent animals and a credit to the Ainscough family. However, times change and with the introduction of lorries and like they have now disappeared altogether, but are not forgotten.

The Hall was subsequently sold by the Ainscoughs in the 1960s to Mr. Alan Bolton, the son of William Bolton who, together with Mr. James Harwood in 1919, founded the Skelmersdale Shoe Factory. After the death of Alan Bolton, the Hall was sold and has since been converted into a residential hotel, which was opened on 12th February, 1970.

Blythe Hall and its associations
The history of Blythe Hall up to 1826

The history of Blythe Hall dates back to the 12th century. In 1189 Blythe was held by Geoffrey Travers whose son became known as 'Henry de Blythe'! The name Blythe was indicated in the charter of Henry when he released it to Prior Benedict (1229-1235), with all his claim to the mastfall in Tarlscough, Greetby and Burscough. The boundaries around Blythe were not fixed until comparatively recently and the boundary mentioned in the foundation charter of Burscough Priory (1189), which existed between Geoffrey Travers and Stephen the Bald (or Calvus), could have been situated somewhere north of the present Blythe Hall. However, Henry also gave what is now called the Ellerbrook to the Priory which he indicated ran through his 'Holme' to the Priory mill of the Bayes. The de Blythes lived here for nearly 200 years and they are mentioned in the various charters (especially Scarisbrick's charters); they subscribed for a stipend of the chaplain at Ormskirk in 1366 and Robert de Blythe's name appeared on the Poll Tax Roll of 1381. The estate passed into the Blackelache (or Blackledge) family in 1488 when Roger de Blythe's only daughter Margaret married John Blakelache of Lathom.

The history of the Blackledge family is varied and at this point a brief outline of their activities may be of interest. When Evan Blackledge died in July 1565 he desired to be buried in Ormskirk Church, 'on the north side of an overlay or stone under which Bishop Blackledge was buried. Evan Blackledge was Bishop of Sodor and Man from 1487 to 1510. In the Check Roll of servants of Lathom House, 13th May 1587, and in a similar roll at Knowsley dated 1st September 1587, the name of John Blackledge appears. This John Blackledge appears to have been the brother of Evan who died in 1565. John Blackledge succeeded his brother Evan and it has been suggested that John re-built or extended the house at Blythe, obtaining his materials from the Priory which had recently been destroyed. However, there is no documented evidence to support this. It is interesting the note the following which appears in the Inquisition Post Mortem, Duchy of Lanc's p. 85:

II Jac. I	Evanses Blackleach		
	Blythall in Lathom	Messuage Terr'	
(1604-5)	Burscough		& co. Lancaster.
	Aughton		

This appears to be the first indication that a Hall existed here called Blythe Hall and that it was there in 1604. Previous documents, charters and the like do not appear to make any reference to a Hall. Blythe Hall as it stood in 1921 was about half the size it is now (1970). The older part of the building is built of brick which has been covered with a fine layer of cement and dates from about the late Tudor period.

The Blackledges seem to have scattered themselves about the country in the past, perhaps because of the Catholic persecutions, but in the Burscough and Lathom area they appear to have compromised their religious leanings. However, be that as it may, in 1631 James Blackledge, late of London, gave £100 to Ormskirk church for distribution amongst the poor of Burscough, and a donation of £1 per annum out of lands in Lathom, in the possession of Mr. John Cave (a recorded tenant of Blythe Hall) for the vicar of Ormskirk. The receipt of William Dunn, the Puritan vicar, is recorded in 1650 for this donation.

Blythe Hall was sold by Evan Blackledge, described as 'of the parish of St. John, Wapping, gentleman and of Blythe Hall', to William Hill of Burscough in 1698. Mr. Hill held over 50 acres of land in Burscough of which 27 acres were freehold. It appears that he kept the estate in Burscough as well, because his son who succeeded him is mentioned in the court books of Burscough in the late 18th century as still holding the land. William Hill junr. appears in the list of justices of the peace for the West Derby Hundred who were concerned with the Lancashire Sessions Act of 1798. In 1761 William Hill jun. conveyed his estate to William Shaw and John Sephton and according to the *Victoria County Histories,* vol III, were probably trustees. However, this appears to have been the case for he was residing at the Hall until about the end of January or February 1800.

The Hall was purchased in 1800 by Thomas Langton but he does not appear to have lived there, for in 1823 the Hall was tenanted by Edward Clifton Esquire. In 1826 the Hall was sold by Thomas Langton to Edward Bootle-Wilbraham of Lathom House.

The Wilbraham Family

The manor of Wilbraham or, as it was called in the time of Henry I, Wilburgham, was in Cambridgeshire and the Wilburgham family had lived there some time before the 12th century. However, about that time some of the Wilburghams settled in Cheshire where they remained for a considerable time. At the end of the 15th century the Wilburghams altered the spelling of their name to Wilbraham. They were amongst the leading gentry of the county of Chester and at court one of them, a knight, was 'Master of The Queen's Revels'. In the time of Henry VIII, Mr. Ralph Wilbraham married a Lancashire lady named Miss Elizabeth Sandford, but the family at that period had no property in this county.

From that date onwards generation succeeded generation without any eventful period being recorded, until the marriage in 1755 of Mr. R. Wilbraham to Miss Mary Bootle, through whom he secured Lathom House and assumed the name of Bootle in addition to his own. His son Edward Bootle-Wilbraham succeeded to the estate in 1796 and in the same year became Member of Parliament for Westbury, and subsequently sat in the House of Commons for Newcastle-under-Lyme and for Dover. This Edward in 1826 purchased Blythe Hall. In 1828, during the ministry of the Duke of Wellington, Mr. Bootle-Wilbraham was created, by George IV, Baron Skelmersdale (peerage of the U.K.) from the manor of Skelmersdale, which descended with that of Lathom. His eldest son Richard Bootle-Wilbraham also took an active part in politics and was M.P. for South Lancashire, but he predeceased his father, dying in 1844. Edward his only son was just seven years old when his father died (he was born at Blythe Hall on 12th December 1837), but fortunately Lord Skelmersdale lived long enough to watch over his grandson's boyhood.

Edward Bootle-Wilbraham became the 2nd Baron Skelmersdale on the death of his grandfather in 1853. Edward was educated at Eton and at Christ Church College, Oxford, where he would have rowed for the University if the doctors had not vetoed his doing so. In 1858 he obtained his majority. There were festivities on a grand scale at Lathom House and at Blythe Hall on this occasion, to which the tenantry of Lord Skelmersdale were invited. It was in 1880 that Lord Skelmersdale, on the recommendation of the Earl of Beaconsfield K.G., was elevated to an earldom by Queen Victoria. On accepting this title, Lord Skelmersdale, thus, resurrected the title of the Lathoms, which had become extinct in the 15th century when a female heir married into the Derby family. Blythe Hall became the dower house of the Lathom family.

The Earls of Lathom at Blythe Hall

Edward Bootle-Wilbraham the first Earl of Lathom married Lady Alice Villiers, second daughter of the fourth Earl of Clarendon K.G. on August 16th 1860 by whom he had four sons and five daughters. Lady Alice died on November 23rd 1897 and the following incident which is often told in varying forms tells of how she met her death. It was Lady Alice's custom to ride in her little trap driven by two ponies to dine with those who had been hunting. On November 23rd 1897, the Earl was ill in bed, and the Countess was returning from the hunt. Some paper had been dropped by some huntsmen, and this caused the ponies to dart off in fury. They dashed into the trees, and the Countess was thrown and killed. As soon as the Earl heard the sad news, he rose from his bed, and had not the patience even to have his horse saddled, but rode bareback to the place of the accident. The tragic incident had occurred on what is now called Lady Alice's Drive. The Earl never recovered after the death of his wife and he died almost a year afterwards (Nov. 19th, 1898), his last request being to be taken the same way as his wife. The first earl was succeeded by his eldest son Edward George, who died at sea off Cape Vincent in 1909.

The 3rd and last Earl of Lathom, Edward William, was a boy of 14 when his father died. He succeeded to the Earldom in 1910, but does not appear to have lived at Lathom House for very long for it soon became a Remount Depot for the cavalry during the 1914-18 War. He became an officer in the Army, and spent his 21st birthday in the trenches in France. After the war he became aide-de-camp to Lord Willoughby, governor of India, and spent a year in India.

When he returned from India in 1920, he decided to give up Lathom House altogether and come to live at Blythe Hall. Dry rot had set in at Lathom. Besides, it was in too bad a condition to be redecorated after it had been used by the cavalry. It was suggested that it could be turned into a hotel, but the idea was subsequently turned down because it was considered to be too far off the beaten track. The earl then decided to knock down a part of it to provide stonework for the new wing he contemplated adding to Blythe Hall. Some of the material from the Hall was also used to repair certain of his properties in Lathom.

As I have mentioned before, the present Blythe Hall is nearly twice as large as it was in 1922. The late Tudor part of the building underwent extensive alteration and decoration in 1921, and at the same time the present main entrance hall was constructed. In order to make way for the staircase several rooms were removed. When this staircase was built, the pillars on the balustrade were made of cut glass and the surrounds of black ebony wood. The resultant effect of the many electric candles (those on the present chandeliers and others over the staircase) shining on the cut glass created an almost fairyland atmosphere.

The new wing was built at the same time. It included an indoor swimming bath, designed in the Greek style, with electric candles round the bath, and further lights on the bath-edges, so placed that no shadow ever fell on the water. This new wing also included the billiard room, and later the library. Now that the new library was built, the old one became the dining room.

A notable addition in the new wing was the private study of the earl (now the monastic choir). The beautifully panelled walls are well worth seeing. Before 1922 this carved woodwork formed the walls of the billiard room in Lathom House and were then painted green and gold (by some barbarian!). One can see on the panels the marks where this paint was scraped off when it was re-erected in 1921.

Another addition was the skittle alley (the present church) built in the grounds behind the Hall. Most of the interior fittings of this, including the special floor, came from the skittle alley of Lathom House. The floor, the wood for which had originally been imported from America, consists of planks about 4-5 inches wide placed on their sides and bolted through.

The cost for all the work done including the addition of the new wing was £36,000 and of this amount £10,000 was spent on the construction of the new swimming bath.

During the time alterations were being carried out at Blythe, the young earl lived at Crane's Hall, which lies on the road from Blythe to Lathom. In 1922 he moved into Blythe.

However, the Earl of Lathom's stay at his newly decorated mansion was fated to be a short one. After less than two years, possibly because of financial difficulties, he sold the estates of Lathom (which covered an area of 4,000 acres and which had a rent roll of about £10,000 per year), and went to live in London. Unfortunately he suffered from tuberculosis (one lung had been removed and the other was diseased); he was only in his twenties. In London he opened an antique shop in a street off Grosvenor Square, almost opposite Claridges. He lived in flats at different times in Portland Place, Park Lane and Mount Street. In 1927 he married Maria Xenia, daughter of E.W. Tunzleman, of Singapore (formerly wife of Ronald William Merison, from whom she obtained a divorce in 1921), and in 1930 he died at the age of 35 years and was cremated at Golders Green.

The third Earl of Lathom was very interested in the theatre, a passion he inherited from his mother. He entertained his friends of the theatre and high society at Blythe, amongst whom were the following: Ivor Novello, Noel Coward, designer Oliver Messel, Gladys Cooper, Marie Tempest, Mrs. Patrick Campbell and many others.

Many stories are told of the high life at Blythe Hall under the Lathoms. However, on the word of some former employees, I can say that it is not true that special trains were hired to bring actors and actresses from London to Blythe to perform in plays the 3rd Earl had written. It does appear that some of the plays of Ned Lathom, as he was called, were so immoral that the censor would not allow them to be put on the London stage. So Ned put them on at the Lathom Club (in the grounds of Lathom House), not at Blythe Hall. As to the transport of these actors, they came from London by ordinary service trains to Lime Street Station, Liverpool, where they were met by a few Rolls Royces and brought to Lathom. Some of them would stay at Blythe Hall, and some stayed at the Adelphi Hotel, Liverpool.

After the Lathoms: St. Gabriels's College.

After the departure of the 3rd Earl in 1924 Blythe Hall remained vacant for five years. The greater part of the estate was sold to Mr. Debenham, who was in the banking business. Mr. Debenham also bought Blythe Hall and merely held on to it until he could find a buyer. In 1930 it was bought by a cotton merchant, Mr. Taylor, who lived here with his wife and children (two sons and a daughter). It was the Taylors who removed the cut glass pillars and ebony surrounds from the balustrade in the Hall and replaced them by the present composition. The glass had been broken too easily (according to Mr. Cox). The long splendid felted damask-covered curtains (about 16 feet long), originally a blue green, were bought by the Taylors, but were removed in 1950 because they had decayed. After about a year the Taylors decided to move and went to live at the Southport Hydro until they could find a buyer for the Hall. After nearly 18 months they sold Blythe Hall to the Passionist Fathers (who were represented in the sale by Fathers Brendan, Keegan and Leo Gribben).

On February 27th 1933 Archbishop Downey solemnly opened Blythe Hall as a College for boys who wished to become Passionist priests.

During the 1939-45 war the outhouses of Blythe Hall were used to house homeless families who had been benefactors of the Order (per Brother Hilarion McGuness) and who had been blitzed in their homes in Liverpool. These outhouses were eventually turned into classrooms. In 1956 they were recognised by the Ministry of Education as efficient. Unfortunately, the expenses of maintaining such a large and elaborate complex of buildings proved to be too much for the Fathers, and in 1973 the Hall was sold for over £80,000 to Mr. David Whelan, the local supermarket owner and former football star.

Lathom House

For several centuries the manor of Lathom was in the possession of the Lathom family, but in the time of Henry IV (1399-1413) it passed to the Stanley family. At this time there is no evidence to suggest that a castle was then on the estate, but some time before 1495 Thomas Stanley, first Earl of Derby, pulled down the old manorial hall, and built what was afterwards known as Lathom House, but which to all intents and purposes was a fortified castle. The second wife of this Earl of Derby was the mother of Henry VII, who in 1495 visited her at Lathom. Seacome describes Lathom 'as surrounded with a wall 6 feet thick upon which were 9 towers, in each of which were 6 pieces of ordnance that plaid three one way and three the other. Outside the wall was a moat 8 yards wide; inside there was a high tower called the Eagle Tower, also two other towers'.

The siege of Lathom has been so often told that I think it only necessary to say that after a prolonged and gallant resistance, on 9th December, 1645, it was surrendered to the parliamentary forces, who straight away razed to the ground the walls and towers, leaving only a few buildings used for domestic purposes. Subsequently a house was built close to where the castle had stood.

After the Civil War the Derby family left Lathom and went to live at Knowsley Park, near Liverpool. However, after the restoration of the Stuarts, Lathom was handed back to the Derby family. The Derbys probably lived here for a short while in the latter part of the 17th century but in 1714 the estate was

Burscough Hall, Chapel Lane, Lathom.

Martin Hall, before it was demolished. The coat of arms of the Breres family was situated in the second window from the right, whilst the initials were in the eleventh from the right, looking from outside.

Another view of Martin Hall before it was demolished.

Briars Hall as it appeared in 1969.

*Blythe Hall, famous home of the Earls of Lathom until the departure of the third Earl in 1924.
In 1933 it was opened by Archbishop Downey as a college for boys who wished to become Passionist
priests.*

Edward William Bootle-Wilbraham, Third Earl of Lathom and Fourth Baron Skelmersdale. In 1920 he removed from Lathom House to Blythe Hall. Stories abound about the high life there under the Lathoms.

The splendid swimming bath at Blythe Hall.

Lathom House in about 1910. The original Lathom House, besieged and brilliantly defended during the Civil Wars, was razed and we are not even certain of its exact location, so completely has it disappeared.

The Remount Depot, Lathom Park. It was calculated that during the Great War over quarter a million horses and mules passed through the depot. In 1919 the complement of staff was 27 officers and 6,688 NCOs and men.

transferred by marriage to Lord Ashburnum who subsequently sold it to Henry Furnese. In 1724 the estate became the property of Sir Thomas Bootle of Melling who had Lathom House built according to the design of Giacomo Leoni. It was begun about 1725 and finished in 1730. Subsequently improvements were made to the house. There were two large service wings of two storeys high, only one of which still survives.

The Remount Depot

Soon after the 1914-18 war broke out the Third Earl of Lathom, through his trustees, offered his spacious park and Lathom House to the Government for the conversion into a remount depot. In a remarkably short time, through the agency of hundreds of workmen, stables and the necessary buildings for the training of horses were erected. Horses came here to be trained for the army from all the parts of the world, and when the Armistice was signed it was calculated that over a quarter of million horses and mules had passed through the depot. The total complement of staff in 1919 was 27 officers and 6,688 N.C.O.s and men.

Unfortunately, many of the records of the Lathom family, together with some valuable information on the surrounding district, which would have helped to fill some of the gaps in the history of this area, were accidentally destroyed by being fed to the furnaces of Blaguegate Colliery in 1925.

Ancient crosses

Many ancient crosses were found in Burscough. On the 1845 Ordnance Survey map no fewer than 18 crosses or their remains were found within a radius of four miles, which included Scarisbrick, Ormskirk and Halsall. The reason why there were so many is not known and the charters of Burscough Priory only seem to refer to crosses cut on trees.

The charters which were preserved at Scarisbrick Hall help to date the crosses because they are mentioned in deeds of the 13th and 14th centuries.

Whether these crosses were erected to mark lands prior to the deeds or whether their origin was devotional is uncertain. Nevertheless when all England was Catholic, the customs which prevailed would be similar to those practices on the Continent at the present time with regard to these crosses, i.e. they use them for devotional purposes. The Crusades also gave impetus to the erection of crosses.

It is possible that the crosses were erected for more than one purpose e.g. the crosses from Scarisbrick Park and Ormskirk church to Burscough Priory could have been placed there as resting places for funeral processions who had the rights at both places of burial, or they may have been placed there purely for devotional purposes only.

During the rise of Protestantism, many of these crosses were destroyed. It is reported that about 120 years ago Roman Catholic funeral processions stopped whenever these crosses or their bases were to be found. The following crosses were erected at Burscough.

Manor House Cross: stood between Lathom and Martin.

Pippin Street Cross: the last cross before reaching Burscough Priory stood near the meeting of lanes with the high road between Ormskirk and Preston. The lanes are named Lord's Gate, Pippin Street and Abbey Lane.

Burscough Priory Cross: to the south of the Priory — only the pedestal remains.

Bath Wood Cross: near the boundary of Burscough and Lathom.

Hobcross: in a north-easterly direction from the Priory — only the pedestal now remains.

Holy wells

These holy wells were in many instances natural springs and in many cases the water was of a chalybeate nature (containing iron) and was used in the cure of rheumatism, inflamed eyes and other diseases. One existed in Lathom in the area now called 'Spa Roughs' and was called Maudlin Well. In 1670, Dr. Borlase of London published a small book about the well. The well was probably dedicated to Mary Magdalene by the monks of Burscough Priory. The well was visited by William Blundell in 1672 and by Nicholas Blundell in 1703. William Blundell claimed that he owed his life to these waters. As far as can be ascertained, the water was similar to that found at Harrogate. However, when mining operations began in the 19th century at Skelmersdale, the waters disappeared.

Placenames of Burscough district

Most of the placenames in the Burscough area are topographical in origin — that is, they refer to physical features and landmarks of the ancient landscape. Many include Old Norse elements, reflecting the extensive Scandinavian settlements in South Lancashire during the 9th and 10th centuries. The meanings of some of the names are unclear or ambiguous, while others are easily interpreted: the list below gives such information as can reliably be accepted.

ON = Old Norse   OE = Old English   OW = Old Welsh

Burscough: 'Wood by the burg': the element 'burg, burug, burig' is OE and meant a fortified place or defended place but could also have a much wider meaning as 'village' or settlement. There is as yet no evidence that there was any form of defended site in the area of the present village. The second part of the name is from the ON 'skogr' (a wood) or the closely related OE 'sceaga', which has the same meaning. The name therefore seems to combine OE and ON elements, which reflects the intermingling of the Norse and Saxon cultures in this area in the two centuries before the Norman Conquest.

Tarlscough: The second element is the same as that found in Burscough. The first is an ON personal name, Thorvaldr, so that the full meaning is 'the wood of Thorvaldr'.

Marsh Moss, Moss Nook, Warpers Moss: All these names relate to the extensive marshes and mosses in the district, originally fringing the shores of Martin Mere. They use the same elements as the modern dialect words, and have been unchanged for many centuries.

Crabtree: This is a simple descriptive name meaning 'the place where the crab-apple tree grows' or even more directly 'the crab-apple tree'.

Lathom: 'at the barns'. The name was recorded as *Lathum* in 1201, and is from the ON word *hlava,* barn.

Langley: OE meaning 'long meadow'.

Martin: OE meaning 'town (i.e. settlement) by the mere (lake),

Sheep Cote Hill: cote is from the same root as cottage and cot, and originally meant simply 'a shelter', so the name is from the OE 'a shelter for sheep'.

Blythe: from the OE for gentle, merry, cheerful. In this sense it probably means gentle, and refers to a stream, so 'gently-flowing stream' is perhaps intended.

Greetby Hill: The name is related to the OE *greote* meaning gravel, and so perhaps indicates a gravelly hill.

Briers Brook: from 'braer, brer' (OE) meaning briers and brambles, so the name probably means simply a brook overhung with brambles'.

Ellerbrook: 'the stream that runs by the elder trees' from OE *eller, ellern* elder tree.

Hoscar Moss: 1332 *Horskar,* 'horse swamp' from OE *hors* and ON *kjarr.*

These placenames are those given for Burscough and district on the Ordnance Survey first edition 6″ map (1845).

Farm names

Many of the farms in this district take their names from the original owners e.g. Rawlinson's Farm, Burscough Town, now occupied by William Dutton Junr.; the original owners were the Rawlinsons who had held the farm from the 18th century until 1893 when the farm was taken over by William Pepper and subsequently by Mr. William Dutton, senior. Other farms have associated their names with the surrounding country, such as Yew Tree and Little Yew Tree, Merridale, Wood House, Marsh Moss House, The Pear Tree and many more. Other farms in the Burscough and Lathom area such as the following have taken their names mainly from the original owners: Dobson's, Richard's, Robinson's, Jump's, Gobin's, Nelson's, Cropper's, Langley's, Haydock's, Rutter's etc., and in some instances subsequent owners have changed the original name and adopted their own on several occasions, e.g. Colburnes to Nelsons.

The Churches of Burscough

The Roman Catholic Church

THE 'old religion' survived the upheavals of the Reformation and its aftermath and continued to flourish in Lancashire despite considerable although intermittent persecution over the following two centuries. Indeed, recent research has suggested that in large parts of the county the Protestant faith maintained only a tenuous supremacy, and that substantial proportions of the population remained Catholic. It has always been known that many of the gentry families of Lancashire were either openly or secretly Catholic but it is now realised that a similar adherence was found among the the ordinary people, many of whom paid only lip service to the new faith.

In the Burscough district, several prominent families remained Catholic and allowed their houses to be used for Catholic worship. There are numerous references to the presence in the area of Catholic priests during the 16th and 17th centuries, a not inconsiderable number of them being sons of South Lancashire gentry families who had gone to Rome to be ordained and had then come back as missionaries.

Undoubtedly many Catholics were imprisoned, fined or in other ways made to suffer for their faith: in 1590, for example, over 900 people were indicted for recusancy in Lancashire alone. Nevertheless, the numbers of Catholics remained remarkably constant and Lancashire continued to be the most Catholic county in England. In the Burscough area it seems that the authorities, except on rare occasions when national anti-Catholic activity was greatest, turned a blind eye to the Catholic worship at houses such as Burscough Hall and tolerated what was technically illegal.

From time to time an attempt was made to enforce the laws on recusancy and fines were imposed for non-attendance at the parish churches. In 1641 no fewer than 52 people were fined at the Ormskirk quarter sessions from Burscough alone for this offence: this represented more than 5 per cent of the total for the West Derby Hundred. The names of those fined from Burscough are as follows:

Marie Maudesley widow, Henry Maudesley, her son, Elizabeth Boydwell widow, Gilbert Gill, Edward Kilshaw & Cicily his wife, Robte Withington & his wife, John Withington & Raph Withington their sons, Gabrill Walker and his wife, Henry Walker their son, Willm Cropper & Elizabeth his wife, Alice and Richard Claypane, Thomas Whytstone & Elizabeth his wife, Thomas Alker, Peeter Vause & Margaret his wife, Jane Vause widow, Adam Vause and his wife, Elizabeth and her husband Roger Lea, Ann Carr widow, George Walker and Dorathy his wife, John Langley, John Flecher, James Burscough and his wife, Ann and Thomas Lea, John Rannet and his wife, Cuthbert Halsall, James Halsall his son, Richard Gill, Thomas Fryth and Ann, his wife, Richard Lathom and his wife and Richard Allerton Junior and Willm Kilshaw Ju. & Ellin his wife.

A close watch was kept on the Catholics during the 17th and 18th centuries in this area and it is interesting to note the following, which appears from time to time in the churchwarden's accounts of the Ormskirk parish church:

'For taking a list of all the 'Papists' in Burscough.'

In 1767 the cost incurred in making up this list was 2 shillings. It appears as though this was a common practice in this area of Lancashire and possibly elsewhere, for in the churchwarden's accounts of the parish of Aughton the following was recorded in 1768:

'To taking the names of 'Papists'...............................4s-0d.'

From the year 1700 till the formation of the present chapel and presbytery, which were built between 1815-1819, services were held in the Mission of the Burscough Hall. This is doubted by some authorities, because of the rebellions of 1715 and 1745 in which Catholic persecution was widespread, and the priest would have required a more secret hiding place than the one quoted above. Nevertheless services were held here from time to time during this period and even in the 17th century Burscough Hall had become a centre to which the priests came secretly to meet the Catholics of the district.

The first priest who is known to have resided regularly at the Burscough Hall was the Rev. James Gorsuch. I have mentioned Father Gorsuch before and stated that he belonged to an old Scarisbrick family of Gorsuch Hall. He studied and was ordained priest at the English College of Douai in France. In 1705 he came to England and remained at Burscough for some years. The tenant of the Burscough Hall in 1712 was Thomas Gorsuch, his brother.

'Aug 22 1714, I came from Preston to the Hall, at Boscow, where Pat Gorsuch celebrated.' (Blundell's *Diary)*

In a 'iist of Papists who registered their estates and the respective values thereof in Lancashire,' in 1714, one of the recusants is 'Richard Burscough £10.' (Baines *Lancs* V. 4 p766).

'Sept 8, 1726, I left Coz Butler at Rufford and came to Pat Gorsuch at the Hall of Boscow, but being too late I staid but a short while and then came through Ormeschurch home.' (Blundell's *Diary)*

Pat was Squire Blundell's contraction for 'pater' — father. The Rev. Gorsuch was of the family seated at Gorsuch Hall, midway between Halsall and Scarisbrick. The Gorsuches were a branch of the Scarisbrick family, 'Adam de Gosefordisiche, sone of Sir Walter de Scaresbrecke being alive in 1189'. Gorsuch Hall was burnt down about 1816 and the family in all old deeds is included amongst the 'lesser gentry'. In 1728 the Rev. Father Gorsuch attended Bishop Williams at Mrs. Ann Woofalls, Moor Hall, Aughton, when 100 people were confirmed in the Roman Catholic faith. *(Lydiate Hall,* p312).

The Rev. Richard Walmsley of Ribchester succeeded Father Gorsuch. He was educated at Valladolid and ordained for the English Mission in 1733 and died before 1752, probably at Burscough. Rev. James Brown succeeded Father Walmsley. He came from Douai to Crathorne in Yorkshire before coming to Burscough, where he remained for many years. When Bishop Mathew Gibson confirmed at Burscough in 1754 Father Brown was still there. In 1759 he prepared and made structural changes in the chapel situated in the Hall at a cost of £80, leaving it much as it is today.

Father Henry Kellet is the next priest mentioned. He was educated and ordained at Valladolid and is recorded as the priest at Burscough in 1793 when

Bishop William Gibson visited the place and confirmed 48 people. Father Kellet died in 1808 at Burscough, but we have no knowledge of his grave.

The earliest baptismal records extant are from the time of Father Kellet, viz. from February 4th 1793 to October 15th 1803. He died at Burscough on August 14th 1808, therefore, it appears that the registers for more than 5 years are missing.

It appears that the Rev. James Dennett of Aughton officiated here for a short while before the Rev. William Coghlan, for the baptismal register begins in January 22nd 1809, the entries being those of the Rev. James Dennett.

After the death of Rev. Henry Kellet the records tell us nothing until the arrival of the Rev. Richard Coghlan, and his first baptismal entry in August 1810. He was the son of the well-known Catholic printer and publisher of London, James Peter Coghlan, who published several books of Bishop Challoner.

About this time it seems that Burscough Hall and its land came into the possession of the diocese after being leased to others for so many years, but just how it became diocesan property is not clear. In 1778 and in 1791 two Acts were passed in Parliament which granted some measure of recognition to Catholics and allowed them for the first time since the Reformation to build churches of a very modest nature. By virtue of this and also because the Burscough Hall property had at last come into diocesan keeping, Father Coghlan decided to build a church alongside the old Burscough Hall. Therefore, the present church and presbytery near the old hall were built by Father Richard Coghlan between 1815-1819, he himself giving about a third of the total cost, £1,520. Its retiring position and plain design are a witness to the difficulties under which Catholics of those days lived. Nevertheless, the congregation began to grow until its number when Bishop Penswick confirmed there in 1821 was about 400.

Father Coghlan died at Burscough in July 1836 and was buried there. Father T. Anderton, an uncle of the late Dean Cooke who opened the 'Holy Family Mission' in Southport, was his successor, retiring in 1849 to a church in the Fylde. On the barn opposite the church above the garner steps a small tablet bears the following inscription:

'T Rev. I. A. 1838'

This probably indicates the date of erection of part of the barn which either belonged to Father Anderton or was dedicated by him. He was succeeded by the Rev. Richard Hodgson who from 1850 to 1871 did great work. He built the school and teacher's house, erected the gallery in the church and paid off the debts which had troubled the parish for so long. In 1871 Father Hodgson left Burscough and went to Carlisle where he became canon of the Carlisle Roman Catholic Cathedral, and for a time was chaplain to Colonel Townley. He was a member of the Carlisle School Board, the last meeting of which was held in his house. On February 13th 1879, he died at the age of 80 and his remains were intered at Burscough Hall.

Canon R. Hodgson was succeeded by Canon James Fisher in 1871, and in 1877 was succeeded by the Rev. John Kelly, who only remained here for a little less than 12 months. In 1878 the Rev. John Daly was appointed and he remained here until 1884.

In 1885 the Rev. James Eager took up his duties here. He was educated at Ampleforth College, later passing on to Ushaw, Durham, after which he commenced his ministry in the Liverpool Diocese. He ministered at St. Vincent's Church, Liverpool, for a period of almost 3 years, and his good work there made it difficult to part with him when he was called to assist the late Rt. Rev. Mgr. Carr in the good work which was being carried out at Formby. He had a short stay at Lea, near Preston, before coming to take over the rectorship of St. John's, Burscough Hall. St. John's, Burscough Hall, was made a rectory in 1856 and the cemetery attached was consecrated in 1890.

During Father Eager's ministry the church and schools themselves underwent little ateration, but still both bore indications of his labours. The church was reseated, and a magnificent new altar rail was erected through his efforts, whilst the organ too did not escape his attention, for it was thoroughly renovated and improved at his instigation. When Father Eager took over the parish there was a debt on the schools, but this he soon cleared off and one marked feature of his life in Burscough had been his unceasing labours in the interests, welfare and education of the parish. In this work he was ably supported by the late headmistress, Miss Connor who, by a remarkable coincidence, came to the parish a few months after Father Eager but died only a week before him. Father Eager by virtue of his being rector was a member of the Ormskirk Education sub-committee, where his educational inclinations found an outlet, and as a consequence he rendered invaluable assistance. He was also a member of the Liverpool Athenaeum library, and was one of the first, if not the first, to own and drive a motor car in Burscough, according to Father Clayton the present priest. Father Eager was buried at Burscough.

Burscough Roman Catholic Priests

1712-1740?	Rev. James Gorsuch. (His brother was tenant of the farm).
1740-1752	Rev. Richard Walmsley
1752-1775?	Rev. James Brown
1775-1808	Rev. Henry Kellet
1809-1836	Rev. Richard Coghlan
1836-1849	Rev. J. Anderton (Initials on Barn J.A.)
1850-1871	Canon Richard Hodgson
1871-1877	Canon James Fisher
1877-1878	Rev. John Kelly
1878-1884	Rev. John Daly
1885-1914	Rev. James Eager
1914-1925	Rev. Joseph Barker
1925-1940	Rev. Patrick Ryan
1940-1950	Rev. Peter Walsh
1950-1958	Rev. Edward Formby
1958-1960	Rev. Charles Winstanley
1960-1961	Rev. James O'Reilly
1961	Rev. F. Clayton

Burscough St. John's Parish Church

Introduction

This church is known as a Waterloo or Million Church and is also sometimes referred to as a Commissioners Church. The various names which have been attached to these churches arise from the fact that they are memorial churches and were named after the Battle of Waterloo (1815) which brought the Peninsular War (1792-1815) to a conclusion. In the preamble of the 1818 Act (The first Church Building Act), it referred to the need to provide free accommodation for the poor; and its first clause set aside one million pounds in Exchequer bills bearing two per cent interest which could be drawn upon by the Commissioners whom the King empowered to appoint for executing the Act. Hence the adoption of the names of 'Million' and 'Commissioners' churches. The grant was given in two parts. The reasoning behind the grants was summed up by the *Quarterly Review* in 1820: 'The edifices which we have erected are manufactures and prisons, the former producing tenants for the latter . . . The only way of making the people good subjects is by making them good Christians.'

In Lancashire at this time the population was growing at an alarming rate and because of this more churches were provided there than anywhere else. The number of churches built before 1830 in Lancashire was 19 and between 1830 and 1856 was 62, these varying in size and cost from the smallest, at Bretherton, which cost £1,058 and provided accommodation for 400 (built 1839-40), to the largest, Foster's St. Martin in Liverpool (built 1825-28 and now demolished) costing £19,948 and providing accommodation for 1,910. Out of the 19 churches built out of the first grant, only 6 were in North Lancashire. However, in the second grant the tables were reversed and North Lancashire received a larger grant than South Lancashire. These churches have often been referred to as 'dreary God-boxes', largely due to their uniformity, being characterised by their tall side windows, usually of lancets or with minimum perp motifs and by aisled interiors and usually containing three galleries. The choice of style was partly influenced by geography and the choice of architect usually depended on the local committee; therefore, a local architect may have been given preference or in some cases a famous London practitioner might have been employed to become the architect for a remote village. During the second grant to Lancashire, the Gothic structures predominated.

Burscough parish church was built with the aid of the second parliamentary grant (½ Million) which was termed the 'Half Million Era'. It is sometimes said locally that there was a parish church in Burscough before the one quoted above, but this is not true. The assumption is based upon references to some old hand-written sign boards which used to be kept at the old Lordsgate Township School, where from time to time in days gone by the Christmas Doles were paid out to the poor of Burscough. Sharrocks Charity of 1730 is the one from which the assumption is drawn and the following quote is taken from one of the sign boards in question:

> 1730 'Thomas Sharrock, late of this town the sum of Fifty-two pounds, the interest to be laid out in bread and to be distributed at the Parish Church every Sunday, of twelve Pence each day throughout the year, amongst the poor of the town, who attend divine service.' £52-0-0d.

The parish church referred to is that of Ormskirk, not Burscough, the following quote from the *Charity Commissioners Report* of 1828, being my evidence:

> 'Thomas Sharrock, by his will, bearing the date 19th June 1729, and proved at Chester, bequeathed to the poor of Burscough, that should attend divine service

at the parish church of Ormskirk, £52 the interest to be laid out in bread for the said poor, and be distributed weekly at the aforesaid parish church, at the discretion of the vicar or curate, and churchwardens.'

'In respect of this charity, six two-penny loaves are placed in Ormskirk Church every Sunday, which are given away by the churchwardens at the church, to poor persons of Burscough.'

The church

As I have said before, since the dissolution of the monasteries there was no place of worship for Protestants until 1832, when the present church was opened at Burscough Bridge. This church was originally built as a chapel of ease (an extra church in a large parish i.e. the parish of Ormskirk), and was mentioned by Baines in 1824, that arrangements were being made for the erection of a chapel of ease at Burscough Bridge.

The land for the church and burial ground at Burscough Bridge was gratuitously conveyed to the Church Building Commissioners by Lord Skelmersdale in about September 1829. The church was built of stone brought from Parbold (probably William Taylor's quarry) and the farmers of the parish voluntarily undertook to do all the carting. I also believe, although I have no documented evidence, that the stone from Parbold could also have been conveyed via the canal.

The building was started in 1829 and completed in 1832. There is no record of how many men were employed in the building of the church, but on making comparisons with churches of a similar size and structure, there would be from about 30 to 40 men employed. Initially the men employed would be mostly masons and sawyers, a few bricklayers and labourers, and as the work progressed, the pattern would change to masons, plasterers, joiners and a few labourers. The contractor for the work was John Twist and the architect was Daniel Stewart. The architect was required to enter into a bond that his estimate would not be exceeded, under a 15% penalty. Daniel Stewart came from Liverpool and later went into partnership with J. A. Picton. They were the architects of St. Matthias's Church, Liverpool, built between 1832-3 in the Ionic style, but unfortunately because of the construction of the Lancashire and Yorkshire railway in 1848, the church was taken down and a new church was built at the Railway Company's expense, with the Commissioners approval, in the twelfth-century Gothic style by A. H. Holme. Burscough Bridge parish church of St. John the Baptist and St. Matthias's Liverpool were the only churches built by Daniel Stewart for the Church Commissioners.

On the Church Building Commissioners' file, there is a return which states as follows:

'the body of the church and the belfry was built of tooled ashlers (hewn stones used for facing of walls) backed with random stone with cornice and moulded base. Iron beams were used to support the belfry and cast iron sash sheets, and the aisles were floored with Dantzic flooring boards, the roof was covered with blue Bangor slates, and the pulpit and desk were made of Dantzic oak and the pews of Baltic firm.'

No mention is made of who supplied the bell, but it was customary at this time with all these churches that a piece of cannon from a battlefield (Waterloo, 1815) would be welded onto the bell.

Burscough parish church actually stands in Lathom, for it is just over the boundary, lying well back from Liverpool Road. When it was first erected there, of course, there was no railway cutting and travellers by road through Burscough then had a clear view of the somewhat plain and quaint edifice in its neat churchyard. Now, the railway line to Southport marches close to the church, and the edifice is partly concealed and sheltered by the road bridge which here crosses the railway lines. From the elevation of the bridge the church has a trim squat look, but in reality it is a massive edifice which is robbed of its impressiveness through lack of a proper tower.

It is built of stone and is styled in the Gothic fashion; the facade has four polygonal buttresses carrying uncouth embattled pinnacles. There is also a bell-turret and two light windows with incorrect perp tracery. This church is very typical of the period and has most of the characteristics which are attributed to the 'Million' churches, including the three galleries which has been preserved. Over the years the stones have become blackened through smoke and other forms of pollution, which have not enhanced its character. This church cost £3,440 and the grant from the Church Commissioners was £3,040, the remainder of the money being raised by public subscription.

The Consecration and subsequent developments

The church is dedicated to St. John the Baptist and on 28th September 1832, Dr. John Bird Sumner, Bishop of Chester, in which Diocese the parish of Ormskirk then was, consecrated the church and the burial ground.

The first officiating minister was the Rev. John Bowman who was supplied by the vicar of Ormskirk and remained here until 1840. Very little is known about him, for the entries in the *Bishop's Act Book* only state the following:

'the commission to qualify issued to the Rector of Aughton and the licence to qualify to the stipendiary curacy on the nomination of the Vicar of Ormskirk.'

They give no further information about him. He is not listed in the surviving ordination papers and his nomination which might have given further particulars was destroyed along with other papers during enemy action in World War II. However, I do know that he was at Ormskirk parish church before coming to Burscough and that initially he met with much opposition in this parish. When John Bowman commenced his ministry in Burscough he made his way to church on Sundays amidst scoffs and insults of the grossest kind and on leaving the church on many occasions had to take a circuitous path to avoid a repetition of the same insults. On Sundays, no respectable female, if she was alone, could enter the churchyard gates without exposing herself to ribaldry and language of the grossest profanity. Even when the Rev. W. Wannop first came to Burscough he too confirmed that the latter state of affairs existed, together with, as he aptly described it, 'streams of drunkards issued from their haunts of debauchery on the Sabbath morning, just as the worshippers were going to the house of prayer.'

The Rev. William Wannop

The Rev. John Bowman was succeeded by the Rev. William Wannop, who became the first vicar when the parish was formed in 1849. The Rev. W. Wannop

The Rev. W. Wannop BA, JP, one of the central figures in 19th-century Burscough. Liberally minded and highly respected, he was at or near the centre of most of the main development and improvement schemes afoot during his incumbency at St. John's.

was the second son of Arthur Wannop of Hillside, near Walton, Cumberland.

In 1835 Mr. Wannop was appointed to the curacy of Ormskirk. Mr. Wannop in 1840 entered on his incumbency of Burscough and preached his first sermon on the first Sunday in May of that year. He was to remain here for 50 years, during which time the parish of Burscough enjoyed advantages similar to those conferred upon Ormskirk.

From his appointment he took an active interest in all that pertained to the welfare of his parish and his parishioners, and was firmly attached to the Church of England. However, Mr. Wannop was liberally minded towards those who differed from the Church of England and during his stay here was very highly respected by the other denominations. Mr. Wannop was an ardent devotee to the Evangelical School of the Church of England and he deprecated any departure from the principles of the Reformation. He adhered to wearing the gown in the pulpit and was a supporter, amongst other societies, of the Society for Promoting Christianity amongst the Jews, the British and Foreign Bible Society, the Church Missionary Society and the Moravian Missionary Society.

The Rev. William Wannop interested himself in many things connected with the parish of Burscough and was responsible for laying the foundations of numerous societies, clubs and the like, some of which are still here today. He was a justice of the peace for the county, having been placed on the committee in 1858 and was senior trustee of the Ormskirk Savings Bank and one of the vice-presidents of the Ormskirk Dispensary. He was the means by which an adult Friendly Society was formed, which was very useful for a great number of years; the Clothing Club and Burial Club were also developed by him. He was the first chairman of the Burscough Bridge Penny Savings Bank in 1860 and was on the first committee of the Ormskirk and Southport Schoolmasters' Association, which was established on June 15th 1854.

The vicarage

Mr. Wannop saw many changes in St. John's parish church during his pastorate. When he first came to live at Burscough in 1840 there was no parsonage and, therefore, Mr. Wannop occupied the house of his predecessor which was situated on the corner of Liverpool Road and Square Lane (called 'The Square'). The same house was in later years tenanted by Mr. Studdart, a former headmaster of the old Lordsgate Township School. (Recently the outside walls of the house have been painted purple). During 1849 the present vicarage house was built on what was called the 'Little Field', an area of just over 1 acre. The Earl of Derby gave the land; previously it had been leased to Jane Jones, who let the land to Samuel Spencer, who was a farmer. The parsonage house was completed in 1850 at a cost of £1,492 and the architect was Mr. Sydney Smirke.

The church (alterations and additions)

The west gallery of the church was erected soon after the church was opened, but the side galleries were not erected until September 1857. The side galleries were erected by Mr. Peet of Ormskirk at a cost of £400, of which sum £150 was given by the Earl of Derby, £150 by the Church Societies, £70 by the Lancashire and Yorkshire Railway Company for land taken from the churchyard and the remaining balance by the vicar and his friends. The congregation were not appealed to for assistance. These new galleries provided accommodation for about an additional 300 persons. The accommodation of the church originally was 749 pews, of which 425 were free; therefore, with the addition of the new galleries, this had risen to 1,049.

The stipend for the ministry was provided by the appropriation of two-thirds of the pews, the rents of which were fixed by the Ecclesiastical Commissioners. The galleries had been erected firstly because of the increase in the population of Burscough, and secondly, because of the great work that Mr. Wannop was doing at the time, both socially and spiritually, and in consequence his church was filled beyond capacity. As I have mentioned before, the church was first built as a chapel of ease to Ormskirk, but in 1849 a district was assigned to it, and in the year 1857, under Lord Blandford's Act, the district attached to St. John's church became a separate and distinct parish for ecclesiastical purposes. In 1868 the incumbency became a vicarage.

The first organ

Before the organ was installed, music for the services was supplied by a string band of musicians who occupied the west gallery. During this time the musicians and choir consisted mainly of the Harriot family from Ormskirk. The Harriot family were also musicians and amateur actors and in the latter capacity, together with other local celebrities of the day, they established a reputation for histrionic powers.

On 18th September 1859 a new organ was installed in St. John's church in the west gallery by Mr. Postill of York, and Mr. Watt's organist at the parish church of Ormskirk presided. The expenses for the building and fitting-up of the organ amounted to £200, the greater part of which had already been raised by public subscription at the time it was installed. This same organ underwent extensive repairs in 1875, the work being undertaken by Messrs. Rushworth of Liverpool. The pedals were lowered and the swell organ enlarged by the addition of bottom octave of principal and stopped diapason, from tenor C. to C.C. It was also thoroughly cleaned and tuned. In addition to the above, the bottom octave of the cornopean was put in at a cost of £10, this being a gift of the vicar and his family. The contract for the whole was £50, forty of which was given by the congregation.

The burial ground

The burial ground was first consecrated in 1832 by the Bishop of Chester, Dr. John Bird Sumner. During Mr. Wannop's time the burial ground was enlarged. The additional land was given by Lord Skelmersdale. A stone wall topped by large stones and surmounted by iron railings was put round a large portion of the burial ground; the stone work being done by Mr. Wells of Burscough and the railings by Messrs. Owen and Sons, Ormskirk. The cost was nearly £300 which had been raised by voluntary contributions from the parishioners. The portion of the churchyard fence which remained incomplete in 1869 was finished in 1877 by Messrs Blaycock and Flaherty at a cost of nearly £80. The whole of the churchyard in 1877 was completely surrounded by an iron fence. The greater part of the stone wall exists to this day, portions being removed when the churchyard was subsequently enlarged in 1907 and again during the 1940s when the new burial ground was added. The iron fencing was probably taken down during the Second World War, as a contribution to the war effort.

Church lighted with gas

One of the last major improvements before the renovating of the church, was the installation of gas in October 1882. This was first time the church had been lighted with gas; previously oil lamps and candles had been used.

Parish magazine

The parish magazine was first published in the 1850s and was printed by T. Hutton, 'Advertiser Office', Church Street, Ormskirk. It was called the 'St. John's Magazine'. The magazine always contained the following: 'The Young Folk's Page', 'The Bible Mine Searched', which was a series of questions on the Bible, the answers to which were given in the next month's issue, and 'Home Words for Heart and Hearth'. There was section on poetry, biblical stories, adventure and travel stories, important hints and the like, and usually varied in size from 22-28 pages per issue. In 1876 120 magazines were issued per month at a cost of 1d each. The magazine was raised to 1¼d in 1877 because a loss of £1-10s-0d had been incurred during the previous year.

The restoration of St. John's church

In April 1877, a meeting of a committee appointed to consider alterations in St. John's church was held. At the meeting it was resolved that the following should be undertaken:

(a)   The roof was to be opened out.
(b)   The church to be re-seated.
(c)   A new chancel should be built.
(d)   A new heating apparatus should be installed.
(e)   and, finally, the organ should be removed from the west end into the chancel.

The last major improvement regarding the accommodation had been done in 1858 and since that time the population of the parish had increased. The need for more room had been becoming annually more urgent, therefore, a meeting of the parishioners was convened in April 1887 to discuss the problem, the resolutions of which I have already outlined. By enlargement of the nave or body of the church, accommodation could be provided for another 100 sittings. Messrs. Waddington & Sons of Burnley were the architects.

By the end of July 1888, the enlargement and re-seating of the church was well under way, and on the 18th September 1888, a grand bazaar took place in the St. John's schoolrooms, School Lane, to help provide the necessary funds.

Re-opening of the parish church, 1889

The church was closed for just over a year while the new chancel was being erected and the whole of the interior decorated and re-seated. Apart from the proposed resolutions it was found necessary to do something to the interior walls, which resulted in the whole of the interior being decorated. Before the restoration of the church the ceiling was low and unsightly and this was removed. The old fashioned high-backed pews were replaced by open benches. On the 22nd

December 1887 the plans submitted by Messrs. Waddington & Sons of Burnley were approved and work was commenced. The work was completed according to the plans and the cost including the heating apparatus was £2,000. Therefore, this was some £300 above the amount envisaged initially, the extra cost being due to the decorating of the church and the repairs to the interior walls. Mrs. Wannop gave a fine baptismal font and brass lectern by Misses Wannop, the latter bearing the following inscription:

'Presented to St. John's Church, Burscough Bridge, for the glory of God by A. B. and C. M. Wannop, June 1889.'

The re-opening of the church was conducted by the Lord Bishop of Liverpool, Dr. John Charles Ryle, on Friday 21st June 1889. The Rev. W. Wannop had, therefore, lived to see his church modernised, although he was not able to take any active part in the work. He preached his last sermon on June 24th 1887, which was Queen Victoria's Jubilee. Since the Queen's Jubilee he had only attended the first two public meetings and opened the bazaar in September 1888, and he attended church for the last time on the 13th October 1889. In November he had a stroke after which his health declined and on 17th February 1890 he died, at the age of 85 years.

When the Rev. gentleman died there were signs of mourning throughout the whole of the village of Burscough. Blinds were drawn and all places of business were closed.

The new chancel of the church (which was erected 2 years before) was re-opened on Sunday 22nd February 1891. In September 1891 a memorial in the form of a reredos was presented to the church to the memory of the Rev. W. Wannop. The reredos shows a painting of the baptism of Christ, the three panels being surmounted by carved woodwork.

After the death of Rev. Wannop there were three short incumbencies in quick succession before the introduction in 1898 of the Rev. Charles Russell. Mr. Russell, like the first vicar, had initially been in education and therefore followed the Rev. Wannop's example by taking a keen interest in educational matters. The Rev. C. D. Russell was largely responsible for the enlargement of the St. John's schools, especially the infant department and the Lordsgate Twnship schools during the period 1901-1903. Both of these schools were overcrowded at the time and in order to meet the requirements of the Board of Education improvements and extensions had to be carried out.

During the Rev. Russell's stay he was partly responsible for the erection of St. Andrew's Mission, Crabtree, which was provided especially for those worshippers (most of whom were canal boatmen and their families from New Lane and Crabtree) living a fair distance from the parish church.

The man who was the founder and developer of this mission was, Mr. Andrew Christian Henriksen. Mr. Henriksen was a lay-missionary of the Mersey Mission to Seamen (founded c. 1857), a society which included within its sphere of operations the boatmen of the Leeds and Liverpool Canal, many of whom had their homes in this district. Mr. Henriksen was put in charge of New Lane and Crabtree. The first mission room was an adapted hay loft at Crabtree, given by Mr. Thomas Smith. The services proved very successful from the start and the room was soon found to be too small and inadequate. New accommodation was sought and eventually a site was provided by the Earl of Derby. The new mission was erected at a cost of £230 by Messrs. Lee & Co., of Manchester,

Two views of St. John's parish church, Burscough. This church was originally built as one of the 'Waterloo' churches. It appears to have been the first church on the site.

The St. John's C of E Bible Class in about 1910. In the centre of the photograph is the late Rev. C. D. Russell (the bearded gentleman) and his wife, together with Mr. and Mrs. Jacques, Master and Mistress of the St. John's Schools.

The former 'parsonage' of Burscough (1832-1849) as it appeared in the early 1970s.

and Mr. J. Tasker, Ornamental Sculptor, Burscough Bridge, laid the foundations, gate and footpath, giving his services from the start. The land was granted by Lord Derby for a small rent. The mission was built to accommodate 140 persons and was opened in 1905 by the Bishop of Liverpool, Dr. F. J. Charasse.

Two years later a small belfry was erected and the chancel added. Subsequent improvements have since taken place — in November, 1933 electric lighting was installed and in 1948 the parish church held a fete which raised £300 for the renovation of St. Andrew's and St. Cyprians.

Rev. C. D. Russell resigned owing to ill health in December 1913 and was succeeded by The Rev. T. S. Stoney, a very hard working minister amongst the parishioners of Burscough. During the Great War of 1914-18 very few, if any, structural alterations were done to the church. However, in October 1918 it was decided by the War Memorial Committee to try to secure the sum of £600 which was required for the War Memorial Window.

The Rev. T. S. Stoney left St. John's for Wavertree in January 1919, but his successor the Rev. W. R. Johnson was not inducted until the 21st March 1919. When Mr. Johnson came to Burscough the population of the district contained something like 4,300 people scattered over some thousands of acres. Since Mr. Wannop's time the population had become more varied: there were the boat people of the canal, soldiers in the near neighbourhood, farmers, some men worked in the mines round Skelmersdale, there was also a certain number of residents who went into Liverpool each day, whilst others had their own business or had retired from them and lived in the parish.

Burscough was claimed to be a difficult parish and the living of Burscough did not provide a sufficient wage. The net income for the vicar at this time was only £274 and after appeals by the Bishop of Liverpool, the stipend was eventually raised to £373 net, and a house. The gross income was derived from the following:

Pew rents £161, Ecclesiastical Commissioners £144, Queen Anne's Bounty £6, Fees £51 and the Easter Offering which varied from year to year, the average being about £24.

When Mr. Wannop came to Burscough the stipend was £200 per annum. It is worthy of note that the church people subscribed a curate's stipend and that they also undertook to remove the vicar's obligation to pay a pension of a former vicar, so that Rev. W. R. Johnson could receive his full stipend.

In July 1919, the Liverpool Consistory Court gave the vicar and wardens of St. John the Baptist Church, Burscough Bridge, the permission to place in the east window a stained glass representing the 'Te Deum'. Permission was also given for the placing of a marble tablet on the chancel bearing the names of men from the parish who fell in the Great War, the cost being defrayed by voluntary contribution. On Sunday 28th June 1920, the church was filled with people when the Lord Bishop of Liverpool dedicated the 'Te Deum' window to the memory of the men from Burscough and Lathom who fell in the Great War.

The window, which is over the altar, is a magnificent portrayal of the 'Te Deum' consisting of five panels. In the central panel Christ is enthroned and around him are angels and the archangels Michael and Gabriel, and a scroll bears the words 'Holy, Holy, Holy, Lord God of Sabaoth, heaven and earth are full of the majesty of your glory'. However, down in the panels is seen the noble army of martyrs, of the different ages of the Church, and in the lower of the three centre panels the Great War is pictured. Directly below the throne, with a dove hovering above with outspread wings, Edith Louisa Cavell and a Red Cross sister are seen ministering to the wounded. To the left of them are three gallant khaki heroes and the panel on the right contains a representation of John Travers Cornwell and another bluecoat, an airman and a colonial. Beneath them are the words, 'They shall be had in everlasting remembrance' and 'Memorial Window, erected 1919'. The lower portions of the panels are filled in with the arms of Lathom, Liverpool, the seal of Burscough, the Ordnance arms and the seal of Burscough Priory. There are also the inscriptions Waterloo 1793-1815 and Mons 1914-1918. On the wall of the church is an alabaster tablet bearing the words 'They died in the Great War 1914-1918', but owing to certain defects, the tablet was not dedicated.

St. Cyprian's Mission, Hoscar

In 1922 St. Cyprian's was handed over to the care of Burscough church by the late Earl of Lathom before he broke up the Lathom estates in 1925. The mission was opened in 1903 and belonged to and was kept by the Earl of Lathom, and was served by his domestic chaplain, the Rev. H. H. Hall B.A. The chaplain, apart from taking or supervising the services, was allowed to do some of the duties of the vicars of Ormskirk and Burscough.

St. Cyprian's was opened mainly through the influence of Mr. H. E. Elkin of Southport, assisted by Mr. James Webster. Mr. Elkin was voluntary lay reader for over 30 years and Mr. J. Webster was superintendent of the Sunday school. It is interesting to note that the building was formerly an old barn, as the large oak beams and round window at the west end indicate. The barn is probably late 18th century and was built about the same time as the farm house which bears the date 1795 and the following letters:

I have not been able to identify with certainty the name of the above, but 130 years ago a Mr. Joseph Hankin occupied the house. The initials might refer to Mr. James Gaskell who was a wheelwright in this area over 150 years ago. The letter P would refer to his wife's christian name.

Additions to St. John's church, Burscough Bridge

During the early part of the 1930s the furnishings of the church were added to. These additions were mainly from generous parishioners who presented a marble font, carpets and an altar frontal. Another altar frontal of blue and gold, which was used on festival occasions, was the gift of the children of St. John's school, who also presented the church flag and staff.

The new vestry

The last major addition to the church during Canon Johnson's stay was the erection of the new vestry. Work was commenced early in June 1933, the new vestry being built to commemorate the first century of the church. The money raised during the century celebrations was used for this purpose.

The foundation stone bears the following inscription:

'This stone was laid by Albert Augustus, third Bishop of Liverpool, to commemorate the 100th anniversary of the consecration of this church. W. P. Johnson, Vicar, canon Diocesan of Liverpool Cathedral; Robert Travis, John Tyrer, Wardens 1932'.

In a cavity under the stone is a metal cylinder which contains two copies of the *Ormskirk Advertiser* for September 29th and October 6th 1932, the centenary period copies of the Burscough parish magazine, one containing an account of the centenary celebrations and the other a full list of church officials and a copy of the centenary service form.

In November 1933, the vestry was dedicated by the Ven. Archdeacon Howson of Liverpool. In 1933 the church was lighted with electricity for the first time. Many improvements have been done since 1947 and some of a major nature such as the improvement of the vicarage in 1963 at a cost of £4,000, the Church Diocese granting £1,000 and the Church Commissioners granted £1,050. The most recent addition is that of the new church hall built at a cost of £16,000 and opened in February, 1970.

The war memorial

The townships of Burscough and Lathom, like many other small villages scattered throughout the country, sent their sons (many of whom volunteered) to do service for King and country in both the Great War and the Second World War. However, in both of these wars many of them lost their lives and, therefore, in remembrance of these gallant men the war memorial was erected in August 1922, at the corner of Junction Lane and Liverpool Road.

The whole memorial was constructed in grey Cornish granite from the famous quarries near St. Stithians, and all the inscriptions were slightly raised lead lettering. The total height of the memorial was 17' 6". The contract for the memorial was carried out by Messrs. James Whittle, contractor, of Ormskirk. The granite steps and cross were supplied by Mr. Samuel Welsby, Sculptor, of Liverpool and Widnes, and the architect in charge of the work was Mr. C. Brighouse of Ormskirk.

Originally the erratic block which I mentioned was going to be used for that part of the memorial which is now occupied by the block of unhewn granite. At the time, however, it was found to be too heavy to move. Mr. James Bromley J.P. the local antiquarian wanted the erratic block to be placed in front of the Stanley Institute, but this was never done.

In June 1949, the memorial was again dedicated to those soldiers who were killed during the 1939-1945 war, their names being added to the memorial. In 1948, £100 was raised by the Burscough British Legion in order to carry out the work on the memorial, the total cost being paid off by July 1949.

The Vicars of St. John's Parish Church, Burscough Bridge

Rev. John Bowman (officiating minister).....................1832-1840

The Vicars

Rev. William Wannop B.A...................................1840-1890
Rev. Benjamin Stewart Darbyshire M.A., B.A................1890-1892
Rev. John Hooley Ella Bailey M.A., B.A....................1893-1895
Rev. James Barnes Brearley M.A., B.A., F.R.G.S.
     F.R.A.S., A.S.L., L.Th., M.A. (Nova Scotia)...........1895-1898
Rev. Charles David Russell M.A., B.A., M.A. (Durham).......1898-1913
Rev. Travers Strathmore Stoney M.A........................1913-1919
Rev. William Robert Johnson M.A., B.A.....................1919-1934
Rev. Herbert Flenley B.A..................................1934-1947
Rev. Frederick Arthur Gadd M.A., B.A......................1947-1952
Rev. Robert James Smith L.Th. (Durham)....................1952-1960
Rev. Arthur Rivers..1960

The rise and fall of Weslyan Methodism in Burscough and district

Introduction

Methodism was first introduced into Ormskirk in 1793 by the Rev. Thomas Taylor and, in accordance with the intolerant spirit of the age, both Methodism and its preacher were received in a hostile manner. The Rev. Thomas Taylor made a record of the situation at Ormskirk and by doing so has given us a glimpse of the feeling that prevailed at that time. He speaks of the humble beginning with a 'place filled with a pulpit and benches' and a 'couple of rooms adjoining for the use of visiting preachers and the caretaker'. He goes on to say:

> 'We also formed a small society. A considerable sum of money was begged for the above purposes, but I am sorry to say it was given up some time after we left the circuit. We had contended with much opposition by mobs and riots, but even these were quelled. A ringleader was taken up and sent to prison, but for sake of his family even our people begged him off, so he was not tried at the sessions to which he was bound, yet after the way was made, and matters in a fair way of being successful, it pained my mind to find that all was knocked on the head and if ever the place is attached again very likely the rabble will renew their opposition'.

Ormskirk provided an admirable centre and the early Wesleyan Methodists, with commendable zeal and courage, carried their faith into the surrounding West Lancashire villages. They were fortunate in having amongst their flock convincing speakers and earnest workers, with the result that the cause was quickly spread in the neighbouring districts.

Wesleyan Methodism was developed in Burscough by Mr. Thomas Bridge, who was practically its founder in this area; he had attained an influence which was equalled by no other layman in the Ormskirk Circuit.

St. Andrew's Mission, Crabtree, in 1970.

St. Crypian's Mission, Hoscar, in 1970.

Left. *The Rev. C. M. Chavasse, voluntary curate at Burscough from 1913 to 1914.*

Below. *The Wesleyan chapel at Hoscar Moss in 1970. It is now a private residence.*

Mr. Thomas Bridge was born at Rufford in 1819 and came of a well-known stock of yeomen. His father, Edward Bridge, who was born in October 1773, was known as the 'hero' of the village and parish of Rufford in its moral and spiritual welfare. A book called *The Hero of Rufford* by James A. Macdonald was published in 1896 which tells of the life of Edward Bridge and his family at Rufford.

The Wesleyan Methodists of Burscough first held their meetings in Mr. Edward Bridge's barn and Jane Moss, daughter of Edward Bridge, opened her house for preaching. Mrs. Moss — 'Mother Moss' as she was called — erected a little mission near her house which was known as the 'little Zion'.

Moss Lane Mission

At the beginning of the 19th century, Mr. Peter Williams of Lathom was converted to Methodism. He held prayer meetings every Saturday evening in his own cottage and at this time was supported by Mr. Edward Bridge. These meetings established the foundation of the Moss Lane Mission in 1813. Mr. Peter Williams before his death made the cottage, now a converted chapel, over to a proper Methodist trust and the little chapel thrived. In the 1840s Mr. Peter Williams lived at a small cottage adjacent to the disused windmill in Moss Lane and the site of the mission was occupied by Mr. Thomas Baldwin. The landowner was Lord Skelmersdale, but whether Thomas Baldwin actually lived at the mission I do not know, because he also occupied other premises as well. On the 1845 Ordnance Survey map and other documented sources of the period I could find no evidence that the mission was being used as a place of worship. In looking through the old directories there is no mention of the Moss Lane Mission after the 1850s and in 1869 the new Wesleyan chapel was opened in Orrell Lane, Burscough, and the Moss Lane Mission was closed, and remained so until about 1902.

Mr. Hugh Staziker was mainly responsible for the re-opening of the mission. When he and his family came to live near the chapel, it was in a very dilapidated state. Nevertheless, he decided to do something about it and, with the help of Rouffignac (the well-respected Wesleyan schoolmaster) together with a group of young men which he brought with him, they cleaned, redecorated and refurbished the chapel.

The old box pews were broken to provide panelling for the walls and new pews were made. Soon after these alterations had taken place, services were recommenced, and the chapel is still in use to this day.

The Burscough Wesleyan Chapel

The first preaching room of the Methodist body in Burscough was situated on the site of what is known today as the Canal Company's Yard, on the canal bank, and was established about 1855. Two cottages had previously occupied this area, which formed the preaching room, and was capable of accommodating up to 200 people. Prior to the preaching room the site was occupied by Mr. James Mayor, timber merchant and boat builder; he also had a timber yard here. However, because of the growing congregation the preaching room was found to be too small and effort was made to secure the erection of a new building.

Dr. Wood of Southport and Mr. E. Holden were interested in the movement and came down to take part in the services. The cause flourished and within a few years the present Wesleyan chapel, the foundation stone of which was laid by Alderman Dr. Wood, was erected. The foundation stone was laid on 20th July 1868 and the chapel was open for divine service on Good Friday 1869. In 1868 the land was acquired as a gift from Lord Derby. Mr. Thomas Bridge junior of Burscough was the architect, and his father Thomas Bridge was the contractor for the work. The chapel contained accommodation for 297 persons and the entire cost amounted to £958. This amount was raised voluntarily by means of subscription and the issuing of subscription lists, the money was soon forthcoming and a shoemaker in the village gave £50.

Description of the chapel as it was in 1869

Several photographs of the chapel were taken at this time and presented to various members of the Wesleyan community but I have so far been unable to obtain one. Nevertheless, I have been able to piece together material from various sources, and the following was the result.

The Chapel was cruciform in its arrangement and was built in the early pointed style of architecture, the material being brickwork of different colours, with ornamental bands and coloured arches to the various windows and doors. Other ornamental brick and stone work was used throughout the building. The windows were chiefly coupled lancets, except in the various gables of the nave, transepts and chancel where well-proportioned triplet windows were used. At the junction of the roofs of the nave and transept rose a spirelet to a height of fifty feet from the ground, and the several gables also had appropriate terminals. Initially only part of the nave was used by the congregation, because a small area was used as a school-room. At that time an ornamental screen was used to separate the congregation from the school-room. The ceiling was enriched with plaster work and divided into bays by arched principals with pierced tracery work in the spandrils and terminated in wood carved corbels. A reading desk was presented to the chapel by Mr. Anthony Darby (Mr. Bridge's foreman). The communion table was very elaborate and was made and presented by Mr. Edward Bridge. Messrs. Meek and Sons of Southport gave the carpets for the chancel. The Misses Wood, of Southport, gave a cushion, Bible and hymn book for the reading desk. The nave was 46' by 36' and the transepts 42½' by 18' and the chancel was 18' by 8'.

Alterations and additions to the chapel

The first alteration to take place was in 1871 when the vestries were altered. In 1877 extensive alterations were carried out and a new organ was installed. Previously music for the choir was provided by means of a harmonium, and Miss Berry from Lordsgate Farm was the organist. The chapel was closed for a short period in November 1877, whilst the alterations took place and was re-opened on 28th November of that year. The new organ was placed at the opposite end of the chapel to the pulpit and the gallery on the left of the pulpit, where the choir formerly sat, was taken out and a stained glass window was placed there. This window was the work of Messrs. E. & I. Holloway of Liverpool. The organ was built by Messrs. Kirtland and Jardine of Manchester.

The chancel was extensively renovated and given a new roof during 1906 and

1907; in 1926 a new organ was provided by an anonymous donor and in July 1943 a memorial window was unveiled in memory of the late son of Mr. & Mrs. Philip Rimmer.

Recent improvements

During the period 1948-1950 the outer wall of the chapel was taken down and rebuilt, the vestries were renewed, and a new boiler was installed and extensive repairs to the roof and windows were carried out. After the above was completed the chapel was redecorated throughout and the total cost was about £2,000.

In 1964 damp and dry rot attacked the chapel, but fortunately the organ and choir stalls were not involved. However, the damp and dry rot had to be removed and the cost of this operation was £2,600 plus £400 for re-decorating. The whole of the communion area was remodelled and renewed during this period and it has been mooted that in the future new pews and a central aisle may be built.

Finally in 1968 a church hall was erected and the intention now is to connect the two buildings by means of a modern foyer.

The ministers

From 1869 when the chapel opened to 1923 there was no resident Methodist minister in Burscough. The ministers who officiated were supplied by the Ormskirk Circuit and in their absence the day to day work of the church was carried on by such people as Mr. T. Radcliffe in the late 1860s and 1870s and subsequently by Mr. F. Rouffignac, the much beloved headmaster, who did great work here. The first appointed minister of Burscough was the Rev. Walter Moore, a probationer, who came here in 1924. At this time there was no 'manse' available for the ministers attached to Burscough, and this remained so until 1931. In 1931 'The Manse' was built by Mr. Fletcher, Builder and Contractor, of Burscough, and the first resident and ordained minister, the Rev. Clifford Crew was appointed. Since 1924 there have been no fewer than 13 ministers at Burscough.

List of ministers

Rev. Walter Moore	1924-1925
Rev. William Cox	1926-1927
Rev. C. L. Brewer	1927-1928
Rev. Charles Staden	1928
Rev. Norman A. Priestley	1928-1931
The first resident Minister was the Rev. Clifford Crew	1931-1934
Rev. Bert Wright	1934-1938
Rev. Maurice Harker	1938-1945
Rev. H. R. Wilkinson	1945-1949
Rev. Ronald Crawford	1949-1954
Rev. A. Edwards	1954-1958
Rev. Lewis F. Lovell B.A., B.D.	1958-1963
Rev. Rodney A. Owen	1963-1970
Rev. Noel Catherall	1970

The Wesleyan Chapel at Hoscar Moss

This neat little chapel, situated near to Hoscar Moss railway station, was erected during 1876-1877. The memorial stone was laid on 23rd October 1876 and the chapel was opened for divine service on Good Friday 1877. The Rev. James Yeames of Bootle preached the first sermon and on the following two Sundays the Rev. J. T. Marquand was the preacher. This chapel was needed by the members of the Wesleyan body who resided at and near Hoscar Moss, for up to 1877 they had not had a building of their own to meet in. Prior to the building of the chapel, services had been conducted on the premises of Mr. William Arnold (farmer, Hoscar Moss) but because the congregation was growing and accommodation was limited, it was decided to build a chapel. Accordingly subscriptions were asked for and the land was procured from Lord Skelmersdale. The memorial stone was laid by Mrs. Farr of Wigan and William Dodd Esq., of Southport, and the contractor for the work was Thomas Bridge of Burscough. A public tea party was held on the day of the opening.

In recent years Hoscar Mission has been acquired by the Burscough Joinery Company who have established their works here, known as 'Chapel Works'.

Conclusion

These churches brought some spiritual comfort to workers, who had been engaged throughout the week in exacting work, on their one day of rest. At this period they were the centre of cultural and social activity. There were Sunday School processions, church concerts, trips to the seaside and Lake District were undertaken (made possible at this time by the railway services available at Burscough Junction and Burscough Bridge) and various clubs, such as clothing, burial and other benevolent clubs were established by all the three churches in Burscough.

The Churches' influence also penetrated into the school and the annual treat of the school children was related to church activities and, on many of these occasions, the parties were held at the vicarage. The Churches tended to support the master in many ways and in a way there was the old parson-squire link, so that even on Sunday, the worker was under the influence of the master. Even at this time when the fortunes of the Non-conformists seemed so high, many historians believed that the whole movement was declining and appeared to be growing more and more middle class, and away from the people. This, however, was not the case in Burscough, because during the 1870s a great deal of enthusiasm and energy was shown by all sections of the community towards the expansion of the Non-conformists and this continued throughout this period into the 20th century.

Much, however, is owed to the Rev. W. Wannop during this period, because of the toleration he showed to all other religious bodies and this is confirmed by the fact that he was welcomed by Non-conformists and Roman Catholics alike, as well as in many other circles connected with the welfare and social life of the township of Burscough.

The Schools and Educational Development with Special Reference to the Period 1870-1902

The schools

Introduction

PROVISION for education was to develop very slowly but before 1836 there had hardly been any provision at all except for an old school which existed in Burscough Town, and the ancient grammar school at Ormskirk, for sons of those who could afford such an education. Subsequent educational development then was to owe little to earlier ages and was almost entirely a result of the new social and economic conditions.

Since the early settlers had built their homesteads along the ancient ridge road (the main Liverpool-Preston road) and had developed farms on what before had been marsh land, which had been drained in the 18th and 19th centuries, the crafts of agriculture, basket-making, spinning, weaving, brick-making, stonemasonry, wheelwright, boat-building and joinery had demanded no formal instruction. These ancient crafts had passed from generation to generation, men living within their trade and class. This established order had been exploded by factory production methods and many of the large industrialists of this new order were confronted by the dilemma of providing an elementary education for the hands who were to understand and run the new methods of production. This problem, however, did not become urgent in Burscough until the first quarter of the twentieth century, when the number of mills increased in the surrounding areas and the population began to expand more rapidly.

Private schools

Only three private schools existed in Burscough in the 19th century that I have any knowledge of and I can only give a very brief description of them because material, i.e. documents etc., on these schools is not available, having either been lost or destroyed. However, there are some references in the St. John's C. of E. school log book which confirm that one of the schools was taking pupils in the 1870s.

The first record of a private school that I could find was at Burscough town. This school was situated near to the Bull and Dog Inn and in 1846 was run by Mr. John Gobbin. This school was only a small school and probably catered for about 20 or 30 children. In 1854 the school is mentioned in Mannex's Directory. John Gobbin appears to have been the only master at the school and it eventually finished as a school in the early 1860s. This building is still standing today and is occupied.

The second school was a small boarding school situated near to Burscough

Bridge railway station and was called 'Miss Teebay's boarding school'. This school was established about 1850 and closed in 1854. The reason why this school closed I do not know, but in January 1855 a Mr. John Garniss of Liverpool opened a drapery store in the building which Miss Teebay had used as a boarding school.

The school was, as far as I could ascertain from various sources, situated where 'Baybutt's' and 'Webb's' shops are today. Older residents will no doubt remember Mr. Stoner who occupied Baybutt's shop from the early 1890s to about 1903. He was a clothier and outfitter and first established himself at Ormskirk in 1887. During Mr. Stoner's stay, the building was known as Victoria House, and he issued a small local railway time-table free to his customers. He was followed by Mr. Henry Kirkpatrick who also took over Mr. Stoner's premises at Ormskirk where 'Johnsons the Cleaners' are today. These shops were known as 'Kirks', he also being a clothier and outfitter. Subsequently, the premises at Burscough became a grocer's shop and this incidentally was what it had been 130 years ago when Mr. Kay occupied this building. The glass verandah in front of the shop originally stood in front of the Corn Exchange, Moor Street, Ormskirk.

The third school was called 'Mary Wilding's School for Girls', and this was situated in the building near to the entrance of the St. John's parish church. The building is now partly occupied by the following:

> 'Jackson's the Auctioneer', 'Ruth's Hairdressing Shop', and part of 'Riley's Outfitters and Drapery Shop'.

This school was established in the early 1860s. In St. John's C. of E. School log book there is the following entry on the 10th May 1875:

> 'Admitted Richard Baldwin, from Miss Wilding's private school a lad of 13 years old — only 1st Standard'.

Therefore, from the above evidence it appears that boys as well as girls, were admitted to this school.

Mary Wilding was the daughter of Mr. James Wilding, who occupied part of the premises facing the Royal Hotel. Mr. Wilding had a saddler's shop, part of which is now occupied by Jackson's the Auctioneer. Previous to Mr. Wilding's occupying the premises, the entire block, which consisted of a house and shop combined, was originally occupied by Mr. Thomas Seddon in 1846, who leased it from the Earl of Derby. This school closed about the year 1890, but Mr. Wilding still continued with his saddle shop and also occupied the premises formerly used as the school.

The above private schools were probably Dame Schools and according to the evidence contained in the Report of the Newcastle Commission of 1861 the great majority were classified as being inefficient. Like many schools today, standards varied but, by and large, these schools only provided a rudimentary education. Fees would be charged to attend these schools.

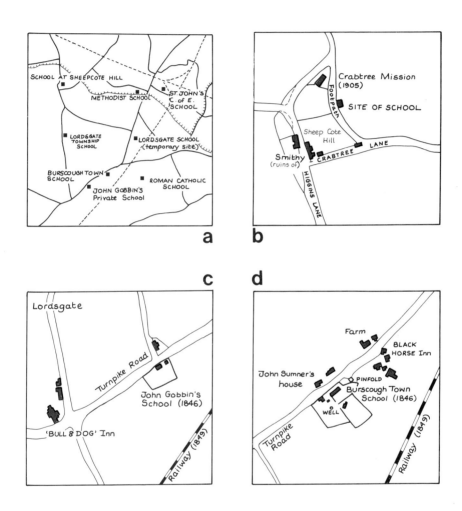

The schools of Burscough during the 19th century

a) General location map
b) The probable site of the school at Sheepcote Hill
c) The position of John Gobbin's Private School
d) The position of the old Burscough Town School
        The sketch maps are based on the 1846 Tithe Map.

First public school
The Old Burscough Town School

From about 1480-1750 Lancastrians poured their money into education in the form of charities to such an extent that the amount was almost double the amount given for all purposes connected with poor relief. Educational charities represented about 42% of all the charities of the county and was therefore the greatest amongst all the other charities. In proportionate terms, the amount of money lent to education was greater than in any other county. The reason for the interest in education is not easily explained. Many men left in their wills money to erect schools; they firmly believed that by educating the children that poverty, ignorance and want of opportunity would be cured. Nevertheless, by the beginning of the 18th century when the continent was increasing its power, it became increasingly obvious that education of the masses was becoming more important, if we were to compete with them in future.

The Burscough Town School or Parochial School was just one of these schools which was founded by a man called John Houghton. In his will dated the 21st March 1732 he gave to the churchwarden and overseers of Burscough £10 towards erecting a public school on the brow or vacant piece of land near the pinfold. This site is across the road from Dutton's Shop and a little to the south of Mr. Guy's house Liverpool Road, Burscough Town. Today nothing remains of the old school and the pinfold, which was used about 100 years ago for holding stray cattle, was used some years ago by the council for refuse, but has subsequently been taken down and a cottage erected on the site. Mr. Houghton made provision for a schoolmaster by giving the churchwardens and overseers £100; the amount was to be invested and the interest paid yearly to the schoolmaster, for teaching such persons' children within Burscough whose parents should not have an estate of the yearly value of £10 within Burscough. He also made a condition in his will respecting the above legacies by stating 'that if they should neglect or refuse to build the public school near the Pinfold within the said town, within twelve months next after his decease, all the said legacies should be void, and he gave the same amongst his relations'.

The sum of £10 left towards building the school was used for that purpose in the following year by the township; and it appears by the accounts that in the year 1734 a schoolmaster received £5 as a year's wages in accordance with the will of John Houghton.

The school was rebuilt and much enlarged in 1818, at the expense of the township; and a house near the school was built by the township, between 1788-1798, which with a small garden was appropriated to the residence of the master. In the constable's accounts for Burscough in 1771 the following entries appear:

April 24th — 'Paid to Abraham Fisher for two Hundred of Brick for a oven at the school...2s. 6d.

April 30th — 'For carting two Hundred Brick from Martin Mare to the School..1s. 0d.

June 20th — 'Paid for making a hoven at Scoole...................3s. 0d.

The master of the school was appointed by the jury at court baron for the manor of Burscough. His income was derived from the following sources: he received £4. 10s 0d. as the interest of the £100 left by John Houghton, which was invested with other charity money, upon the security of the tolls of the Leeds and Liverpool canal.

The amount of £4. 10s 0d. is confirmed by the constable's accounts of Burscough in the year 1772 where the following entry appears:

Thomas Smith constable of Burscough for 1772 — Nov 19 'Paid George farriment for this years salary...£4. 10s 0d.

He also received £2 10s. 0d. from Thomas Tasker Esq., being the interest of £50, bequeathed in 1803 by the will of John Tasker, for teaching the children of such persons in Burscough as should not be possessed of an estate or farm of £10 a year.

In 1828 the master let the school-house, which was intended for himself, at £6 a year, and a small cottage adjoining the school was repaired and filled up at the expense of the township, to increase the schoolmaster's salary, at £3 10s. 0d. a year.

In respect of his income, and a gratuity of £2. 2s 0d. which he received from the Earl of Derby, he taught free any children who applied provided they belonged to the township, and their parents did not live on a farm of £10 yearly value; the number of scholars of this description varied from 15 to 25. They were taught reading without any charge, but if they were taught writing they had to pay the same as other scholars. The master also took other children who paid and usually had from 60 to 80 or 90 scholars.

The following which appears in the will of John Houghton and is subsequently described by the Charity Commissioners is also of interest educationally:

'He (that is John Houghton) gave to the churchwarden and overseers of the town of Burscough, and their successors £80, to be invested, and the interest to be applied towards binding out such poor children apprentices as they, with the substantial inhabitants of the said town should think fit; and he directed that, if any time there should be no poor child, boy or girl, to be bound in any one year, the interest should be applied for the use of the next apprentice, that should be loose of his or her apprenticeship, towards buying him or her apparel or other necessaries as should be thought proper by the inhabitants.'

Regarding the sum of £80 given for apprenticing, boys were occasionally bound out apprentices. During 1853-1863 six boys were placed out for apprenticing, with premiums of from £4 to £5 each. If in any one year no boy had applied for the benefit of this branch of the charity, it was agreed that a greater number of applicants might be admitted in the following year, but the directions of the testator, that the interest of this money should in such case be disposed of in supplying clothes for those who had passed through their apprenticeship, was not attended to, apparently.

Regarding the running of the school and the kind of tuition given I am afraid I have no knowledge as it appears that the records which might have given some insight into its workings have been lost. Nevertheless from what I have been able to find it appears that the variety of subjects which were taught in the early years was very limited indeed. However, by the 1870s it appears that the range of subjects had increased. I say this because of the following announcement made on the 18th April 1861:

Mr. John Strickland, Master.

Begs to inform the Inhabitants of Burscough and the surrounding neighbourhood that he has been appointed master, of the above school, and has now entered upon his duties: and trust by assiduity and attention in the school, and kindness to his Pupils to secure a good attendance of pupils and the support of Parents.

The branches of Instruction will be, Reading, Writing, Arithmetic, Geography, History and Grammar.

Terms may be known on application at the School.

With reference to the above I also have three books which were used in this school in the III, IV and V Standards. These books are mainly concerned with reading, spelling, English grammar, vocabulary, with reference to geography, travel and history in the form of stories; there is also poetry introduced in the fifth standard reader, but no arithmetic.

The name of the first schoolmaster is not known, but his successor appears to have been called George Farriment, and to have commenced his duties in 1758. On 12th May 1758 an advertisement appeared in the *Liverpool Chronicle and Marine Gazetteer* for a schoolmaster at Burscough. Certainly, in 1765 George Farriment is recorded as being the master and it would be reasonable to suppose that he was the man appointed in 1758, although of course this is not definite. He continued at Burscough until 1772, from whence until 1850 the position was held by members of the Sumner family, their precise relationship to each other being unknown.

It was during James Sumner's time as master of the school that the school house was let, and he (the school master) went to live at a house just across from the school. The school house was occupied by Mr. Henry Meadows in 1846. In 1850 the position of master of this school became vacant, and Alfred Armstrong applied for the post. This is the only master for whom I have any evidence of his qualifications. He points out in his letter that preference would be given to an applicant who had been accustomed to class teaching. Whether he was a pupil or a teacher at Bispham is not clear in the letter, but it seems to me that he was the latter. He mentions his brother at Bispham who, incidentally, became the headmaster of Bispham (Parbold) Grammar School, a position which he held for 20 years. His brother's name was John Armstrong, who was born at the 'New Inn' (now called the Manor House the residence of the late Bruce Smith) in the year 1822. Both brothers lived here, but John Armstrong left to live in Wigan. Their father was an amateur actor of no mean ability, and belonged to a local company known as 'The Ormskirk Amateurs'. He was also a volunteer in the Ormskirk and Leyland Militia, which was disbanded in 1815.

In 1854 Alfred Armstrong was joined by his wife Maria, she being the schoolmistress. The Armstrongs continued until March 1861, when they were succeeded by John and Caroline Strickland, who were master and mistress of the school until it closed in 1877. John Strickland was only 26 when he became master of this school and after its closure he would only be 42 years of age; therefore, initially I would have thought that he would have been a candidate for the position of master, at the new Lord's Gate School.

However, this was not to be; whether he was not suitably qualified, or his health had given way is not disclosed. Nevertheless, the latter seems to have been the case, because on the 30th August 1883 after being in poor health for over 12 months, he was found in a pit full of reeds and unfit for swimming. He was only 48 years of age and had one daughter Jane Eliza Strickland. John Strickland was staying with his daughter at Blackpool for his health, when the unfortunate incident occurred. He appeared to be a well liked man in the district and I can remember as a boy my great uncle, William Farrington, always spoke of him with great respect. When the school closed, John Strickland left teaching, and took up the position of collector of the Queen's tax.

The Old Burscough Town or Parochial School

List of masters

1773 - 1758? not known.
1758 - 1772 George Farriment.
1772 - 1850 The Sumners. James Sumner was the master from
about 1810 - 1850.
1850 - 1861 Alfred Armstrong (he was joined by his wife in 1854, she being the Mistress of this school, her name was Maria).
1861 - 1877 John Strickland and his wife Caroline.

Public elementary education between 1870-1902

Introduction

Before 1870 and throughout the period under discussion, religious differences between Nonconformist, Anglican and Catholic were acute in most areas of England. However, in Burscough although a great deal of tolerance was shown by all the three religions, this being as I have mentioned before due to the work of the Rev. W. Wannop, nevertheless when certain educational progress was to be established by certain Acts of parliament, then all the intolerance and acrimony that could be roused were present during the 19th century in Burscough. This is difficult to understand today to a certain degree, but examples of intolerance still exist in the world and I do not think I need to repeat them here. Non-interference by the State in elementary education and the right of denominational schools to conduct religious instruction were the only issues religious bodies ever agreed upon. The nature of public education in Burscough for the next thirty-two years was to be decided by the religious leaders of the township.

W. E. Forster's Elementary Education Act of 1870, which was a compromise, was the first step in the struggle to develop a national system of education that bore some fruit. Even this compromise was rejected in Burscough, the very thought of having a School Board being considered repulsive. The School Board schools were regarded as 'Godless' places, but more important they were a great drain on the rates. This point will be made clear when I discuss the origin and development of the Lord's Gate School. During the whole of the period the voluntary schools in Burscough were never very rich and one nearly failed altogether because it had run into debt. Money was raised for the running of the voluntary schools from bazaars, school sermons, collections in the form of subscription lists and the like. The equipment and buildings were unsatisfactory and deficiences in staff was also great problems.

Forster's Act did not furnish the country with a national system of education neither was the problem of school attendance solved nor the religious difficulty overcome, but Forster did establish through the Act the chance for every child to secure some form of elementary education.

A dual system was instituted by the Act; on the one hand, the Board Schools, undenominational and supported by government grant, the rates and fees, and on the other the denominational school with no rate and dependent on government grant, fees, subscriptions and, in the case of one school in Burscough, endowments. The general condition throughout the country of most denominational schools at the end of the century is described by most writers and historians as being at a great disadvantage with the Board Schools with whom they could not compete. In Burscough and district the opposite was true to a certain extent, as shall be seen when I refer to the School Attendance Committee.

Lord's Gate Township School, Burscough Town

With regard to this school all the information has been received from secondary sources and it appears as though the school log books were lost during the war when the school was demolished in Lord's Gate Lane to make way for the aerodrome. The school was carried on in temporary buildings off Liverpool Road during the war. The foundation of the present school was laid by the Bishop of Liverpool on November 2nd 1951 and opened the following year. It is built on the land which adjoined the temporary school at a cost of about £35,000.

The forerunner of the Lord's Gate School was the old Burscough Town School, which I have previously discussed. The Burcough Town School, under the 1870 Education Act, was in 1876 declared to be unsuitable with regard to accommodation; therefore, the township of Burscough was ordered by the Education Department to build another school. They were given six months in which to decide what to do, the choice being either:

(a) They could build their own school, in which case the township of Burscough would have to depend on subscriptions and donations from the people of the township. Or

(b) A School Board School would have to be erected which would have to be paid for out of the rates, which would have been between 5d and 9d in the pound.

The land for the school was given by Lord Derby by a deed dated 19th June and enrolled in Chancery 2nd July 1877. The plot of land was 1,450 square yards and was conveyed to the Rev. W. Wannop and Robert Edge under the authority of the School Sites Act of 1870.

Under an order from the Charity Commissioners dated 28th August 1877, the trustees sold the old schoolhouse and cottage and dwelling house & Co., and their site containing 920 square yards for £430, which by a further order dated 1st September 1877 they were authorised to apply towards the cost (which was £573-10-0d.) of the new school built on the site given above.

Regarding the building fund it may be proper to state that in addition to the £430 — the proceeds of the sale of the old school property of Burscough Town, and the donation of £60 from the Earl of Derby — there remained to be raised the sum of £180, which was required to cover the extra work not included in the builder's contract, such as out-offices, fences, walls, school desks and other school materials and also the architect and lawyers fees. The question that next presented itself was : how was this sum of £180 to be realised? The rate-payers, in lawful assembly had answered — and answered as one voice 'by a voluntary rate of 3d. in the £1'. It had been the unanimous opinion of the meeting that to have attempted to collect the money in any other way would have been fruitless and unavailing.

The committee, therefore, left the matter with confidence in the hands of the ratepayers. They had uttered no threat nor did they use one word of intimidation, but they knew that the school must be finished and they could not close their eyes to the only alternative that met them in the face, an alternative which the committee deprecated and dreaded as strongly as any resident in the parish: the infliction of a School Board.

On the 29th September 1877 a meeting of the ratepayers of the township of Burscough and of that part of the township of Lathom which lies within the ecclesiastical parish of St. John, Burscough Bridge, was held in the school room, Burscough Town, for the purpose of considering the best means of raising the money still required for completing the new school in Lord's Gate, inclusive of fence, walls, out offices, school desks and other school furniture (the estimate for the above was about £180); the vicar was in the chair, and the following resolutions were unanimously adopted:

1. It was decided that because the Legislation had imposed upon rateable property the obligation of providing sufficient school accommodation for every parish or district throughout the land that they resolved that a Rate of 3d. in the £1 be levied on all the rateable property in the Township of Burscough and the portion of the Township of Lathom which lay within the Ecclesiastical Parish of St. John, Burscough Bridge, for the purpose of completing the New School in Lord's Gate Burscough.

2. That in the event of the above Rate not being paid, it was the opinion of the meeting that another meeting of the Ratepayers should be convened as soon as practicable to consider the expediency of applying to the Education Department, for the appointment of a School Board.

> Signed William Wannop,
> Chairman.

The above caused discontent amongst the people of Burscough and Lathom and for many weeks a great argument arose about the religious question as to whether the school was to be a denominational school or a non-denominational school. The imposition of the 3d. rate was also questioned and was the cause of much controversy. I think the following extract from a ratepayer's letter will give the mood at the time:

'Sir, — In reply to your notice regarding the one or two resolutions passed at a meeting held in Burscough, presided over and presumably called together and advised by the vicar, laying a rate for the raising of (I think) £180, to complete a certain school building and threating recusant and non-paying parishioners with some very terrible thing in the shape of a School Board to be thrust upon them for their daring unpliancy. But if the chairman advised the meeting, I wonder who advised the chairman. Something is said about obligations imposed by law on lands for the education of the people. But is there any law authorising a public rate for a denominational school, or empowering the Burscough meeting to vote and inforce it? I think there is none and indeed this seems to have been felt, and is tactitly acknowledged in the threat of a School Board in case of non-compliance.

But neither can a School Board be forced on unwilling ratepayers, or certainly not for building purposes if there be already a sufficiency of suitable school accomodation with efficient teaching and as to compulsory attendance, that may be well enough looked after by an attendance committee without the necessity of a School Board, or further if a School Board were formed, and built its own schools, they would be board schools, not denominational. This arbitary attempt at coercion is too flagrant and offensive; and it is just thus, that some, if they could have their own will, would trample out all non-conforming Christians, and all proper and praiseworthy independence of mind and character and action. But let there be a true practical catholicity of spirit all round, and then things will go well with us all.'

To the above the Rev. W. Wannop replied in the following manner which virtually sums up the case and within it answers the above correspondent's question:

The writer of the above should have known that the new school in Lord's Gate had been erected to supply the defective school accommodation in the township of Burscough; and that it had been erected under the pressure of a "final order" from the Education Department, and also in pursuance of a resolution adopted about two years ago, at a meeting of the ratepayers of the Township, legally convened. The scheme had at the time, and still had the fullest approval of the Earl of Derby, who not only gave the site of the new school, but added a liberal donation of £60 to the building fund'.

'The building of the school had been superintended by a committee appointed at the meeting referred to above and it was at the instance of the same committee that the meeting of ratepayers called on the 29th September, when the two resolutions were unanimously adopted which formed the object to the ratepayer's criticisms in his letter.'

'The school in question had not been built for a denominational school; nor was it to be the property of any one denomination. It was to be the property of the township at large or, rather, of the ratepayers of the township, wholly and entirely irrespective of political or religious considerations. The site of the school with the building upon it had been conveyed to the official trustees of charitable funds on behalf of the rate-payers and would remain the inalienable property of the township forever'.

School Scheme of 1878

The school was appropriated solely for a public elementary school for the labouring, manufacturing and other poorer classes in Burscough. The vicar of St. John's Church Burscough was to be in charge of the religious instruction (The Rev. W. Wannop in his reply to the ratepayer had stated, 'that the school was not to be denominational nor was it to be the property of any one denomination'. It would seem, therefore, that the first part of this statement was not altogether true). The management in other respects was under the control of a committee which consisted of the vicar or his curate if appointed and 12 other persons; they had to contribute £1 each annually to the funds of the school and had to be resident in the district.

In 1880 Lord Derby also gave to the Rev. W. Wannop and Robert Edge a plot of land containing 466 square yards adjoining the school site for the purpose of erecting a house for the schoolmaster or mistress of Lord's Gate School in accordance with the above scheme.

On 4th June 1880 authorisation for the erection of a master's house was given by the Charity Commissioners. The cost of the house was £300 and this was met by applying £200 of the endowment of the educational charities of John Houghton, John Tasker and Richard Prescott on the understanding that the remainder should be provided by private subscription or from other sources, and it was ordered that part of the £430-7-7d. consols mentioned above, should be sold to provide the £200. The amount of consols sold was £203-11-3d.

The school

The site for the school was chosen because it was within a fair distance for the children of Burscough Town, Crabtree and New Lane. It was a compact and well-built structure, with picturesque gabled roof. Unfortunately no photographs appear to exist of this school. It was opened on 18th February 1878, and the number of children attending in that year was sixty-eight. The school was opened by the Rev. W. Wannop, who was chairman of the managers and by the first headmaster, Mr. H. Coleman. Mr. Ralph Tomlinson J.P. of Burscough was the treasurer of the school. On the second day of opening the following entry was made in the log-book:

> 'Some parents complained that the fees were too high, and in some cases a reduction was made'.

Other extracts from the log-book cast interesting side lights on those times. It was recorded that 'children who passed Standard 3 may be kept at home by their parents', and an entry of December 5th 1880 stated that a certain girl 'returned to school after an absence of over three months. She does not know a letter or a figure , and will be nine years old next May'.

Attendance

Unlike the other schools in Burscough, Ormskirk market day always appears to have adversely affected the attendance, as the following extract which appeared in the log-book dated 26th March 1885 suggests:

> 'The attendance is always bad on Thursdays and many having missed school on that day, do not come again until the week following'.

The proximity of Ormskirk to this school at that time would probably be partly responsible for this state of affairs. In those days one must remember that transport facilities were not as good as they are today, and the children were evidently kept at home, not only to help carry eggs, butter and garden produce to market, but to carry home big baskets of provisions for the week. Ormskirk's 'Fine Fairs' also adversely affected the attendance and frequent mention was made of this fact in the log-book. The 'Fine Fair' was held on the Thursday following the horse and cattle fairs at Whitsun and in September, and on these occasions the stalls were gaily dressed and all the country folk for miles around gathered in the town.

In 1891 the average attendance was 111 and in 1898 the average was 116 according to a report of the Education Committee and in 1902 the average attendance had risen to 150 and the total number of children on the books was 230.

Transfer of pupils from one school to another went on, but with regard to the pupils of Lord's Gate School the transfers seem to be few and far between.

The following two entries appear in the Weslyan School Log-Book:—

Nov. 22nd 1888 — 'Three have gone to St. John's some to Burscough Town School'.

June 11th 1902 — 'Admitted one new scholar Alice Berry from Lord's Gate School'.

The first concert to be held in the Lord's Gate School was on 31st December 1880, and its aim was to raise funds for the school. These concerts usually consisted of persons of known local musical notoriety with one or two well-known actors, humorists and the like from Liverpool in the case of the first concert it was a Mr. William Bennet, a well-known humorist and elocutionist from Liverpool.

Lord's Gate School also received money from St. John's Church, Burscough Bridge. School sermons were preached on many occasions such as the one in 1882, when the money was collected towards liquidating the debt of £30 on the master's house, Lord's Gate School.

However, not all the concerts were held in aid of paying the school debts. For example, in April 1891 a concert was held by the scholars and friends to raise funds for the formation of a free library. A concert held in November 1890 proved so successful that the money provided the Lord's Gate day and Sunday school with their annual treat in September 1891. This school treat was something special for they went by train from New Lane Station to Southport having first assembled at the Lord's Gate School. Competitions took place on the sands and 99 prizes were distributed, after which the children, parents and teachers sat down to a meal at the Messrs Thorpe's refreshment rooms in Neville Street. They returned home about 6 p.m.

Free Education

In 1891 the Lord's Gate School was again to run up against financial difficulties, because although the Lord's Gate School was declared free like all the other schools in Burscough, it meant the managers lost £15 per annum. This deficiency was met by soliciting small subscriptions from the parents and thus making the purpose of the Act seem ridiculous, because instead of making education free in this case it had caused an increase in fees for the parents.

By 1893 the debt on the school had still not been paid and the Rev. J. H. E. Bailey tried very hard to wipe out this debt. However, by 1896 the Lord's Gate School was in financial difficulties to such an extent that it was thought that the school would have to be closed. A meeting of the ratepayers of Burscough was called on Friday 18th September 1896 at 7 p.m. The object of this meeting was to decide what steps should be taken to get Lord's Gate School out of debt and carry on the same as a voluntary school, so as to avoid a School Board in Burscough. It was suggested that the two schools, i.e. St. John's, Burscough Bridge and Lord's Gate School, become merged into one.

The above proposals were rejected and eventually they agreed that a committee be formed with Mr. Peet as chairman. It was also suggested that the debts of the above schools be merged and a joint bazaar undertaken to raise money. The committee also had to undertake to solicit subscriptions from persons residing in Burscough. It was also agreed that a rate of 2d. in the £ be levied

EDWARD'S SERIES.   ST JOHN'S CHURCH, BURSCOUGH BRIDGE.

This photograph was taken in 1900 and shows the building formerly used as a 'private school' by Miss Mary Wilding. The shop which faces the Royal Hotel was Mr. Wilding's saddle shop.

A photograph showing the noticeboard advertising the St. John's School Procession in 1913.

on all ratepayers in the parish of Burscough. The above was subsequently carried out and the school continued as before under the voluntary principle.

To try to throw a little more light on the school, I was very fortunate in being able to get hold of one or two of Her Majesty's Inspectors reports and I include a summary of the report for the year 1893:

> Report on the School: Mixed School 'The condition of the school seems to be full of promise. The handwriting, neatness of papers, together with the high character of discipline and work in the lower standards have evidentally rewarded the mistress's efforts. In the higher parts of the school the children still show some innaccuracy and a lack of cheery desire to intelligently do their best. While mentioning this it must be distinctly understood that I attribute it entirely to the past history of the school, and anticipate that it will disappear. The needlework shows painstaking, but care should be taken to avoid unduly small stitches.'

The school house which adjoined the school was erected two years after the opening of the school in 1880, and the infants department was not added until 1902. Various improvements were made to the school as time passed and equipment added, notably a 'museum', which occupied an entire cupboard. This 'museum' was introduced by Mr. Studdart and consisted of all kinds of samples and materials by which small experiments could be performed.

Mention was made in the log-book of the visits by H.M. Inspectors to conduct examinations under the old 'payments by results' method, and it was also recorded that Miss Wannop, daughter of the vicar, and Miss Tomlinson, daughter of Mr. Ralph Tomlinson, came into the school to help with the teaching of needlework. Miss Wannop and Miss Tomlinson also taught needlework at St. John's C. of E. School.

Closure

In April 1943 the school was closed and, as I have mentioned previously, because of the war the land was required for an aerodrome, and the school was demolished. A temporary school was erected off Liverpool Road, which consisted of three Nissen type huts, with classrooms and corridor built alongside.

This therefore completes the history of the Lord's Gate School, in which I have tried to show how it began, developed and how it was nearly closed in 1896. I hope I have made it clear that the people of Burscough did not want a School Board school and I have tried to show what a strong influence the Church had upon the activities, both inside and outside of the school, and just how these were woven into the fabric of the local government of the district. Charities also played an important part in assisting the voluntary schools, but in the case of the Lord's Gate School neither charities, subscriptions nor donations were to save the school, so the imposition of a rate upon the ratepayers of Burscough was found to be the only solution. In 1902 the school came under the Lancashire County Council, who paid all expenses except those incurred in the upkeep of the buildings of denominational schools.

Headmasters

1878 - 1881 Mr. H. Coleman.
1881 - 1884 Mr. H. Preston.
1884 - 1893 Mr. George Bentley.
1893 - 1898 Miss Mary Taylor.

1898 - 1925 Mr. A. J. Studdart.
1925 - 1943 Mr. John Barrow.

Other early elementary schools

Two other elementary schools are known to have existed in Burscough in the 18th and 19th centuries, although almost nothing is known about them. The first seems to have been founded in about 1770, and to have had a Mr. John Tasker as its master in the late 18th century: it was owned and occupied by him in the 1780s. It was situated at Sheepcote Hill near New Lane. There is a suggestion that it may have survived into the 1860s, for in December 1870 it was said that 'the Earl of Derby has intimated through George C. Hale Esq. to the Rev. W. Wannop, Vicar of Burscough, his lordship's intention of erecting at his own cost a new school-house at Sheepcote Hill, near New Lane'.

The other school was situated near to the canal at New Lane, and was nothing more than a converted house. It was established in about 1840 when the Rev. W. Wannop became minister of St. John's parish church at Burscough Bridge. This was a day and Sunday school and was run by Wannop and his daughters, who did much of the teaching. The premises were owned at this time by John Campbell who leased the land from the Earl of Derby. The Rev. W. Wannop was a teacher before he entered the ministry, and was very aware of the need to improve the elementary education of ordinary people.

Both of these schools closed in February 1878 when the new Lord's Gate Township School was opened, and it is doubtful if the school building at Sheepcote Hill was ever replaced. The buildings of both schools have long since disappeared.

St. John's School, Burscough Bridge

Introduction

In the first half of the 19th century and after the Churches had a monopoly in education in Burscough. Churches had been connected with education through the Sunday Schools. In 1785, churchmen and nonconformists had joined together to form the Society for the Establishment and Support of Sunday Schools. However, Church and Dissent were split through two men. Bell, a churchman, and Lancaster, a Nonconformist, who introduced the system of teaching called the Monitorial System. Bell's method was adopted by the National Society, founded in 1811, and Lancaster by the British Society, founded in 1803.

The School

St. John's School, Burscough Bridge, was erected in 1836, the site having been given by Lord Skelmersdale. St. John's School adopted Bell's system of teaching and was known as the 'St. John's National Schools', up to the year 1906, when the title of the schools were changed to 'St. John's Church of England Schools, Burscough Bridge' by order of the Board of Education. Information about the running of the school before 1870 is very sketchy, because there are no log-books, manager's reports etc., to refer to.

The first schoolmaster was William Walton (1836-1854) and the first mistress was Elizabeth Wilding (1836-1849), who was followed by Catherine Irving in

1849. In 1854 they were followed by Mr. and Mrs. Saywell who were respectively master and mistress of the school, but gave up teaching altogether because he did not agree with the new educational scheme, which had been introduced by Forster's Education Act of 1870.

Apart from government grants and the fees from scholars, the school had to rely on subscriptions and donations from the people of Burscough and the money raised from the anniversary sermons at St. John's Church. These anniversary sermons were conducted once a year, and in 1856, £35 was raised for the schools.

St. John's National Schools between 1870 and 1902
The buildings and facilities

In 1870 the schools comprised the following: boys' school and infants' school. During the period 1870-1902 the school buildings remained largely unaltered, the only alterations taking place being of a minor nature, more in the form of repairs and modifications of existing buildings. The construction of a new classroom and gallery in 1881 was the only significant exception.

The schools were built to accommodate about 300 pupils, and in 1903 the schools were enlarged so as to take 480 children. The above schools still remain much as they did in the 19th century, but additions and alterations throughout the school have been undertaken during the last 20 years which have resulted in a major change in appearance both within and without the school.

The playgrounds have also been modified and washing, toilet and cloak-room facilities have been much improved and added to. As late as 1900 the H.M.I. commented on the insufficient cloak-room accommodation in the boys' school. Toilet facilities for both the boys and girls remained in a deplorable state until the 1950s. Water closets were not erected until 1911; prior to this dry earth closets had been used and it was the duty of the caretaker to empty the closets and remove the contents to the ashpit at the rear of the school. In 1896 the managers proposed that water should be laid on to the school, but because of a shortage of funds it was not completed until about 1912. The school was heated by open fires throughout the period of 1870-1902 and, according to the log-books, the caretaker on quite a number of occasions when ill did not light the fires, in consequence the children had to commence work in a cold school. In March 1904, 5 fire-guards were provided. This was done because the H.M.I. had complained about the safety of the children, especially the infants. The school was probably lighted with oil lamps throughout the period because there are several entries such as the following in the log-books:

> December 22nd 1874, 'During the holidays an entertainment will be given in this school for the purpose of raising funds to light the school with gas'.

However this does not appear to have been carried out, because the following log-book entry states that on the undermentioned date:

> December 14th 1886, 'The school room becomes so dark it is impossible to work according to the time-table'.

The only major activity that went on in the playground was drill, and this was either conducted by the headmaster, or an ex-sergeant from the army and in the early part of the 20th century St. John's Schools and the Wesleyan School drilled together.

Many attempts were made to improve the playground, but the work done was only in the nature of patching up the holes by filling them with cinders and the like. The drains in the yard were often blocked and it was this that caused the playground to flood during wet weather. However, in 1876, a Mr. Joyce gave the school 3 swings and 2 horizontal bars, which were erected in the boys' playground. In December, Mr. Joyce distributed prizes as an encouragement to the boys who had shown proficiency in the use of the above apparatus. The swings and horizontal bars were subsequently removed because several boys had hurt themselves. In 1909 Lord Lathom let a plot of ground behind the infant school at a rent of 10/– per annum — this land was subsequently used as a school garden.

It can be seen from the above that the conditions in the school during the 19th century and early 20th century must have been frustrating to teacher and pupil alike. It is also evident that money was the main problem, as always, in effectuating improvements, but there also seems to have been a certain amount of complacency on the part of the managers in attempting to improve the school in accordance with the various Acts of Parliament and Health Regulations. The H.M.I.s were important in this respect in that they could bring the manager's attention to certain things and, although they had no direct power to enforce their wishes, they could bring pressure to bear upon the managers and so effectuate certain improvements.

Without the registers of the period the number of pupils is difficult to assess and one has to rely upon the spasmodic entries in the log-books, which give the average number of pupils, but very frequently omit the total number on the books. One frequently comes across the remarks 'Poor School today' or 'a thin school today' which do not indicate how many pupils were present. The following are the averages that I have been able to calculate:

Mixed School	Total number of children on the Books	Average Attendance	
1870s	about 150 – 180	115 – 120	117
1880s	about 200 – 240	130 – 210	170
1890s	about 220 – 250	130 – 205	167
Up to 1902	about 250 – 300	240	240
Infants			
1870s	about 30 – 40		
1880s	about 40 – 55		
1890s	about 60 – 80		60
Up to 1902	about 110 – 120		80

It will be seen from the above that by the 1890s the school population had risen to over 300 pupils and having only been built to accommodate 300 pupils originally, the school must have been overcrowded. It was, therefore, because of overcrowding that the schools were enlarged in 1903.

Under Bell's system severe punishments were deprecated, nevertheless certain masters dealt in different ways with the pupils, and gave varying types of punishment which they thought would be sufficient to make them understand their wrong actions. Throughout the entire period I could not find any suggestion that severe punishments had been used on any occasion. Children were often deprived of certain privileges and by and large received greater punishment for playing truant than for any other kind of misbehaviour. The cane was used on the pupils from time to time and occasionally they had their ears pulled. Below I have extracted several entries from the log-books, so as to give the reader a more vivid impression of what happened:

1872, 17th Oct. — 'Clarkson playing truant again'.
1872, 24th Oct. — 'Clarkson kept without dinner for playing truant'.
1885, 29th Nov. — 'Caned 8 boys for playing truant'.

Subjects taught, 1870-1902

The three main subjects were reading, writing and arithmetic. It was upon the performance in the examinations of these subjects that the annual grant to the school was made. This 'payment by results' method had been introduced under the Revised Code of 1862, and was mainly responsible for the introduction of mechanical learning; it was discontinued in 1897. The grant was based on attendance as well as on the above examinations. For each infant (that was a child under 7) 6/6d was paid on attendance only, but this was also subject to the inspector's report. The older children (over 6) were grouped in six standards according to ability. The 3 Rs as noted above and needlework were the only subjects tested. A child could earn up to 4/– for good attendance and 8/– for a pass in the 3 Rs. A failure in one subject cut this to a third. Over the age of 13 the grant was 2/6d for attendance, and 5/– for examination. Teachers' salaries depended upon the annual grant and therefore they would be tempted to use any means to get successes and regular attendance.

The above had the effect of reducing the number of pupil teachers and also the number of candidates for the training colleges dropped. The national average was about 1 pupil teacher to 90 children in place of 1 to 50 before the Code. Thus, the large class was introduced.

The class in the boys' school at St. John's in 1873 contained about 80 pupils. Before the examination the children were drilled for many weeks, and were given tests and revision continuously and throughout the year they were subject to weekly and fortnightly tests.

The following is the summary of the inspector's report for the above:

'I regret to see no progress in sound instruction here. The examination passed by the boys although as many as 25 scholars qualified as regards attendance were withheld shewed that their knowledge of spelling and arithmetic was radically defective. In these subjects only 16 and 18 passes were respectively made. The reading was more successful, but was not characterised by intelligence. The discipline was very fair and the registers seem to be very carefully kept'.

In the 1870s at Burscough St. John's Schools, class subjects were introduced, e.g. geography, history and grammar; the following are some log book entries which give one an idea of the way they were taught and what they learned:

May 1871 'Commenced the Geography of England this morning with the 1st two classes'.
May 1871, 'Geography lesson: Six Northern Counties of England'.

Sept., 1871 'Geography lesson: Seas, gulfs, straits and Capes of Europe, learned by heart, and position put on map'.

To the above subjects drawing, singing and later object lessons were introduced. Home lessons were given in vocabulary, arithmetic and several other subjects. It is noticeable as the 1880s are approached that the scripture lessons become less frequent and the following type of entry appears time and time again: 'discontinued the Scripture lesson — have substituted arithmetic lesson instead', therefore making the religious controversy appear ridiculous. Poetry and literature were introduced in the 1880s and each year a reading list was produced giving the books to be read for each standard, such as the following:

1889 Poetry Standard I Mother and Babe in the Snow.
　　　　　Standard II Casabianca.
　　　　　Standard III The Wreck of the Hesperus.
　　　　　Standard IV-VII Lays of Ancient Rome.

The first pupil teacher that I have any knowledge of at Burscough St. John's School was a Mr. Thomas Greener. Therefore, I think if we follow his career it will give us an insight into how he became a pupil teacher, what he did, and how he was taught.

Thomas Greener commenced teaching as a candidate for pupil teacher on June 5th 1871. At the beginning of his career he was absent from school on many occasions because of illness. He received one hour's instruction per day and he had to sacrifice his dinner time to do it, but by 1874 this did not prove very practical because many children were staying in school and proved a nuisance. The alternative that was adopted to suit everybody was that he received his lessons from the master from 7 p.m. to 8 p.m. at his house. The master would give a lesson with the pupil teacher observing, and the day after the pupil teacher would either repeat the lesson or continue on from where the master had left off. He eventually gained a Queen's scholarship in 1879, and he left Burscough to go to St. Mark's College, Chelsea, for three years in order to continue his studies and become a certificated teacher.

As one approached the 1890s the turnover of pupil teachers increased and more women enter the school at St. John's to become pupil teachers. In 1900 the staff consisted of the headmaster, three assistant teachers and two pupil teachers in the 'mixed school' in contrast to the headmaster and one pupil teacher in 1870.

The headmasters

After Mr. Saywell left in February 1871 (he had been at St. John's School for 17 years) he was followed by a Mr. Thomas Lodge and Mrs. Susan Lodge, being master and mistress respectively.

In July 1874 Mr. J. K. Winter became master and he did much to improve the school and the reports of the H.M.I. were very favourable. It was through his endeavours that the school floor was transformed from a flagged floor to a wooden floor in 1875 during the summer holidays. The school rooms were also wainscoted (wooden panels put round the walls.) round 4 feet high and the rooms were painted and whitewashed throughout.

In July 1877 Mr. H. J. Wadeson took over as headmaster and during his period re-introduced the night classes for young people, which had been commenced by Mr. Winter. An additional classroom with a gallery was also built under Mr. Wadeson's influence in 1881. The school population was now growing and Mr. Wadeson apart from the mistress in the infants' school had three pupil teachers. He terminated his duties in December 1884, due to bad housing conditions.

W. H. Prestwood became master in 1885 being assisted by three pupil teachers. During his period very little developed, but the H.M.I. reports were very favourable. However, be that as it may, the managers requested Mr. Prestwood to resign after the Inspector's report of 1896.

Mr. E. J. Jacques took charge of the school in January 1897, and under his guidance and supervision the school was to develop and improve in many respects.

The three masters from 1871-1884 appeared to be at variance with the H.M.I. and because of this variance, it eventually resulted in them dismissing themselves. Five different headmasters in the course of just over thirty years is quite considerable and would, therefore, have a profound effect upon the establishment of some kind of foundation upon which to build the school's organisation in those early years.

Other uses of the school buildings.

The school was used mainly on Monday afternoons either by the clothing club at which the headmaster always appeared to be present, or the burial club which incidentally is in operation to-day. On the above occasions the children received a half-day holiday. Occasionally the school was used by the Provident Club and quite often for dances, school concerts, bazaars and the like, all held mainly for the purpose of raising money for the school. The school was also used for 'penny readings' which were discussions about certain popular books, and were quite common throughout the district during this period. The school was also used for local government elections.

In 1891 the managers consented to allow the use of the school for Technical Instruction lectures, which provided valuable information for the pupil teacher. Burscough St. John's School became a local centre for these lectures.

Finance and control

Apart from the government grant, money was raised by subscriptions, school sermons were preached, donations given to the school and there was the school pence. The school pence could range from 2d to 8d per week per pupil, and amongst large families could prove to be a great drain on their financial resources (labourers only received from 15/- to 18/- per week during this period), and more than anything else was responsible for the poor attendance of pupils. If the child did not bring his school pence to school he was usually sent home. The following is an extract from the log book:

1877 April, 'Sent Henry Sutton (3rd Class) home for his money (1/6d for 9 weeks)'.

It also appears from the following school log-book entry on 21st September 1883 that labour and materials were on occasion accepted as well as money in payment of the school pence:

'Grates and fireplaces rebuilt by a parent who has been in arrears of pence'.

St. John's School was accepted and taken under government in February 1871. In 1891 the schools, with the unanimous consent of the managers, accepted the free grant of the Assisted Education Act 1891 and were declared free on September 1st 1891. Thus ended the paying of the school pence to a certain degree.

Until September 30th 1903, the manager's accounts had been annually examined by the Board of Education, but on October 1st in accordance with the 1902 Education Act the Lancashire County Council took over the schools paying all expenses except those incurred in the upkeep of the buildings of denominational schools. The managers of these were required to keep their buildings in proper repair in return for retaining the right to give their own religious instruction, and St. John's managers spent the money in that way.

St. John's C. of E. School, Burscough Bridge

List of Headmasters

1836 – 1854 Mr. William Walton.
1854 – 1871 Mr. Joseph Saywell.
1871 – 1874 Mr. Thomas Lodge.
1874 – 1877 Mr. J. K. Winter.
1877 – 1884 Mr. H. J. Wadeson.
1884 – 1897 Mr. W. H. Prestwood.
1897 – 1924 Mr. E. S. Jacques.
*1924 – 1952 Mr. Isaac Jenkinson.
*1952 Mr. Norman Briggs.

List of Headmistresses of the Infants' School

*1836 – 1849 Elizabeth Wilding.
1849 – 1854 Catherine Irving.
1854 – 1871 Mrs. Maria Saywell.
1871 – 1874 Mrs. Susan Lodge.
1874 – 1884 Miss Mary Jane Edwards.
*1884 – 1887 Mrs. Wadeson.
*1887 – 1897 Miss A. E. Ward.
*1897 – 1898 Miss Emma Stephenson Edwards.
1898 – 1920 Miss A. E. Ward. (Miss A. E. Ward married Mr. Jacques
about 1915, and continued as headmistress until her death in 1920).
*1921 – 1927 Lucy E. Bruce.
1927 – 1952 Miss E. Smith.
1952 – 1966 Miss Wright.

*Approximate dates.

Regarding the infants' school, the log-books are missing, therefore, some of the dates on which the headmistresses commenced and finished are only approximate. There is no information about the earlier headmistresses, except for brief references in the headmaster's log-books. There was no log-book at this school before 1870.

The Roman Catholic School 1870-1902

The school

This school was erected in 1852 on land belonging to the Roman Catholic mission of Burscough. The property was leasehold, £10 rent being paid for the whole of the mission property, but none on the school separately. In 1700 Peter Lathom was granted this land on a lease of 999 years at a rent of £10, and that this was in trust for the St. John Roman Catholic mission. In 1850 the Sunday school was established in the Burscough Hall and from this developed the day school in 1852. The school was managed by one manager. There was no committee throughout the period.

In 1865 the school was known as the Burscough Roman Catholic School, the correspondent for the school being the Rev. Richard Hodgson.

The building and facilities

The school was built of brick with wooden floors and a slated roof. The classrooms appear to have been of the Prussian type which were usually small and contained one larger room, called the schoolroom, which was usually partitioned off from the other smaller room.

The school building remained unaltered until 1884 when a third room was added and attached to the principal school room; this room was 50 ft. in length, 22 ft. in breadth and 17 ft. in height. During 1884 the following internal alterations occurred: the gallery used by the infants which was in the junior school was removed into what had been the 'principal school room' and three cloakrooms were added, one each for the boys, girls and infants. Prior to the above the school had consisted of only two rooms as previously mentioned and the only alteration of any consequence before the above was done was in 1872 when windows were placed in the large door leading from the junior school into the 'principal school room', so that the teacher could keep her eye on the infants.

From the plans it can be seen that the school was heated by means of two open fires, but if one looks in the third room which was added, there are no fireplaces. Toilets were provided in the school, but there were no out offices for the boys. These toilets would be the dry earth kind and their contents would have to be removed by the caretaker to an ashpit. In 1911, however, 10 toilets were erected (5 for the boys and 5 for the girls and infants) together with a urinal for the boys, and at the same time piped water was laid on for the first time. There were two playgrounds, one for the boys and one for the girls. The school had been originally built to accommodate about 65 children but, similar to St. John's C. of E. School, the population increase has necessitated an enlargement, and in 1885 the recognised accommodation for the school had risen to 165 pupils. The school was divided as follows in 1885:

Accommodation for large room	100 pupils	(new building
Accommodation for class room	21 pupils	erected 1885)
Accommodation for infant room	44 pupils	
	165 pupils	

Finance

The annual income of the school in 1866 was the following:

Voluntary contributions......................................£48-0-0d.
School pence.. 9-4-0d.

Total　　£57-4-0d.

The school pence, rates of weekly payments and number of children paying at each rate in 1866 were as follows:

23 children at 1d and 12 at 2d. Different rates were determined by the older children. The annual expenditure for 1866 was the following:

Salary of teacher...£42- 0s.-0d.
Books.. £2- 5s.-0d.
Fuel and light... £3-10s.-0d.
Repairs.. £3- 0s.-0d.
Other expenses... £4- 5s.-0d.

£55- 0s.-0d.

Money was raised in the same way as at the other schools in Burscough in order to keep the school running, such as school sermons, bazaars and the like.

Number of pupils in the school at different times

The number of pupils on the books in 1866 was 50, in 1873 it had risen to 60 and by 1885 there was about 100. In the 1890s the number varied from 105-128 and at the end of the period there were 132 pupils on the books.

From the above it can be seen that in the early 1880s another school room was necessary because of the increased school population, however the new school room when built was large enough to last them into the early part of the 20th century, and was, therefore, by and large less crowded than the other schools in Burscough during the period in question.

This school was a 'mixed school' from the time it was established, and in the early days of the school, the boys, girls and infants were taught in the same building under one teacher.

Regarding punishment, one of the main methods employed was that of depriving the children of some of their privileges such as the following which appeared in the log-book:

1872 — 'On Wednesday several children were detained half an hour after the others for coming in after morning prayers without giving any written cause as required'.

Subjects taught, 1870-1902

The Catholic school, similar to the other schools in Burscough, received the government grants on the same basis, namely 'payments by results'. Therefore, the main subjects taught were reading, writing and arithmetic and in 1874 literature was introduced as a special subject. Geography, history, drawing and needlework were offered about the same time as class subjects. However, the class subjects did not last for long as can be gathered from the following log-book entry of 1875:

> 'Because of the dropping off in the upper standards the extra subjects have been given up and more time devoted to writing and arithmetic'.

By the 1880s class subjects were re-introduced and were continued, with success.

In 1866 the books and apparatus consisted of the following:

> 1 doz., copies of the Catholic series, 4 doz., Nelson's Step by Step, 1 set of New Reading Cards, 60 slates, 2 boxes of slate pencils, 2 blackboards and easel, 2 large framed slates one of which formed a lesson stand, 6 rulers, 10 packets of Davis' Arithmetical Cards, 1 Davis' Arithmetic with key, 6 doz., copies, 1 Box of chalk and a sufficient supply of foolscap and blotting paper.

Therefore, in the early years of the school it can be seen that the range of lessons and work was very limited and that the emphasis was on the 3 Rs. One can also sense a certain amount of pressure that must have been applied as the annual examination drew near. Religious examinations had also to be completed, but the Catholic school was fortunate in one respect in that there was only one manager: to judge from the log-books of the schools with more than one manager their very frequent visits must have seriously interfered with the daily running of the school!

By 1900 the range of subjects taught had increased, but nevertheless much can be seen in these lessons that echoes back to the method of 'payments by results', which was abandoned in 1897. There was still the emphasis on the 3 Rs and, if anything, very little flexibility within the subjects themselves. The introduction of physical exercises was nevertheless an innovation and something regarded as progressive in this district at the time.

The teachers and pupil teachers.

It is difficult to attribute the progress and development of this school to any one teacher, because there were about three teachers who were responsible for improving the standards and organisation at various times within the period. Unfortunately, when a teacher left, the school became unstable for a while and, therefore, spoilt the work that had been done before. The rate of turnover of teachers was higher than in any other school in Burscough, and in 1885 no fewer than five teachers held the position of mistress. In 1885 the H.M.I. said the following:

> 'There has been including the present mistress, no less than four teachers in this school during the year. Good results cannot be expected under such circumstances and it is creditable to find such excellent order and improvement rather than retrogression in instruction'.

All the teachers including the head teacher were women throughout the entire period, and this is only peculiar to this school in Burscough, all the other schools having a headmistress and a mixed staff of men and women.

Pupil teachers were recruited from the school on some occasions, usually starting as a paid monistress at about a 1/– per week. The first pupil teacher commenced duties in 1870 and was trained by the teacher during school hours, the teacher giving a lesson, which was observed by the pupil teacher. The method employed varied from teacher to teacher as the following log book entry will make clear:

1874 — On Wednesday the Mistress listened to a lesson given by the pupil teacher on the 'Goat'. These object lessons are always prepared by E. Dillon the evening before — she is supplied with 'Anecdotes of Animals and Birds' and the Natural History of Birds, Plants, Fishes and Insects'. These lessons are intended not only for the children, but also for E. Dillon's own improvement and to excite a taste for reading.

Quite a number of candidates for pupil teachers only remained in the school a few months and then gave it up, the main reasons being ill health and domestic troubles. Very few pupil teachers were recruited locally; some came from Liverpool, Wolverhampton and even further afield on occasions.

On several occasions when the teacher was absent or on holiday the assistant mistress in 1877 allowed assistants from other schools to help her in running the school. This again was peculiar to this school only.

This school was a mixed school and remained an all-age school until July 18th 1956. From September 1956, the older pupils attended St. Bede's, R.C. Secondary School, Town End, Ormskirk.

In 1961 and 1968 a new school was erected adjacent to the old school. This school is equipped with modern educational aids, the instruction is progressive and a great interest is shown in drama. The old school is still used and has been much improved.

St. John's Roman Catholic School, Chapel Lane, Lathom.

List of Head Teachers.

1852 — 1866 Miss Elizabeth Dunsford? (I am not certain of Miss Dunsford's appointment.)
1866 — 1871 Miss Esther Dagliesh.
1872 — 1877 Miss M. Keating.
1878 — 1885 Miss M. Woodward.
1886 — 1914 Miss Margaret Connor.
1914 — 1915 Mrs. Atkinson (temporary).
1915 — 1953 Miss Brennan.
1953 — 1963 Mr. P. P. O'Brien. Died July 17th 1963.
Sept. 1963 — Dec 1st 1963 Mrs. Fairclough, acting head.
Dec. 1963 — Mr. A. C. Evans.

The Methodist School Burscough Bridge.

Its history and development from 1870-1902.

Its foundation.

The memorial stone was laid on Monday 17th October, 1870, by James Wood Esq. LL.B. of Southport. The land was given by Lord Derby for the purpose of the school and it was agreed that the new school would stand on the south-east side of the chapel and would accommodate about 200 children. Mr. Thomas Bridge senior, was the contractor for the work and Mr. Thomas Bridge junior was the architect. The cost of building the school at this time, including alterations in the chapel, amounted to £540. The school was opened on 9th January, 1871.

Originally the chapel was divided into two parts, one for the congregation

A photograph of St. John's C of E Schools Walking Day, taken about 1925 with the Rev. Canon Johnson in the centre.

A boys' class during the early 1900s, taken at a school in the district, and unfortunately damaged.

The Roman Catholic School, Chapel Lane, Lathom, erected in 1852. Apart from certain improvements, the building remains much as it was in the 19th century.

The old school house, Chapel Lane, adjacent to the Roman Catholic School. The end view of this building can be seen in the photograph of the school above.

Angelic faces at the Burscough Wesleyan School in 1892.

And another group photograph at the same school, this time in 1919.

and the other for the school; but the congregation had got so large that the children were pushed out. They were thus forced to build a school. At this time about half of the children who attended the Sunday school prior to the building of the new day school, could neither read nor write, therefore it was hoped that the new day school would remedy this state of affairs.

The Wesleyan Sabbath School was established in 1856; the superintendent of the school was Mr. T. Radcliffe and the number of children attending in the 1860s was about 100. Before 1856 these children had never attended any Sabbath school. The Bible, singing and listening to sermons from various ministers in the circuit appears to have been the only form of teaching that they received. In 1870 only half of the children could read or write, and it requires much imagination to try to envisage just how these 100 children could have been taught in the chapel; it must have been almost impossible. The Education Act of 1870, which stressed the importance of accommodation, had to a certain degree influenced the development of the day school. The idea of a School Board in Burscough was to be avoided at all costs, and so the Wesleyan Methodists had to remedy the situation themselves.

Similar to all the other schools in Burscough, the Wesleyan Methodists raised the money from school sermons, the issuing of subscription lists, bazaars, glees and above all they were specially favoured with several large initial donations from interested parties in the area of Burscough, and the surrounding district, particularly Mr. Woods of Southport. When the school was erected the school fund already stood at £340 towards the £540 required and this debt was removed about three years later.

The building

Again similar to all the other schools in Burscough the school was built of brick, the rooms were small, the floors were of wood and the roof slated. It was heated by open fires until 1891 when hot water pipes and a boiler were installed. Initially the school was probably lighted with lamps, but in 1871 gas fittings were put in the school, therefore making this the first school to be lighted by gas in Burscough. Adequate toilet, washing and cloakroom facilities were only supplied in the 1940s. Toilet facilities would be the dry earth closets similar to those at St. John's School until 1911, when flush toilets were installed. It was between 1902-1911 that most of the area of Burscough was connected to the sewerage plant at New Lane. Throughout the period there were no out offices for the boys. The playgrounds again were similar to the other schools in Burscough and were in need of much attention and the repairs were only in the nature of patching up holes with cinders here and there, this making the surface dangerous for the children. Very little was done in the way of enlarging the school during the period, and it was only in 1899 that any major enlargement was effectuated by the construction of an infant school. Alterations were carried out in 1888 and in 1896 a classroom was added. Prior to 1899 the infants and senior children had been taught in the same school. The infant school was erected to accommodate 100 children and it was opened by Lord Derby on September 12th 1900.

The numbers of pupils in the school at different times

As I have stated before, this is a difficult task without the registers, and the undermentioned list will give the reader only an approximate idea of the increase in pupils during the period:

	Number of Pupils
1870s	43 – 80
1880s	80 – 165
1890s	165 – 200
1902	220

By the 1890s the school was overcrowded and the inspector warned the school under Article 84, that the school was overcrowded and not properly furnished. Therefore, this precipitated the managers to raise funds and build the infant school in 1899.

Children were admitted at the age of 3 during the period 1870-1902. Most of the children left school either at 12 or 13, but after 1886 some remained until they were 14 because they had not completed the required number of attendances. The school was first divided into a mixed and infant school in 1885. When the infant school was erected the pupils transferred to the mixed school at seven years of age.

There is very little evidence of punishment in the school log-books and apart from the occasional reprimands and detaining children either during lunch or after school, there appears to be very little else recorded on this aspect.

Transfers to and from other schools were rather more frequent in the Wesleyan school and they took place from and to the St. John's schools, Roman Catholic school, Lathom school and the Lord's Gate school. However, the Wesleyan school effectuated more transfers to other schools outside Burscough, than all the other schools put together. I attribute this to the fact that the greater proportion of the children were from canal boat families, and in the course of their parents' occupation they moved to other localities and established roots elsewhere. The other reason for transfers appears to have been caused by the establishment of the Ordnance Stores in Burscough in 1890. Some of the population of Burscough who worked there became soldiers and were moved to different areas from time to time by the War Department, and in consequence the children moved with them. It is likely from evidence contained in the log-book that during this period most of the people who worked at the Ordnance Stores sent their children to the Wesleyan School.

School pence at the rate of about 2d per week, per pupil, was in force, but was discontinued in 1891 when the school was declared free. Lathom school was a free school before 1891 and in some instances this is the reason why some children left the Wesleyan school to go there.

The subjects taught

Again reading, writing, arithmetic and needlework were the most important subjects which were taught in the early years; however, in the 1870s object lessons were introduced, and geography was also taught. From 1880, examinations were held nearly every fortnight and marks taken. During the 1880s and on into the 1900s, the school subjects began to expand and progress with a little bit of experimentation here and there. By 1900 the following subjects additional to the 3 Rs were being taught: English grammar, geography and map work, history, physiology, elementary science, scale drawing, a very wide range of object lessons (in 1896 samples were sent to the school from various branches of industry in connection with these lessons) and a fairly large number of songs were learned by the pupils as well.

Regarding the supply of books, the following log-book entry is of interest:

1884, April 4th — 'Received some new "Geographical Readers" the "World at Home". Propose selling them to the children who can pay for them at the rate of a 1d. per week.'

The above indicates that the children had to pay for the school books they would use while in class. This was common to all schools in Burscough, and the above did not only apply to text-books, but to copy-books as well.

Pupil teachers were employed at the Wesleyan Methodist school from its opening in 1871, but the system used was different. Unlike either St. John's school or the Roman Catholic school, the headmaster taught the pupil teachers at his own house. In 1887 when the school was short of another pupil teacher, two monitors were employed and the headmaster instructed them at his home as well. The headmaster at this time was Mr. Rouffignac and he was most concerned about doing the best he could for the education and instruction of the pupil teachers. In September 1892 the following appears in the log-book which I think will confirm this:

1892 Sept. 9th — 'Received a circular letter from the Secretary of the Harris Institute, Preston concerning Pupil Teachers classes about to be re-commenced. I should like our Pupil Teachers to attend, but I fear the expense of travelling twice a week will be too great.'

However, because the pupil teachers could not attend the above Institute, they took a correspondence course instead, supplemented with the 'Technical Instruction Classes' at Ormskirk (the pupil teachers attended these classes for drawing). The above together with the instruction from the headmaster was proving to be a big strain on the pupil teachers, as will be gathered from the following entry in the log-book:

1899 March — 'The pupil teachers have had so much study and answering questions for the correspondence class and so much extra work in connection with the Ormskirk class that they have not been able to prepare any notes of lessons.'

Until March 1879 only women teachers had been in control of the school; the first mistress being Janet Craven. Very little was done in the way of establishing a system within the school before Mr. F. H. Rouffignac came. Mr. Rouffignac was appointed the first headmaster. He came straight from Westminster Training College and was of Cornish French Huguenot extraction. He stayed in Burscough throughout his career and certainly gained the affection and respect of the people of the district. Mr. Rouffignac retired in 1921.

The school was enlarged and developed under Mr. Rouffignac and he was also responsible for extending the range of subjects and was for ever ready to help the pupil teachers all he could. Therefore, in contrast to the other schools in Burscough, only one headmaster was in control of the school, throughout the entire period under review.

During the Second World War, half-time instruction was introduced and the building was shared with Walton C. of E. (Girls) and Evered Avenue (Boys) Schools from Liverpool.

The general condition of the building, playgrounds (of mud and cinders) and toilets were deplorable and unsafe; therefore, the school quickly achieved controlled status in 1947. The county authority renewed the roof and toilet accommodation and gradually other improvements came, including new floors, the temporary classroom, screens, resurfaced playgrounds and finally staff toilets.

The all-age period ended in January 1959 and the character of the school changed. The highest number on the roll had been 291 pupils.

List of Head Teachers
1871 – 1873 Miss Janet Craven.
1874 – 1875 Mr. James Catterall.
1875 – 1877 Miss E. A. Aspinall.
1877 – 1879 Miss Storer. (supply mistress left in March 1879).
1879 – 1921 Mr. F. H. Rouffignac.
1921 – 1922 Mr. J. Cockroft. (supply teacher).
1922 – 1945 Mr. J. F. Robinson.
1945 –   Mr. E. B. Todd.

List of Heads of the Infants Department
1900 – 1901 Miss E. Greenwood.
1901 – 1903 Miss C. Veevers.
1903 – 1919 Mrs. Mary L. Hoyle.
1919   Miss Florence May Woodhead. (temporary).
1919 – 1930 Miss F. Bannister.

In 1930 the school was merged into one school and the position of headmistress of the infants school was brought to an end.

The attendance problem
Although there were many other difficulties confronting elementary education in the early years, perhaps the greatest was the acute problem of attendance. The 1870 Education Act was the first real attempt to tackle the problem. In this Act, the principle of 'permissive attendance' was adopted; this meant that if a child reached a certain level of educational attainment which was recognised by Her Majesty's Inspector, the child could leave school.

The half-time Factory Acts accepted the principle of compulsory attendance and by and large they saw that this was enforced by their factory inspectors. There are recorded in the log-books of every school in Burscough visits by the factory inspectors who made periodical checks of the schools to see that those children who were working half-time held recognised labour certificates to do so. A fine of £2 was imposed upon the parents if a labour certificate was not produced. In 1900 the children had to have an examination at Ormskirk in order to obtain their labour certificate. However, the problem of child labour involved social and economic factors. Children who were earning money were an asset to their parents and therefore their parents would encourage their children to go to work instead of going to school. The following entry in St. John's School log-book of 1877 will make this clear:

'The irregularity of attendance, which is the serious drawback to this school seems incapable of improvement. The root of the evil lies in the fact that the greater part of the parents have not the least desire to see their children educated. The lower the parents are in the social grade the more is this apparent'.

It was not until 1876 that the problem of compulsory attendance was tackled. In this year Lord Sandon's Elementary Education Act was passed its aim being to set up school attendance committees in those areas that were without a school board. Where no school board existed, the school attendance committees were to be appointed by the Town Council, Urban Sanitary District or the Guardians of the Poor Law Union. With regard to Burscough and the surrounding districts, with the exception of Skelmersdale, all the schools were voluntary, therefore there had been no need to erect any school board schools, and in consequence there was no school board in this area.

In August 1877 a Guardian School Attendance Committee was duly formed under the chairmanship of Mr. Roper and in accordance with the provision of the Act for enforcing the regular attendance at schools of all children within the Union, Mr. James Dixon was appointed school attendance officer. Incidentally Ormskirk formed its own School Attendance Committee to deal with Ormskirk schools only.

The Board of the Union School Attendance Committee consisted of nine members. Mr. Dixon was appointed as school attendance officer at a salary of £120 per annum and this was confirmed by the Education Department in September 1877. This Committee met at the board-room of the Workhouse in September 1877 when the bye-laws were made concerning compulsory attendance. The Committee met alternately once every month at the board-room of the Ormskirk Workhouse and at the Birkdale Town Hall. In 1878 Mr. Dixon furnished returns showing the number of children on the books of the elementary schools in the Union and the average attendance for the years 1877 and 1878. The total number on the books in 1877 was 5,277 and in 1878 it was 5,975. The average attendance in the former years was 3,100.7 and in the latter 3,708.19, an increase of 19% which was very satisfactory and showed that the amount of work that must have been done by the S.A.O., in accordance with the Education Act of 1876, was very great indeed.

On November 24th 1881 a special meeting was held by the Ormskirk Union School Attendance Committee for the purpose of appointing officers of the three divisons into which the district had been formed. Mr. Roper (chairman) presided and the following were appointed:— No. 1 district, Mr. David Cundliffe, post office, Maghull; No. 2 district, Mr. John Strickland, Burscough; No. 3 district, Mr. James Blundell, Banks.

The following attractions and occupations were responsible for a great deal of truancy during the period in all the schools in Burscough: hay-harvest, potato-setting (in March), potato picking (in October), circuses, rush-bearing, the 'Ormskirk and Rufford fairs', wash-day, picking sticks for the basket-makers, working in Isherwood's brickfields, coursing and working on the canal boats with their parents were some of the reasons or excuses for not attending school. Potato picking and working on the canal boats could affect school attendance for up to 8 or 9 weeks in the year, and after a fall in attendance it took weeks to make up a good school.

The canal boat people of Burscough (who represented the greater proportion of the people of Burscough at this time) and throughout the country in general were left pretty much to themselves. They were considered outside the pale of local and educational authorities. They were permitted to live in their boats as they pleased, to employ what labour they chose and to bring up their children without interference from school authorities. Having no fixed habitation, but being constantly in motion, they were outside the jurisdiction of any local authority. However, the Canal Boat Act of 1877, which was mainly the result of the work of George Smith, in drawing attention to these people did help to improve their conditions. The Act required all boats to be registered, the number of people of either sex, number and age were laid down that may be allowed to dwell on a canal boat, having regard to cubic space, ventilation, provision for the separation of the sexes and general cleanliness to prevent the spread of infectious diseases. It was not unitl the Canal Boat Act of 1884 that local authorities were required to make annual reports to the Board upon the action they had taken, and instructing local authorities to make sure that the children attended school. After 1885 the attendances in school by and large improved in Burscough as a result of the S.A.O.s. having the authority to enforce the compulsory school attendance clause contained within the Canal Boat Act of 1884.

Not only did the above effect attendance, but inclement weather, rain, snow and the like cut attendances drastically. Epidemics could close an entire school for weeks on end, the main infections being measles and scarlet fever. These two infectious diseases were very prevalent in Burscough during the late 1880s and early 1900s and all the schools were closed many times, from four to seven weeks at a time. Whooping cough, mumps, chicken-pox, diptheria, scarlatina, influenza and skin diseases were also responsible for reducing the school attendance. The undermentioned extracts from St. John's log-books indicate the problem:

1887, May 23 — 'Much sickness still prevails particularly measles'.

1887, June 2 — 'The Wesleyan School and Lord's Gate School are both closed on account of measles'.

1887, June 3rd — 'Medical officer called and looked at Schools'.

1887, June 16th — '40 children away with sickness, 75 absent altogether'.

After having looked at all the old schools in Burscough it only remains to say a little about the educational facilities which exist in Burscough today.

All the old schools in Burscough which were originally all-age schools catering for children from the age of 5 to 15, have now all become primary schools. The following is a list of all the primary schools in Burscough:

C. of E. Primary School, School Lane.
Lord's Gate Township, C. of E. Primary School, Liverpool Road.
Methodist Primary School, Orrell Lane.
Roman Catholic Primary School, Chapel Lane.

Burscough County Secondary Modern School, Trevor Road, Burscough

This Secondary School was one of the first to be built in Lancashire under the Ministry's scheme for reorganisation of secondary education in rural areas, and was officially opened on 10th June 1958 by the Right Hon. The Earl of Derby M.C., Lord Lieutenant of Lancashire. The school, which had been talked about and discussed for many years before if came to fruition, was opened for children on June 7th, 1959, and was built at a cost of over £100,000. Initially the school was to take 300 boys and girls, but would later cater for between 350-400 pupils.

The children attending the school were initially drawn from the pupils attending St. John's C. of E. School, Lord's Gate township school, the Methodist school, Newburgh and other local districts.

In comparison to the older schools in Burscough, this school is but an infant, having only been in use for just over 10 years at the time of writing. Nevertheless, times change and there have been alterations and additions to the school. Changes are necessary in order to keep up with the demands of technology, and the like and, therefore, the school has got to play its part. Courses have got to be flexible and need to be able to expand in order to embrace as many variations as possible to enable every child to have a chance to become involved. Commercial courses covering a variety of subjects have proved to be very popular, and of recent years have been well attended.

Although this school to some people may seem grand and to others not so grand in comparison to other schools and institutions, it is nevertheless a great stride forward from the first school which opened in 1733, on the brow of the pinfold. It has taken a long time to reach this position of secondary education, but much more needs to be done and in the future the comprehensive school may or may not provide the answer to the problem. It must be remembered that throughout the history of education, there has never been one system which has been able to satisfy the entire needs of a country, because change, competition from other countries, economic frictions and political and social differences have either enhanced or held back the evolution of educational thought and ideas. Therefore, toleration, co-operation and eventual unity among all nations and men is probably the only solution.

The Development and Administration of Burscough

FROM 1786 onwards Burscough village grew along the main road from Liverpool to Preston, and only in the years since the late 1950s has the shape of the village begun to alter from a simple linear one. In the past the high quality of the agricultural land to the west of the main road, and its tendency to flood or to be damp, have discouraged development for housing and industry, while to the east the land was extensively used for clay extraction in association with the brick and tile industry, and this, too, prevented building on any significant scale. During the Second World War the Government commandeered land from six local farmers to construct an airfield on the flat land west of the main road. The airfield remained derelict for some years after the Admiralty finally gave up its interest in 1961, and large parts of it are still in this condition, although some light industry has been established in the area of the airfield recently. Since the war, too, the abandonment of the old brickyards and clay workings has been followed by some filling in and reclamation, while the growth of Burscough as a residential area for workers in other towns has led to house building away from the old line of the village, to cover the area between the main road and the railway line and out towards the Skelmersdale road.

Most of the property which has been built since the 1950s has been private housing, with some council housing and council flats, and a number of new industrial buildings as Burscough acquired a range of small scale light industrial concerns. The village has thus grown rapidly in both population and area since the war, until it now has the scale of a small town. The next section reviews in more detail the changes in building types and the physical growth of Burscough over the past two centuries.

Types of Building

Up to the latter half of the 18th century many of the buildings in this area were constructed of wood with walls of wattle and daub and roofs thatched with reeds. Very few of these now remain in this area and, although many have been demolished in recent years, it is refreshing to see the 'Thatched Cottage' in Moss Lane (between Burscough and Rufford) which has been rebuilt by Mr. and Mrs. Carter on the site of a former cottage. Some of these sites have been occupied by cottages for over four centuries, and whilst most of the cottages have now gone, subsequent buildings have been erected on their sites. Gradually, some three hundred years ago, the pattern of building began to change from wattle and daub to brick.

Owing to the good supply of clay in this area, houses were built of brick from the 17th century, but it was not until the 18th century and especially during the early part of the 19th century that brick began to supersede the traditional building materials of wattle and daub in this area. During the 1840s to 1870s

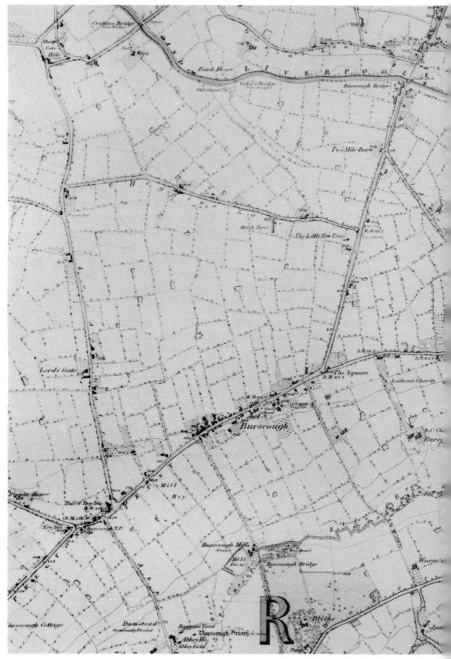

A section of the first (1845) six inch OS map, showing

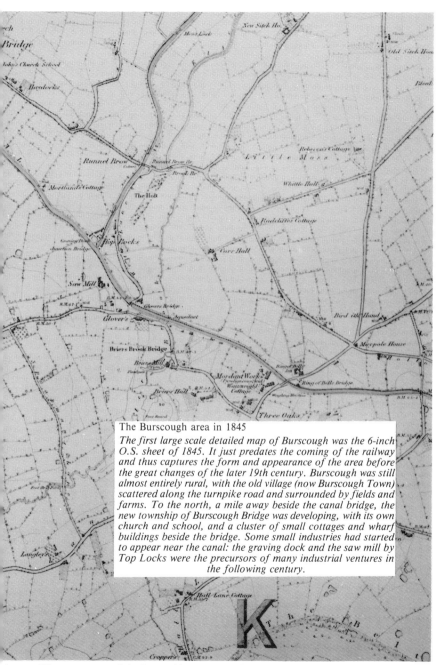

The Burscough area in 1845

The first large scale detailed map of Burscough was the 6-inch O.S. sheet of 1845. It just predates the coming of the railway and thus captures the form and appearance of the area before the great changes of the later 19th century. Burscough was still almost entirely rural, with the old village (now Burscough Town) scattered along the turnpike road and surrounded by fields and farms. To the north, a mile away beside the canal bridge, the new township of Burscough Bridge was developing, with its own church and school, and a cluster of small cottages and wharf buildings beside the bridge. Some small industries had started to appear near the canal: the graving dock and the saw mill by Top Locks were the precursors of many industrial ventures in the following century.

h area. Photo courtesy of the Lancashire Record Office.

several brick and tile works emerged in this district and the building activities of Thomas Bridge are evidence enough to show that brick was the predominant building material by the 19th century. By 1801 in many of the leases and bills of sale at that time the principal buildings were described as being of brick with slated roofs. It is also interesting to note that although building regulations were not in force during the 18th century and early part of the 19th century, specifications were issued regarding the building of houses in the 18th century in this district which were quite detailed for that period. A building specification concerning a house to be erected by a Mr. William Mawdesley at Higgins Lane in 1804 distinctly stated that it had to be built of 'Good Brick and slate and the front to be sashed with stone'.

As time marches on there is a gradual transition from the old to the new methods, but there is always a little of the old that seems to linger on and this can be seen in the buildings surrounding the Burscough area. Today in the township of Burscough the majority of houses are built of brick. Very few buildings are constructed throughout of stone and of these the number are mainly farms, the vicarage and the parish church. Other structures which are the mark of a former era that are, or were, constructed mainly of stone are the Burscough Priory, the canal and railway bridges and some of the railway stations, which were largely constructed from local stone. Breaking away from the local and traditional materials was the construction of Iron Bridge over the canal by Joseph Butler & Co. of Stanningley near Leeds in 1848 which is adjacent to H. & R. Ainscough's Flour Mill. Definitive details concerning the dating of all the property of Burscough could be done, but this would be more suitably achieved on a geographical rather than historical basis.

Growth of building

Between the years 1580 to 1720 from information contained in parish registers, the population remained fairly static by today's standards. However, by the end of the 17th century the plague had left England and there was some recovery and slight increase in the population which continued to gain momentum in the latter half of the eighteenth century. By 1773 the population of Burscough would lie approximately between 750-850 persons (there was no census at that time) and the number of inhabited houses was in the region of 170-180. A large number of these houses were centred along the turnpike road at High Lane, Burscough Town and down Moss Lane, and others were situated down Martin Lane (now demolished), Sheepcote Hills and the remainder consisted of the odd farm house dotted here and there. By 1801 the population of Burscough had risen to 1,139 and the population continued to increase until 1851 when it reached 2,480 persons and, correspondingly, the number of houses had risen to over 400. However, from 1861 to the 1880s the population declined owing largely to the development of coal mining in the Skelmersdale area. As I have mentioned before the population of Ormskirk in particular increased appreciably in the late 1840s which was mainly due to the flood of Irish immigrants who entered many parts of Lancashire as a direct result of the Potato Famine of 1845. By 1855 there was a great demand for houses in and around Ormskirk, and in 1861 the Ormskirk and Southport Building Society was established with Mr. William Mawdesley as secretary.

During the late 1880s the population of Burscough began to increase and in

1887-8 several improvements were effectuated. In the area of what is now Moss's Electrical Shop, Eastwood's Shoe Shop and the Burscough Tyre Company's premises near the canal bridge, a number of old and delapidated properties were taken down in 1887. Part of this area was taken over by the Leeds and Liverpool Canal Company who built stables and a provender warehouse on the site. They also installed a seven horse power gas engine which was put down for the purpose of mixing provender. This 'station' (subsequently called 'Canal Company's Yard') was originally built to enable the horses coming from and going to Liverpool to be changed there. On the opposite side of the road, between Orrell Lane and the Southport-Wigan Railway (Mart Lane was only established at this date), Mr. James Martland Ltd. had his warehouse built as well as erecting 16 cottages. He also had two shops built fronting the Liverpool and Preston Road and between these and the warehouse he had a further 6 cottages built.

A railway siding was also constructed which ran to the warehouse and was at that time capable of holding 60 wagons. A pierhead was also built from which the produce could be deposited into the wagons. The basement of the building was intended to be used as a potato store and a heating apparatus was provided to keep the frost from attacking the potatoes. In the heating room, experiments were carried out with trial seeds, mainly for buyers. On the first floor was the saleroom, the weighing-up room and the bagging room. At that period a large number of potatoes were being exported to America. The second floor was the sample room. The houses comprising Stanley Street were also built during this period, but they have since been demolished and replaced by the car park adjacent to the old Canal Company's Yard. A number of houses were also built in Orrell Lane (then known as Gobbins Lane) in 1897 to mark Queen Victoria's Diamond Jubilee. During 1894-1895 a number of terraced houses were erected in Square Lane.

By 1901 the population had risen to 2,752 and in 1900 Mr. John R. Bissett, builder of Mill Lane, Lathom erected 30 cottages in what was subsequently called Victoria Street.

From the 1860s to 1890s a number of fairly large residential houses were built in the Burscough and Lathom districts, e.g. Howick House (built 1870 renamed Ordnance House), Richmond House built about 1870 (now demolished), Sefton House (built in the 1890s, the largest house in Burscough and now used as an old peoples' home), Florida built in the 1860s, Clayton House (now turned into flats), Brooklands (now demolished) and several more which marked, in most cases, the rise in this area of the middle classes.

During the 1880s and 1890s several small builders and contractors were established in Burscough apart from Mr. Thomas Bridge:

> Henry Darby, Builder, John Ross Bissett, Joiner, Builder and Contractor, Mill Lane and Mr. Charles Wells J.P.

In the late 1890s Mr. Charles Wells built some property in Burscough and his father Mr. Robert Wells built Richmond House and outbuildings in 1870. In the 1860s he became proprietor of an extensive stone quarry at Bootle, but when the latter town made an arrangement with the city of Liverpool for the supply of water from Lake Vyrnwy, it resulted in his quarry becoming flooded and he had to discontinue operations. Subsequently, Mr. Wells purchased stone quarried at Higher Bebington, Cheshire. He returned to his old home of

Richmond House, Burscough, in 1896 and, to the great benefit of the community, erected a number of houses in Burscough.

In 1885 Mr. James Tasker, who was a monumental mason and sculptor, established his business at Liverpool Road, Burscough, adjacent to the Burscough Bridge Garage. His workshop was situated there and still remains to this day in a delapidated state, and on a tablet in the wall is an inscription bearing his name. He was joined in the business by his son in 1895 and he supplied monuments, headstones, tombs and crosses in marble, granite or stone. During the excavations of Burscough Priory in 1886, Mr. James Tasker was the foreman of works under the direction of Mr. James Bromley J.P., the local antiquarian. The memorial stone of the Wesleyan Infant School at Burscough was the work of Mr. James Tasker.

By 1901 the number of houses in Burscough had risen to 577, but for the next 15 years very little building appears to have been done, and with the intervention of the 1914-18 war, both men and materials became scarce. However, following the First World War, building began to pick up again and, in the next ten years, another 250 houses were built in Burscough. Prior to the First World War, most of the houses in Burscough had been built by private speculators, but after the war, the private sector was found to be inadequate and, as in many other areas, the Government was forced to step in and a number of council houses were built in Red Cat Lane. Building was again brought to a standstill during the great depression 1930-1935 and, as a result, wages and prices of building materials fell with the result that there was a revival of the private non-subsidised building. From 1936 to the outbreak of the Second World War in 1939, there a housing boom and in Burscough houses were erected at Trevor Road, Lord's Gate Lane, Mill Lane and Mill Dam Lane. In 1936 a survey was made under Section 1 of the Housing Act, 1935, and the number of working class houses in Burscough (excluding council houses) was 718 of which 30 were overcrowded. The survey also revealed that there were 80 council houses in Burscough of which 9 were overcrowded and in the whole of the Ormskirk Urban District, there were 155 working class houses (which nearly represented 5% of the total) overcrowded. Over 30 houses were empty at that time and, therefore, the problem was one of re-housing, which was mainly met by private contractors in this area.

The Second World War intervened and progress was again halted and many of the builders and contractors in Burscough during and towards the end of the War did much repair work to bomb damaged houses in Liverpool. It was during the 1940s that the council houses were erected at the Manor Road site which was followed by the erection of more council houses in Richmond Avenue and Elm Road in the 1950s. During the Second World War a Fleet Air Arm camp was built along Higgins Lane (it also occupied part of the Vicarage Field) and adjacent to Trevor Road, and after the War was over the huts were vacated by the W.R.N.S. and other naval personnel, but the property was subsequently invaded by squatters in 1946 and 15 families took possession of some of the disused huts. Subsequently more people came from Liverpool and the entire Camp was eventually occupied by squatters. Many of these huts were converted and improved by the occupants, but during the late 1950s council houses were erected on this site, the Nissen huts were gradually taken down and many of the squatters were re-housed. The plan of the roads changed very little and today Truscott Road follows the same route as Nelson Road did when it was the Fleet Air Arm camp.

During the 1960s the building of privately owned residential houses increased appreciably in the Burscough area and reflects to some degree the increased prosperity and higher standard of living enjoyed by some of the inhabitants since the War. During the 1960s the main concentration of private buildings were erected off Junction Lane, e.g. Glenroyd Drive and associated roads, Gower Gardens, Alexander Drive and Ellerbrook Drive and associated roads. These have since been followed by Almond Avenue, off Red Cat Lane, Colbournes Close, off School Lane, Rivington Drive, off Liverpool Road, Christine Crescent and Peters Avenue, off Higgins Lane, Windsor Close, off Richmond Avenue and at the time of writing, property is being erected by the Sefton Building Company just off Moss Lane and several other private residences have also been built in this district in recent years.

In 1963 proposals were put forward by the Council to build Stanley Court and, subsequently this was done and, for the first time, flats have been built in Burscough.

Much of the building during the first half of the 20th century was undertaken by local builders such as the following:

Robert Hesketh, Henry Trafford, James Billington, Ben Turner and Mr. Fletcher and Mr. Ward.

In 1904, Mr. Trafford's business premises were situated down Moss Lane where Alty's are today. However, in 1926 the premises were occupied by Mr. Ben Turner and subsequently by Mr. Ward and in 1960 the premises were taken over by Alty's Ltd., builders merchants from Hesketh Bank.

Many of the local builders had originally been joiners and Mr. Fletcher (now retired) of Briars Lane, initially worked for Lord Lathom, but after the First World War he went to work for Mr. Trafford. Unfortunately due to the Great Depression, Mr. Trafford met with financial difficulties and subsequently Mr. Fletcher took over his business. Mr. Fletcher's premises were situated down Stanley Street and during his career he has built numerous private houses in this district and has improved and modernised many as well such as the Manor House along High Lane, residence of the late Bruce Smith, Dr. Pearson's house and the late Dr. Pitt's surgery in School Lane. He has also carried out many repairs to council houses and during the Second World War carried out many repairs to bomb damaged houses in Liverpool. In 1933 he built the manse along Liverpool Road, and in 1926 carried out extensive alterations to the Wesleyan chapel in Orrell Lane.

It was during the 1930s that two more builders emerged in this district, namely J. & R. Woods, and Berry and Hellowell. The late Mr. Ernest Hellowell came from Yorkshire and initially started in business as a building contractor with Mr. Berry in the Southport district. His original business premises were situated in Trevor Road, Ainsdale, but after undertaking many large housing and other contracts, his business soon grew. Subsequently in the late 1930s he moved his headquarters to Burscough where he found employment for many people. During the 1930s he built the houses in Trevor Road, Burscough, and at Ryburn Road and County Road, Ormskirk. The firm still continues and in recent years has erected houses in Glenroyd Drive and their associated roads. Mr. Hellowell lived at the 'Homestead', Junction Lane, the former home of Mr. James Bromley J.P., the antiquarian. Mr. Hellowell was interested in the welfare of Burscough and did much to promote the development of the Old People's Club. He also concerned himself with many activities in Burscough which are too numerous to mention at this point, and throughout his career was very much respected by the people of this district.

Since the 1950s numerous other builders have erected property in Burscough, such as the following:

G.C.T. Contractor Ltd., of Blackburn (Colburnes Close); Thomas Construction of Ormskirk (Almond Avenue); First National Housing Trust Ltd., and several more.

Parks and gardens

In the June issue of the *Burscough Parish Magazine* of 1936, the late Rev. H. Flenley dealt with the question of playing fields for children in connection with the King George Memorial. He said, 'We have at present the Vicarage Field for organised games (not chiefly for children), Victoria Park for organised games for children, and a small piece for children's games near the council houses, Red Cat Lane.' He envisaged the time when Burscough would be more built up than it then was and he proposed the following:

'What we need now is a playing field between the bottom of School Lane and Runnel Brow; one at the corner of Square Lane and Liverpool Road; another at the corner of Lord's Gate Lane and Liverpool Road; and another that would be available for the children of New Lane and Crabtree Lane. In this way the children of the parish could go to play in safety.'

However, times change and Mr. Flenley could not have forseen the great impact that the motor car was going to have on the life of a future generation, neither could he have forseen the development of television in all its aspects, nor the improved sports facilities at schools and other diversions which are created in the world of today.

For a time it appeared in Burscough as though the trend towards developing parks and other outdoor recreational facilities was on the decline, for by the end of the 1950s there were fewer facilities for outdoor recreation than in Flenley's time. The vicarage field had been sold for building purposes and the tennis courts and croquet pitch were abandoned and have remained in a disused state until this day. By the beginning of the 1960s the position was acute and subsequently in 1962 land was obtained off Junction Lane for the purpose of developing a park. The park was named Richmond Park which possesses a bowling green, tennis courts and other facilities. Therefore, the immediate needs have been satisfied to a degree but, as times change and the population grows, who knows Mr. Flenley may be proved right.

Gardens

In July 1938 a public garden was opened in School Lane, Lathom (at the rear of the Royal Hotel) by Mr. William Sephton who was chairman of the Parks Committee and Mr. Clucas of Ormskirk gave most of the plants. This has now been done away with and has been replaced by a car park. Subsequent to the removal of the old property in Stanley Street, another small garden has since been developed and recently a number of rose trees have been planted along the entrance to the old Canal Company's Yard.

Burscough Palais de Danse and the Market Scheme

On December 2nd 1926 the Burscough Palais de Danse was opened which was a new feature added to the social life of Burscough. The building was situated at the rear of the old brewery (near the Packet House Hotel) and was erected by Colonel Wallwork, who was the sole proprietor. The building was well equipped as a dance hall and was fitted with every convenience. On the opening night special celebrations took place and valuable prizes were awarded for dancing during the evening. It is of interest to note that there was parking accommodation provided and cars could be garaged free of charge. The entrance fee to the dance on that occasion was 2 shillings. Subsequently dancing was held every Monday (admission 1 shilling), Wednesday and Saturday (admission 2 shillings). In March 1928 the Palais de Danse was transformed into the 'Burscough Market Hall' on Fridays only and was open from 9 a.m. to 9 p.m. Stalls were let for confectioners, greengrocers etc., and a cafe was also envisaged. A large room was also provided free of charge for farmers to transact their business, but it appears from the information available that this was never used.

In 1927 Mr. Wallwork also erected some shops in front of the Brewery and altered and improved some of the existing buildings, flanking the Liverpool to Preston main road. However, in April 1928 Mr. Wallwork went ahead with his project of a covered market and he appears to have abandoned his first project of the dance hall, for on April 19th 1928 he opened Burscough's first covered market. A number of stalls were taken by Burscough, Ormskirk and Southport tradesmen and on the day of the opening special prizes were awarded to lucky purchasers at various stalls. There were over 30 stalls ranging from drapery to motor cycle accessories and the market remained open until 8 p.m. In 1929 he was joined by his son and the market at that period was open every weekday until 6 p.m. However, in March 1930 Mr. Wallwork anticipated improving and extending his existing premises, but for reasons unknown he postponed the venture and the business subsequently declined and eventually closed.

The reason why this enterprised failed is not fully known, but at the time the population of Burscough was probably not sufficient to maintain the market. It was also the period of the Great Depression when wages and materials fell, and he would have had opposition from traders in this area no doubt and the competition from the established market at Ormskirk would always be there.

Conditions in Burscough before the 20th century

It is difficult for us today to realise just how life was for ordinary people even at the end of the last century. If we think of life without such facilities and amenities as piped gas, water supplies, electricity, the regular removal and disposal of refuse, metalled roads, streetlights, sewage disposal, medical services and welfare facilities, then we will perhaps appreciate how difficult life was for our forefathers. Burscough was no exception to the hardness of life and the conditions which existed here before this century make fascinating, if sometimes disturbing, reading.

Public health and disease

In earlier centuries the disease which was perhaps the most feared was the plague, because of its devastating consequences. There were of course many other diseases which regularly ravaged communities and numerous infectious diseases which were so widespread and so regular in their appearance that contemporaries often make no remarks or comments about them. Infectious diseases spread rapidly during the Middle Ages largely owing to the widespread malnutrition amongst the people caused by the famine pestilences; the insanitary conditions of the times, especially in the removal of sewage and the prevention of contamination of wells and other sources of drinking water and the lack of scientific knowledge to check their spread. Disease is no respecter of persons and the nobility and clergy also fell victims to the plague and other diseases but owing to their numbers not being so great as the poor people and by and large because they were better fed and in some instances isolated from the community, their chances of survival were greater in certain areas. Tuberculosis was known as the King's Evil and since the Dark Ages it was thought that the disease could be cured by the royal touch, and it is supposed that Charles II touched nearly 100,000 persons. In 1676 Richard Aspinall of Burscough asked for an order 'that the overseers of the poore may allow some reasonable sume of money towards carrying the poor child,' which he described as being 'about fowre years of age' and 'well nigh consumed with the King's Evil,' to London. The Justices of Peace at Ormskirk allowed £1 which was recorded by the clerk as follows:

'To pay 20 shillings into the hands of Mr. Chorley to be payed when it gone or if it dye or does not go then to be returned.' L.R.O. (QSP 452/1)

It appears that the plague visited Ormskirk parish (which then included Burscough) in 1558 and 1559 for the number of deaths recorded in those years was respectively 174 and 115 which was above twice the normal death-rate at that time. In July 1590 there were 20 deaths in Ormskirk parish and in 1591 from August to December 77 burials were recorded: both of these figures were well above the average death-rate. Ormskirk parish was affected again in 1623, 1642, 1644, 1648 (was badly stricken) and in 1653 nearly 400 people were confined to their homes, they either being infected or suspected of having the plague.

The number of people that died of the plague in Burscough is not known for although Burscough was within Ormskirk parish, the early registers do not specify the residence. Unfortunately, the later registers from 1644 to 1656 do not exist from which relevant information concerning the number of deaths in the Ormskirk and Burscough area could have been ascertained. In the Ormskirk churchwarden's accounts for 1665 and 1666 there are numerous entries concerning the destruction of vermin, i.e. rats, moles etc., and it is interesting to note that even during the 19th century there was a voluntary rate of 1d in the £ laid for the destruction of moles in Burscough.

Poverty and poor relief

Before the development of workhouses and later hospitals there were very few places except monasteries where the poor could obtain some relief from their suffering. At the Dissolution some of the monasteries were found wanting, but there were many that did good work in alleviating the suffering of the people and I believe that in this connection the Burscough Priory, although not free from faults, did much work in this direction. I have already mentioned that there was a leper hospital at Burscough and there was no doubt an infirmary there, but during the excavations in 1886 the area associated with the infirmary, together with the great hall, chapel of the Prior's house and the chapter house, were not fully explored.

When the monasteries were dissolved much hardship was inflicted on the poor, which in turn resulted in a great increase in vagrancy. At Burscough when the Priory was dissolved a certain amount of hardship must have been experienced for as we know up to 40 people were employed at the Priory, and each year the monks distributed £7 (in the form of wheat every week) for alms to the poor in Burscough, but this was disallowed by the Commissioners in 1536. The monks of Burscough Priory during their stay at Burscough no doubt took care of the sick and infirm and this burden would also be added to the township's numerous problems when the Priory was dissolved. This burden was relieved a little with the introduction of the Elizabethan poor laws, which also helped to arrest to some degree the increase in vagrancy. In 1531 an Act was passed which permitted licenses to be issued for begging and for the first time a distinction was made between 'vagabonds' and 'poor, aged and impotent persons'. With regard to the latter persons, which also included soldiers who had been wounded in the wars, the justices of the peace had the right to grant them licenses to beg. Another Act was passed in 1536 which prohibited the issuing of begging licenses and in essence contained much of the basic material of the Poor Law Act of 1601, but unfortunately because of the great reliance on private charity the law remained ineffective.

Subsequently, numerous Acts were passed in an attempt to organise the collection of alms and from the compulsory levy instituted in 1572, the basis of the poor-rate evolved. However, the Act of 1576 made the first attempt to deal with the problem in practical terms. The parochial authorities were to purchase material whereby employment might be given to the workless and 'Houses of Correction' were to be set up in every county for those who refused to work or were committed to them. The first 'House of Correction' in Lancashire was established at Preston in 1617 and in this connection the following entries in the constable's accounts of Burscough may be of interest:

'October 27th - 1707 Paid to Mr. Orme High Constable for the master of the House of Correction as appears by a receipt......1/10¼d.'
'August 17th - 1718 To bringing of Ann Spiley (or Spibey) to House of Correction.....5/– d.'
'Paid the same day to Mr. Coubon for putting and loosing Ann Spibey into House of Correction......7/d.'

Although Houses of Correction initially served as workhouses, lunatic asylums, infirmaries and gaols many of them subsequently became gaols. The original county gaol was Lancaster Castle and there are references to its upkeep by the numerous townships in Lancashire and Burscough was no exception. In 1707 William Green, Constable of Burscough, recorded the following:

'Paid to Edward Darwen high constable for the repair of Lancaster Castle and dungeon......4s-7d'.

A House of Correction was built at Kirkdale in 1819 and was followed by Walton Gaol in 1855, which in 1884 was enlarged by Mr. Thomas Bridge of Burscough.

Poor Law, 1601

In 1601 the famous Poor Law Act was passed which was based on the experience gained from the working of the previous Acts. Therefore, there was very little that was new in this Act except that it was a codification of the existing laws. This Act formed the basis for the poor law administration for over two centuries. The main points of the Act were as follows:

(a) Each parish was to be responsible for the maintenance of its poor.
(b) The infirm were to be maintained, and work was to be provided for the able bodied.
(c) The destitute were to be compelled to work in the houses of correction.
(d) The children of paupers were to be apprenticed so that they could play their part in the life of the community.

The money for the poor-relief was obtained partly from fines such as recusancy and partly from the poor-rate which was levied by the overseers on the householders of each parish.

The overseers' accounts for Burscough in the early part of the 18th century indicate that the money was collected from the householders of the parish in sums varying from a few pence to over £2. The wealthier landowner or farmer paid more, e.g. during the first half of 1729 the occupiers of Martin Hall paid £2 5s. 0d. into the poor-fund. Relief was paid out in various ways and the following are a few extracts from the overseers' accounts of 1717-1718 and 1759 and 1771:

'1717 Clogs for Mary Fletcher –/8d.'
'1717 Paid for sherts for William Houcroft 4/– d.'
'1759 Oct., - Thos. Culshaw for the Coffin 5/6d.'
'1771 April - Paid Martin Wilson for relief 1/6d.'
'1771 August - To reducing a fracture for Forshaws sons arm 10/6d.'

This last entry indicated that medical treatment was costly business even for what we would term minor injuries.

The undermentioned were the amounts collected by the overseers of Burscough, partly in 1771 and 1772:

From 9th April — 25th October 1771

	£	s.	d.
Total Cash received from Ley or Rates and others.....	35	4	8
Total Cash Disbursed..............................	35	3	8
Cash due to Town	—	1	0

20th April 1772

	£	s.	d.
Total Cash received from Ley or Rates Book..........	53	3	6
Total Cash Disbursed..............................	40	8	7
Cash due to Town (from Mr. Hill)..................	12	14	11
Cash due to Town from John Culshaw...............	—	1	0
Total due to the Town by both officers..............	12	15	11

Act of Settlement, 1662

This Act was intended to operate against or prevent persons from other parishes drifting into an area and, as each parish was responsible for its own poor, this law was carried out very rigorously. A newcomer might be removed within 40 days unless he or she could give some security that they would not become liabilities on the parish. Subsequently certificates were issued by parishes which acknowledged that the worker's own parish would be liable for his support if he became destitute. The only way that a person could acquire settlement in a new parish was if he became wealthy enough to rent a house worth £10 per annum.

The Law of Settlement was carried out in Ormskirk parish (which included Burscough at that time) and evidence exists in the parish registers and settlement papers of its enactment. In some instances the settlement concerned persons coming into this area from elsewhere and *vice versa,* and the following accounts concern the former:

'1699 - Upon hearing the difference between the overseers of the poor of Burscough and Burtonwood in the said County touching the settlement of Ralph Darbyshire, his wife and Joseph his son who are lately come to inhabit and reside in the town of Burscough aforesaid not having acquired a legal settlement there, but being poor are likely to become chargeable to and burthensome upon the inhabitants of the said township. And it appearing unto us that the said Ralph Darbyshire was born in Burton Wood aforesaid and lived a considerable time there and no proofe being made that the said Ralph Darbyshire hath gained Legal Settlement elsewhere since that time. We therefore two of his Majesties Justices of Peace one being of the Quorum of and for the said county doe hereby declare and adjudge the last settlement of the said Ralph Darbyshire to be in Burton Wood aforesaid and doe order the overseer of the poor of Burscough aforesaid to Remove him thither his wife and son and the overseers of the poor of Burton Wood are hereby required to Receive and provide for them according to law Given under our hands and seals this eighth day of Feb: 1699.'

Signed C. L. Stanley

John Entwistle

(L.R.O. 1257PR)

It is interesting to note in this connection that illegitimate children that became the responsibility of the parish had to be maintained by the father, who paid from 1/ − to 1/3d per week during the 1760s-1820s to the churchwardens and overseers of the poor in this area. These payments continued so long as the child remained chargeable to the township of Burscough and the father was also responsible for paying for the lying in of the mother, and the doctor's fees which varied from about £1 to £2-10/ − during the period 1760 to 1820.

Apprenticeships

The majority of indentures concerning apprenticeships in Burscough are connected with poor or pauper children and, under the Elizabethan Poor Law, each parish was made responsible for the poor in its own district or area. There are some 56 apprenticeship indentures extant for Burscough covering the period 1725-1832. In appearance and content one indenture differs little from another except concerning the trade or craft that the apprentice was to follow and the period of his or her apprenticeship, which usually terminated at 21 years of age, but in certain circumstances was extended beyond this period.

The trades to which they were apprenticed were numerous; for example in 1729 John Tongue a poor child of Burscough was apprenticed to John Maudsley of Rufford for a period of 9 years in the occupation of a tailor. Others were apprenticed to weavers, blacksmiths, shoemakers, plasterers, basket makers and even as housewives.

The Settlement Laws do not appear to have affected the movement of apprentices as the following and, many other indentures confirm:

> '5th December 1725 Joseph Rawsthorne son of William Rawsthorne of Burscough being a poor fatherless child of ye said town and apprentice unto ye said Thomas Tatford with leave to Dwell from this Day of ye date thereof, for swearing the term of four whole years.'

The reason why the apprentice could move in this manner was no doubt due to the fact that the responsibility of looking after the boy or girl fell upon the master. In this connection the charities of Burscough should not be overlooked for by the will of John Houghton in 1732 he left £4 per annum for apprenticing, if claimed. This money was claimed on several occasions, and in 1832 was claimed by John Harrison as the following apprenticeship indenture confirms:

> 'In 1832 John Harrison a poor boy belonging to the township of Burscough of the age of 13 years son of Betty Harrison as an apprentice to Henry Rothwell with him to dwell and serve from the Day of the date of these Presents, for, during and until the said John Harrison shall attain the age of twenty one years. A sum of £4 was by the Churchwarden and Overseers out of a charitable fund for binding poor children belonging to the said Township of Burscough unto Henry Rothwell a roper.'

After the term of apprenticeship it would be customary for the person concerned to return to his or her original township, but no doubt this would be deviated from, and just how many original inhabitants of Buscough became settled elsewhere as a result is not known.

Workhouse Act, 1722

Poor houses or workhouses, although not called such, were established before 1722 in some towns, but by this Act they were extended. The parish or parochial authority were empowered to provide them and paupers who refused to enter the workhouse were refused relief. This became known as the 'Workhouse Test' and in Lancashire, especially in the north-east, it was vigorously opposed, which eventually resulted in able-bodied persons being able to receive out-relief.

Burscough being situated in the parish of Ormskirk did not have a Workhouse, but in Ormskirk there were two workhouses; one situated at the lower end of Aughton Street and one on the corner of St. Helens road in Moor Street, now occupied by the Beaconsfield Buildings.

The Moor Street Workhouse

Originally this workhouse was responsible for 17 townships, but the Poor Law Amendment Act which was enforced in 1827 at Ormskirk altered this state of affairs. The Aughton Street Workhouse closed in 1837-38 and the 'Ormskirk Union' was subsequently formed which comprised twenty-one townships:

Altcar, Aughton, Hesketh-with-Becconsall, Rufford and Tarleton, the townships of Bickerstaffe, Birkdale, Bispham, Burscough, Downholland, Formby, Halsall, Lathom, Melling, North Meols, Ormskirk, Scarisbrick, Simonswood and Skelmersdale; and the chapelries of Lydiate and Maghull.

The first meeting of the Board of Guardians of the Ormskirk Union was held on Friday, February 3rd, 1837 at the Town Hall, Ormskirk. The following appointments were made:

Messrs. Rev. Joshua Thomas Horton, chairman of the Board; Mr. Edward Boyer,vice-chairman and Mr. Wright, solicitor was appointed clerk to the Board as well as being the superintendent registrar.

Subsequently application was made to the Registrar General to divide the Union into 9 districts and in this connection Burscough came under the Scarisbrick District and Mr. James Sumner of Burscough, schoolmaster (at the old Burscough Town School), was appointed registrar of the Scarisbrick District and Mr. Richard Holcroft was appointed Guardian for Burscough in 1837. Initially two relieving officers for the Union were appointed in 1837.

In 1853 a new workhouse was built in Wigan Road at a cost of £4,000. The architect was a Mr. Culshaw and the contractor was a Mr. Richard Balshaw. Initially there was some delay in the building of the new workhouse and it was not opened until November 24th 1853.

The Moor Street workhouse was put up for sale in 1853 and was demolished in 1855. The site was purchased by Mr. Lax (Resident Surgeon at the Ormskirk Dispensary) who subsequently had his house built there in September 1856.

Subsequent developments took place and in 1871 it was suggested that the workhouse be enlarged to accommodate 100 inmates. However, in 1873 an order of the Local Government Board required extensive additions to the workhouse, involving an expenditure of £12,000, or more than three times the cost of the original workhouse. The separate cell system for tramps was also suggested.

It is interesting to note that various anomalies existed with regard to the application for relief. For example, William Forshaw who was described as a 'professional beggar' in 1870 who had moved from Southport to Burscough because the police were making Southport too warm for him, obtained 2 shillings in relief per week until further notice. However, when a widow woman who had two young children applied for relief in the same year she was only awarded 4 shillings per week until further notice, and some other individuals in similar circumstances were only awarded 2 shillings and 1/6d. per week.

The workhouse and its connection with public health.

In 1866 the Sanitary Act was passed which compelled local authorities to appoint sanitary inspectors and to suppress nuisances. It was due to this Act that conditions began to improve but initially when it was implemented there were too many authorities whose work overlapped, and in this connection the Guardians of the Poor of the Ormskirk Union acted as a rural sanitary authority under the Public Health Act of 1872.

The reports of the inspectors give one an insight into some of the conditions which prevailed just under 100 years ago in this area and the following inspector's report which I quote in full from the minutes of the Ormskirk Rural Sanitary Authority for 1872 will make this clear:

1872 Burscough (A Case of Overcrowding)

'I beg to report a case of overcrowding here. A portion of a cottage is let off to Thomas Baybutt. The place is only 13ft. × 9ft. yet in this small space lives a father, two daughters and one infant. There is only one bed for all and all sleep together in it. There is no privy accommodation whatever. There is also a quantity of ashes and filth at the back which wants removing. The eldest daughter has lately been confined. I am of the opinion that the place is too small for a family to live in and that the landlord be called upon to turn them out. I am informed that Mr. Richard Reynolds, New Lane is the owner.'

'Resolved that notice be given to both landlard and tenant.' (L.R.O. S.A.O.).

Other nuisances of overcrowding, manure wharves, fever, stagnant water and gastric fever and the like are recorded and instances of property being fumigated, disinfected (nearly always with carbolic acid), burning of bedding and the white-washing of walls both inside and outside of the house was often carried out, and in some instances the property was pulled down.

In the first decade of the 20th century various reform measures were introduced which heralded the beginning of the welfare state, such as the Unemployed Workers Act of 1905, which was followed by the Labour Exchange Act of 1909 which established employment exchanges throughout the country, the Old Ages Pensions Act of 1908 and the National Insurance Act of 1911, all helping to relieve the workhouse of some of its responsibilities.

The last meeting of Ormskirk Board of Guardians was held in April 1930 at the Union Offices, Wigan Road, and Mr. John Bailey Gorst of Burscough was chairman.

The Ormskirk Dispensary

The Ormskirk Dispensary was a valuable asset to Ormskirk and the surrounding districts, and the pioneers of this institution did much to relieve the sufferings of the people in the 18th and 19th centuries, before hospitals as we know them today were established.

The Dispensary was founded about May 1705 and the institution at that period and until 1829 was of very modest proportions, but its pretensions and aims were as brilliant as those of hospitals today, namely to relieve suffering humanity. In the early days the Dispensary was situated in what was then known as Lydiate Lane, now styled Derby Street, and a cottage on the right-hand side approaching Burscough Street was utilised for the purposes and objects of the institution.

The Ormskirk Dispensary was a charitable institution and its purpose was to supply medicines, medical and surgical advice and assistance to the poor gratuitously. On 23rd April 1830 the foundation stone of the New Dispensary in Burscough Street was laid by Mr. Thomas Brandreth, son of the famous Dr. Joseph Brandreth. The sum of £300 was left by the widow (Catherine) of Dr. Brandreth in her will of 1827 and this was donated by the son Thomas Brandreth to the purchase of a new Dispensary. The Earl of Derby granted the land for the Dispensary and Lord Skelmersdale (1st) gave the stone which forms the front of the building which was obtained from the Round O Quarry on the east side of Lathom Park.

The Dispensary was maintained largely by subscription from the numerous townships surrounding Ormskirk and donations were received from Peter Lathom's Charity and up to 1874 a collection was made at the Almonry, Lathom in aid of the Dispensary. After 1874 Hospital Sundays were established (the first Hospital Sunday took place in May 1875) at over 20 churches, chapels and missions in the adjacent townships. All denominations contributed and the Burscough St. John's parish church was amongst the foremost of contributors and the Rev. W. Wannop of Burscough was for many years vice-president of the Ormskirk Dispensary. A donation of £1 was also given annually to the Dispensary out of Reynolds Charity of Burscough, according to the will of Robert Reynolds of Southport dated 25th January 1878.

From the information available the number of persons seeking assistance from the Dispensary during the 19th century varied from 800 to over 1,500 per annum. The Dispensary was used by people living within a six mile radius of the institution.

Charities

Numerous charities were developed during the 17th, 18th and 19th centuries for the benefit of the poor of Burscough and these were mainly the result of legacies being left either in money that could be invested, or property and land from which a rent-charge could be obtained.

Some of these charities were given for schools, books, and apprenticing and others were given in food (bread and beef) cloth and in money. Over the years the distribution of these charities has been modified to meet the changing times, and subsequently most of these charities were united, and today the payment of these charities is given in money, mainly to the old people of Burscough.

Several of the Burscough charities laid down certain conditions respecting the persons that were eligible to benefit from them. For example, Sharrock's Charity, which was distributed in bread at the parish church of Ormskirk every Sunday by the churchwardens of the church, was only distributed to those poor persons of Burscough attending divine service there. Tasker's Charity which was distributed in beef at Christmas was restricted to those persons who were not receiving any relief from the township of Burscough. The distribution of the charities would also vary with the vicar in charge and it would also depend upon the honesty of the churchwardens, and from time to time, if any deviation from the will of the donor of the charity occurred, the Charity Commissioners tried to rectify the matter, and as times changed they were largely concerned with the amalgamation of these charities. In many cases these charities helped to supplement the work of the Poor Law, but because they were not united and contained certain restrictions and were distributed in many areas initially their effectiveness was not as great as it could have been.

Blackleech's Charity

The origin of this charity goes back to the year 1633 according to the Charity Commissioners' report of 1828 and at this stage I can only give a brief outline of its development. Initially a feoffment (a gift or grant of land held by military tenure) was drawn up in 1633:

Between Edmund Smoult and Ellen his wife, and Thomasin Smoult, widow, of the first part and Abraham Blackleech and Thomas Browne, executors of the will of James Blackleech, the Rev. George Walker, and the Rev. John Broxop, overseers of the said will, and ten others of the other part, paid by the said Edmund and Thomasin Smoult, in consideration of £100, paid by the said executors, granted and enfeoffed to the said Abraham Blackleech and others, parties of the second part heirs and assigns &c.

This was a common form of mortgage at the time and the trustees never entered into possession. In connection with this feoffment Edmund Smoult covenanted to pay the interest on £100, but the document under which he agreed to pay the interest was not forthcoming. For two years previous to an indenture which was drawn up in 1640, Edmund Smoult failed to pay the interest, and this was shown by the sum of £10-16-8d., which was paid by Richard Case, accordingly the trustees were enabled to enter upon the premises. However, the premises were found to be worth £202-17-9d. and the balance of £102-17-9d. was paid to Smoult by Case, to whom in consideration of his paying the arrears the trustees sold the premises by way of demise or lease to secure a rent charge of £6. From the information available it does not appear that the feoffment of 1633 was intended to be an absolute purchase, but was merely the first step in the process of securing an investment by way of rent charge of Blackleech's bequest.

By an order of the Charity Commissioners dated 18th November, 1861 the vicar and churchwardens of Ormskirk were appointed trustees *ex officio* and the real estate belonging to the charity was vested in the Official Trustee of Charity Lands.

The site now occupied by the ordnance depot and owned by the War Department are the premises which are subject to this rent charge of £6 per annum. In 1899 according to the Charity Commissioners' Report £5 was paid to the churchwardens and £1 to the vicar of Ormskirk. The £5 was distributed during the winter, in the form of bread and provisions to the value of 5/– to 10/– each among 40 or 50 persons of whom no record was kept. The distribution of the charity was initially intended for the whole of the ancient parish of Ormskirk, but in 1899 was confined to the township of Ormskirk. This charity is still operative today.

Peter Lathom's Charity

A full description of this charity can be found in the Charity Commissioners' Report of 1899 on Croston and for the reader who requires further information on the history of Peter Lathom, an interesting account is given in Vol. 97 of the *Transactions of the Lancashire and Cheshire Historic Society* by Professor R. J. A. Berry.

The charity was founded by Peter Lathom of Bispham (described in his will as a yeoman, but locally referred to as 'Peter Lathom the pedlar') by his will bearing the date 2nd April 1700. According to the Charity Commissioners' Report of 1899 the charity was endowed with lands in Skelmersdale, Wrightington, Heskin and Newburgh, containing about 260 acres, let at £264-10-0d., a ground rent of £10 from the Burscough Hall and £43,734-14-0d. consols, producing yearly £1,202-14-0d., the total income in 1897 being £1,486. It was owing to the great increase in the endowment caused by the development of the coal mines underlying the estate that the Charity Commissioners implemented a scheme in November 1879 whereby the income could be regulated. It was under this scheme that the charity was placed under the management of 13 trustees who were resident in each township. In accordance with this scheme the trustees were authorised to distribute the income in a variety of ways including subscriptions to cottage hospitals or dispensaries (e.g. The Ormskirk Dispensary) or to funds of provident clubs or friendly societies, gifts of money, clothes, bedding, tools, food, medical aid etc., and also payments of reward or prizes for school attendance upon receipt of a written certificate from the principal teacher; subscriptions were also given for the provision of school libraries and evening classes.

Mr. Holcroft was appointed the trustee for Burscough under the scheme of 1879 and the money was mainly given out in doles varying from 10 shillings to a half crown. During the 1790s and first half of the 19th century Peter Lathom's donation to the poor was given in linen and the total distributed varied between £17-£22 in total. The number of recipients varied between 60-95 and each person received from 3-14 yards of linen each, and in 1798 the amount donated was £3-12-1d. According to the Charity Commissioners' Report of 1899 up to £9 was distributed at Michaelmas and £18 at Christmas since 1881. Grants of £5 were also given to the Ormskirk Dispensary and £4 was given to Lord's Gate School, Burscough, for the purchasing of book prizes which were awarded to children for the best record of attendances and good conduct on the recommendation of their teacher.

Peter Lathom also made provision in his will for part of his charity to be donated to poor prisoners of Lancaster Castle. In the report of 1820 the annual sum of £6 was set apart according to the directions of the decree of 1744 for the poor prisoners in Lancaster and was sent at that time to the gaoler there. After making payment to Lancaster the residue was divided amongst the 17 townships specified in the donor's will (except that of the Burscough Hall estate). The townships were as follows:

Bispham, Mawdesley, Ormskirk, Newburgh, Burscough, Dalton, Rufford, Wrightington, Parbold, Ulnes Walton, Croston, Welch Whittle, Scarisbrick, Skelmersdale, Bickerstaffe, Eccleston and Heskin. Lathom was subsequently added to the list.

The rent of £10 payable from the Burscough Hall estate was at that time received from James Tasker, the occupier of the Hall, by Mr. Richard Prescott of Lathom, one of the trustees. Upon receipt of the £10 Mr. Prescott distributed the money in small amounts amongst the poor persons of the townships of Lathom, not receiving relief, with the exception of the hamlet of Newburgh.

The Burscough Hall rent was not brought into the general account of the charity, but a separate account of the disposal of it was kept by Mr. Prescott. It is also of interest to note that two old cottages were rented by James Tasker from the trustees which were situated on a small slip of land adjoining the Burscough Hall estate. All the buildings on the charity estates were repaired by the trustees except the two cottages rented by James Tasker. At that time Chapel Lane was an outlet road from the Burscough Hall and this belonged to the estate.

The Burscough Charities in 1870

Date of legacy	The charity	Interest £.	s.	d.
1732	*The Old Burscough Town School.* John Houghton left £10 to build a school, and £100 to support a master whose salary was, by legacy and gratuity.	18	12	0
1749	*Charities for Books* Wallas and Hill left per annum (paid to schoolmaster for obtaining books)	1	2	0
1793	*For Cloth* Platt's Charity (left per annum for the purchase of linen, distributed to 20-25 poor persons).	2	10	0
1732	*For Apprenticing* Houghton's Charity per annum, if claimed.	4	0	0
1638	*Rent Charge* Sutch's Charity per annum to the poor. Was up to 1803 £3-10-0d. £1 was paid by Mr. Hill up to 1803, but this rent-charge on the meadow was discontinued.	2	10	0
1729	*Charities for Bread and Beef.* Sharrock's Charity (six twopenny loaves were placed at the Ormskirk parish church every Sunday).	2	12	0
1732	Houghton's Charity (Distribution in beef at Christmas).	1	0	0
1768	Parrpoint Baldwin's Charity (Distribution annually in beef).	1	3	9
1799	Richard Berry's Charity (the elder) (distributed in beef at Christmas).	—	10	0
1801	Robinson's Charity (Five shillings worth of two-penny loaves distributed at Christmas).	—	5	0
1801	James Berry's Charity (Distribution in bread at Christmas).	—	5	0
1802	Alty's Charity (Distributed in beef annually).	—	14	0
1803	Tasker's Charity (Distributed in beef at Christmas to poor persons receiving no relief from the township of Burscough).	1	0	10
Will examined 1692	Scarisbrick's and Walker's Charity (Distributed in beef at Christmas to 14 of the most needy and indigent poor within Burscough, who should be constant goers to the parish church of Ormskirk).	1	0	0
1821	Charity of Richard Berry the younger (distributed in bread at Christmas).	—	6	0

All the above subsequently became part of the United Charities of Burscough.

In 1880 Robert Reynolds of Southport bequeathed to Richard Sephton and Henry Reynolds £1,700 upon trust for investment. After deduction of legacy duty a sum of £1,530 remained, which was paid to the Official Trustees of Charitable Funds in 1881 and £1,505-10-8d was invested in consols, the annual income then being £41-8s.-0d. This account was placed to the account of Mr. Richard Sephton at the Ormskirk branch of the Manchester and District Banking Company Ltd., who, after deducting £1 for the Ormskirk Dispensary, sent the remainder to the vicar of Burscough. The money was mainly distributed in doles to the poor of Burscough and a proportion of the charity was also distributed in doles to the poor of Lathom. Today this charity is mainly distributed to the old people of Burscough and Lathom.

Before the Charity Commissioners' Report of 1828 the following payments that were made in 1826 may be of interest:

	£.	s.	d.
Candlemas distribution	11	0	0
May distribution	11	0	0
In beef	8	15	11
Schoolmaster	4	10	0
Books	1	0	0
Platt's	2	10	0
	38	15	11

Benevolent or Friendly Societies

Originally these societies developed from small groups of people who got together and contributed regular payments to a common fund from which payments could be made to members in times of sickness, to widows and children of deceased members or to cover funeral expenses. There was very little progress during the agrarian and industrial revolutions against these hardships and even burial clubs (such as the one developed by the Rev. W. Wannop and subsequently improved by the Rev. C. D. Russell of Burscough which were developed primarily to provide funds to cover funeral expenses, were important when their cost was large in relation to income.

During the first half of the 19th century many friendly societies developed and the abstract of parochial returns shows that in Burscough there was approximately one friendly society member for every family in the 1830s.

The first friendly society which appears to have provided the people of the Ormskirk and Burscough districts with any real provision against the hardships due to economic frictions and the like during the early part of the 19th century, was the Manchester Unity of Oddfellows, which was established at Ormskirk in 1831. The name of the first lodge was the 'Good Intent' and three years later the 'Temple of Peace' Lodge was founded. Subsequently on 27th August, 1838 'The Loyal Rose of England' Lodge was established at Burscough and the first meetings were held at the Red Lion Inn, Burscough Town. In 1842 'The John Bull' Lodge was established at the Bull and Dog Inn, Burscough Town.

Some of these friendly societies grew and prospered but many others failed during the early years, mainly as a result of faulty actuarial valuations. The

Oddfellows were one of the societies that prospered in this district and, by the beginning of the 20th century, 12 lodges had been established in the Ormskirk district, with an adult male membership of nearly 3,000.

Other friendly societies have developed in this area notably the following:

The Royal Lathom and Burscough Tontine Friendly Society, which was established at the Junction Hotel in 1883; the 'Loyal Order of Ancient Shepherds' established in 1870 at the Cambridge Hotel, Burscough. There have been other societies such as the 'Ancient Order of Foresters' which was very strong in the Ormskirk district during the 1830s-1850s and the 'Independent United Mechanics' and the 'Loyal Society of Druids' were also developed in the Ormskirk district during the 1830s.

Today the usefulness of the old charities and some of the benevolent societies has been largely superseded by the National Insurance Act of 1911 and especially by the Act of 1948. One of the main drawbacks to the old charities was the fact that they were largely restricted to the principal or capital amount of money invested, and unless mineral wealth etc., was found on the land which was left by the donor (as in the case of Peter Lathom's Charity) there was no appreciable growth as time went on and, as the population increased, their demands became greater. Therefore, although they helped to alleviate the distress of the poor in the past, their value today is minute. Some of the friendly societies on the other hand were much better organised and during the 19th century did much good work in alleviating the suffering of the poor. However, with the growth in population and the need for a more centralised authority to co-ordinate the activities and reduce the cost of administration of the poor law the Acts of 1911 and 1948 were passed which greatly curtailed the activities and usefulness of the friendly societies.

The Burial Club

Under the supervision of the Rev. C. D. Russell the burial club was put on a sound footing and in 1907, after all payments had been made, the balance in hand stood at a little over £4,031, and showed an increase of £78 on the previous year. He revised the organisation of this club and implemented a new scheme by which benefits were both increased and extended. This club is still in existence today. The several funds and clubs in operation such as the 'Sick and Poor Fund', 'Clothing Club' and the like were in a sound financial position, and at the time were very useful to the poor, sick and old before the introduction of the Welfare State.

Taxation and the constables

There were numerous taxes levied on all manner of things from servants down to dogs, and in 1662 a hearth-tax of two shillings was levied in respect of each hearth above a certain stipulated number, although cottages were exempt from it. In the Health-Tax Return of the Ormskirk parish in 1666, which was applicable to houses with 3 or more hearths, Burscough was listed as having four such houses. One of these houses belonged to James Starkie of Martin Hall which then possessed 12 hearths, the other three are not named but it is possible that they were the Burscough Hall and two farms, one in possession of the Berrys and the other belonging to the Johnson family.

In the Middle Ages another kind of tax called the poll-tax was introduced, but was bitterly resented and by and large was evaded. Each village was assessed at a certain amount per head of its adult population, but within the parish the amount was graduated according to the means of the inhabitants which usually resulted in the richer people paying more than the poorer people. Alice and Isolda of the Cross (of Cross Hall) are named in the Poll Tax Roll of 1381. The poll-tax was introduced again in the 16th century and a last attempt was made to revive the poll-tax in 1608.

Land Tax was also imposed and in this connection after the Act of 1780 it was declared that none should vote at county elections who were not assessed to the Land Tax. The constable's accounts of Burscough bear witness to the imposition of the land tax as follows:

'1718 May 19th - Paid the same day for Warrants
for Land Tax and Window.....................................9s.-9d.'
'1758 August 4th - Spent at Thomas Culshaws at regalating
the Land Tax...1s.-3d.'

William Hill contributed to the Land Tax in 1792 and in the 18th century James Berry, John Tasker and Thomas Johnson were the three principal inhabitants of Burscough who no doubt also contributed to this tax.

The constable also appears to have been responsible for looking after the township's arms and in time of trouble, war or other calamity he would probably command so many men to protect the township. On 12th January, 1708 the following entry appears in the constable's accounts for Burscough:

'1708 12th Jan., - Paid to James Barton for cleaning of the towns armes.'

The following entry is also of interest:

'1758 August 3rd., - Paid for the melisha Act of Parliament...........-11d.

In medieval times and up to the 18th century the lesser gentry and yeomen often held their lands by military tenure and in time of war they fought for the lord of the manor, and in some instances supplied men and horses. The early occupiers of Martin Hall originally held the lands by military tenure and such families as the de Burscoughs, Gorsuches, Bridges and others in this area served the lord of the manor in this way. During the threat from the Spanish Armada in the 1580s, the arms for this district were kept at Cross Hall by Stanley of Cross Hall, muster master. Again during the Napoleonic Wars the Ormskirk and Leyland local militia was formed in 1809 and disbanded in 1815. Mr. Thomas Brandreth J.P., who died in 1857, was the last surviving officer (captain) of the local militia. John Armstrong, brother of Alfred Armstrong the master of the old Burscough Town school, was also a volunteer in the Ormskirk and Leyland militia.

Police

The police force was introduced in London by Sir Robert Peel in 1829, but the Lancashire County Constabulary was not established until about 1840. The position of town constable virtually came to an end after 1840 and their work was taken over by the police force. During the 1840s the police station as such was situated in Burscough Street, Ormskirk, and the site is now partly occupied by a new block of flats facing the Hant's Lane and Burscough Street car park. However, in 1850 a sessions house, magistrates' rooms and police offices were built at a cost of £2,200 in Derby Street, and the Court's jurisdiction extended over the twenty-one townships of the Ormskirk Union.

The present police station at Burscough was not opened until 25th March 1895, but before this date from about the 1860s a small house which was situated on the corner of Square Lane and Liverpool Road nearly facing Yew Tree House and on the same side as Superwood Products Ltd., was used by the police. This house was owned by Anne Welsby in 1846, but was occupied by a Mr. John Gill before being used as a police station and subsequently by the Bromley family (no connection with James Bromley the antiquarian), of Burscough. The house has been demolished in recent times.

The reason for the police house originally being situated at Burscough Town was most probably the fact that until the 1880s the greater number of the inhabitants lived there. Before the 1860s there does not appear to have been a police station as such in Burscough, but the police were there in the late 1850s because in 1858 I came across several cases of assaults against the police at Burscough, one of which involved a curious case in which the constable had his ear bitten off by his assailant.

The police force at that time used to rent houses for their constables and the house already mentioned may have been occupied by the police constable for Burscough, but at that time there is no evidence to suggest that it was being used as a police station. In 1947 two police houses were built at Mill Dam Lane and two more were also erected in Richmond Avenue; the latter houses were built several years before the Richmond Avenue and Elm Road properties were erected.

In 1897 the Burscough police station was equipped to deal with the adjusting and stamping of weights and measures, and a small building at the rear of the police station was built for this purpose. The inspectors of weights and measures were available at Burscough on the fourth Monday in January, April, July and October from 10 a.m. to 3 p.m., but over the years both the dates and times were changed.

Minor cases were dealt with at the Ormskirk petty sessions and from the reports drunkenness in the 1850s to 1890s appears to have been the major offence. Cases of breaches of the Turnpike and Highway Acts were quite common and numerous people were fined from 5-10 shillings for sleeping or riding in their carts without reins. Other cases concerned stray cattle, assaults and affiliation cases.

Local administration

Burscough came under the Ormskirk Local Board of Health and subsequently the Ormskirk Rural Sanitary Authority, but did not come under the Ormskirk Highway Board. It was decided at the Kirkdale quarter sessions in July 1863 that the best way of carrying out the provisions of the Highway Act in those parts of the Hundred of West Derby which had not adopted the Act in connection with the Ormskirk police division was that it should be divided into two districts, namely: the Ormskirk Highway District and the Southport Highway District. In 1864 they became the Highway Boards and under this arrangement Burscough was attached to the Southport Highway Board until

1894 when Burscough joined with the Lathom Local Board (formed 1873). The adjustment of the accounts was done by Mr. George Kay of Liverpool. It was in 1894 that the Local Government Act was passed which abolished the Highway Boards.

Lathom and Burscough Urban District Council

After Burscough broke away from the Southport Highway Board they joined the Lathom Board to become the Lathom and Burscough Urban District Council, the elections for which took place in December 1894. The district comprised two wards, namely: Burscough ward and Lathom ward. Mr. F. C. Hill was the returning officer and there were two polling stations, one in the Wesleyan schoolroom, Burscough Bridge, and the other in the schoolroom in Hall Lane, Lathom. The wards, especially Lathom, were very large and in consequence there was much inconvenience caused to the voters owing to the distance they had to travel to record their votes. Mr. James Bromley said that on future occasions more polling stations would be available. There were 6 seats on the district council in the Burscough ward and there were 10 candidates; whilst for the nine seats on the Lathom ward there were 16 candidates. The counting of the votes took place in St. John's C. of E. schoolroom, Burscough Bridge, on Tuesday morning, the 18th December, and at noon the returning officer announced the results. There were 21 spoiled papers and the result was as follows:

Burscough Ward	Votes	Lathom Ward	Votes
Thomas Peet	184	Richard Ainscough	345
James Martland	179	George Roper	337
William Tyrer	175	Robert H. Leach	313
Edward Bridge	146	Martin Culshaw	259
Henry Banks	134	Henry Holland	254
William H. Denham	121	James L. Shawe	254
Not Elected		James Thorougood	235
John Whittle	96	Thomas Samples	234
James Lyon	84	Edw. Wainwright	207
Henry Sherrington	61	*Not Elected*	
James Travis	58	John Banks	186
		Thomas Stoner	119
		James Bromley	95
		Daniel Harrison	84
		Isaiah Piggot	67
		William L. Smith	36

The above members formed the first Lathom and Burscough Urban District Council. For fourteen years the Council did not possess any permanent offices; the meetings of the old Lathom Local Board were held in the schoolroom at Hall Lane and after amalgamation the joint council met (by the courtesy of the law clerk, Mr. F. C. Hill) at Mr. F. C. Hill's offices in Ormskirk. However, it was decided in 1907 to build the new council offices in Mill Lane, Lathom (now used as a clinic and library). The new premises were more central and convenient for everyone concerned. The building in Mill Lane was erected by Messrs. J. Robinson & Son of Ormskirk at a cost of £2,000 and the architect was Mr. C. S. Beeston, of Ormskirk.

The building is of commanding appearance and originally was railed round

A local omnibus known as the 'Flying Post' with a party of South-West Lancashire councillors at Halsall in the 1920s.

The first Council for Greater Ormskirk (1931). Fourth from the left on the front row is A. J. Studdart, late headmaster of the Lordsgate Township School; third from the left in the middle row is J. B. Gorst, last Chairman of the Poor Law Guardians.

(these being taken down during the Second World War) and when it was used by the Council, the meetings took place in what was known as the Council Room on the first floor.

The new council offices in Mill Lane were not only built to hold Council committee meetings, but to provide suitable offices for the surveyor, collector and other officials besides storage accommodation which had long been felt necessary. The first surveyor of the Lathom and Burscough Council was Anthony Darby. He was also sanitary inspector and collector of the Council and previously when he was surveyor to the old Lathom Local Board he was amongst other things a draper. About 1906 he was succeeded by Thomas Burrows, but for some months it appears that Mr. Darby remained as his assistant. Mr. Burrows remained surveyor to the Council until 1931 when the amalgamation with Ormskirk took place, after which he joined the Ormskirk Urban District Council.

The amalgamation with Ormskirk in 1931

The amalgamation originally arose out of an application to the Lancashire County Council by the Ormskirk Council in 1928 for an order to be made extending the boundaries of the Ormskirk Urban District. Ormskirk's proposal was to annexe a portion of Lathom and Burscough, together with the whole of Aughton and portions of Scarisbrick and Bickerstaffe. In 1928 the Parliamentary Committee of the County Council held a lengthy inquiry into the proposed scheme as put forward by the Ormskirk Council, but refused to give it their sanction. The Local Government Act was before Parliament at that time and, although it was felt that there were alternatives to the scheme which might prove to be better, it would be easier to implement them if the Act became law. Therefore, immediately after the passing of the Local Government Act a conference was called on June 10th 1929 of all the local authorities affected by the proposals. It was subsequently announced by the County Council representatives at the conference that they had come to the conclusion that some extension of the Ormskirk Urban District was desirable. At a later date suggestions were put forward and, as a result, agreement was reached and it was proposed that Lathom and Burscough should, together with portions of Aughton, Scarisbrick and Bickerstaffe, be added to the Ormskirk Urban District. A scheme on these lines was submitted to and adopted by the County Council. The scheme was then submitted to the Ministry of Health and in order to come to an agreement a further conference of the local authorities was called in November.

Burscough had been under a misapprehension about the scheme because they thought that the small authorities were going to be abolished under the Local Government Act of 1929. There was very strong opposition to the scheme, but the County Council on considering the position finally resolved to proceed with but with certain minor amendments. Some of these amendments concerned the revision of acreage and boundaries. However, the scheme was accepted and took effect from 1st April 1931.

Many of the local residents resented the amalgamation and even this connotation was disputed by many, saying that the word 'added' should be used instead. It was feared that the individuality of Burscough would be lost and according to Mr. Studdart (late headmaster of the Lord's Gate School who was then a local councillor on the Lathom and Burscough authority and a bitter opponent of the amalgamation), 'We are given no chance, we are simply wiped off the map'. If this has been so I leave it to the reader to judge.

From 1931 Burscough remained under the authority of the Ormskirk Urban District Council: in 1974 this became part of the new district of West Lancashire.

The introduction of gas, water and electricity services

Gas

In Mannex's Directory of 1854 he states the following concerning the introduction of gas at Ormskirk:

> 'Gas Works were established in 1833, and the town was first lighted with burning vapour on Easter Monday 1835. They are situated in Aughton St., and the Company is now legally incorporated with powers to light four adjoining townships. There are two gasometers, one capable of holding 12,000 and the other 10,000 cubic feet of gas, which is made from cannel; and the numbers of public lamps in the town is between 50 and 60.'

The formation of the Ormskirk Gas Light Company, as it was known, goes back to a meeting of the residents of Ormskirk which was held at the Town Hall on September 13th 1833. A Mr. John Fairhurst presided at the meeting, but it was adjourned until October 2nd, when it was agreed to accept the articles which were embodied in a deed of settlement. This venture was a private one and by the deed the Ormskirk Gas Light Company was incorporated as a joint stock enterprise.

The initial capital to be raised as stated by the deed was £1,500 in 150 shares of £10 each, and it was stipulated that 'no individual shall hold more than five shares'. The objects of the Company were defined as 'lighting the streets, shops, houses and other places in the Town of Ormskirk' by means of 'inflammable air or gas extracted from coal and conveyed by means of pipes', and to 'divide amongst themselves the profits to be gained thereby'.

Subsequently the Company developed, but just how it progressed in the 1830s and 1840s is not very well known. However, it was not until 1858 that the Ormskirk Gas Light Company resolved to extend their mains to Burscough. In August of that year the directors of the Ormskirk Gas Light Company decided to extend their mains to Burscough Bridge upon the recommendation of the shareholders, there being several interested parties in the Burscough area.

On 17th November 1858 Burscough was first lighted with gas and Mr. William Holcroft of High Lane Burscough was the first consumer. This gas was supplied direct from the works by a 5 inch pipe.

By the 1870s the demand for gas was growing and this is indicated by the amount of gas sold in 1871 which was 10,046,300 cubic feet, which brought in £2,593. At that time gas was sold to private consumers for 5 shillings and sixpence per 1,000 cubic feet. The Local Board paid 5 shillings per 1,000 cubic feet for gas used in public lamps.

Steady progress was maintained during the 1880s and most of the coal required for the production of the gas at Ormskirk was obtained from those mines in the Wigan area whose shafts had been sunk by Mr. Piggot of Burscough, namely the Arley and Park Mine and Ince Hall from which cannel was obtained.

The 1870s saw gas introduced into the Wesleyan School, Burscough and by 1883 the parish church at Burscough was lighted by gas for the first time and during the 1890s gas was installed in many households in Burscough. By 1892 the amount of gas sold had risen to 28 million cubic feet per annum.

In 1900 the public lamps of Burscough Junction and Burscough Bridge were first lighted with gas. At that time gas was supplied at 3s-5d per 1,000 cubic feet and the lamps were fitted with meters. The cost of installing the gas mains was £160 and this was paid for by the Lathom and Burscough U.D.C. who agreed to erect and light 98 lamps for ten years. In 1912 the scheme of public lighting continued and the Lathom and Burscough U.D.C. completed the lighting of the turnpike road (now High Lane) from Burscough Bridge to the Ormskirk boundary. The lamps on the last section from Burscough Town to the boundary were completed in November 1912 and were lighted for the first time during that month. At that time a number of oil lamps were also placed in various areas of the village.

As the industries of Burscough were developing during the latter half of the 19th century they started to utilise more and more gas and by 1901 6,200,000 cubic feet of gas was being consumed by Burscough alone, the chief consumers being Burscough Bridge and Burscough Junction railway stations, Ordnance Stores, Isaac's Laundry Company, Stanley Institute, Martland's Mill and Thorougood's Brewery. Industrial use of gas increased in the Burscough area and by the 1930s the chief users became Outram's Bakeries and Lavery's Biscuits.

In November 1945 the amalgamation of the Ormskirk and Leyland Gas Companies was approved. This amalgamation was mainly due to the increased demands made by consumers in 1941 and extra capital and facilities were needed to meet the demand.

Finally in 1949 the Ormskirk Gas Company was nationalised and, in 1948, was producing 278 million cubic feet of gas per annum. Today gas is supplied in this area by the North Western Gas Board which has local offices and showrooms in Aughton Street, Ormskirk. In 1970 natural gas was introduced into this area for domestic use and has largely replaced gas produced from coal and the like in this area of Lancashire.

Water and sewerage

Unlike the supply of gas the facilities for providing a pure supply of drinking water were not as easily or as readily implemented.

In the 1840s there were over 60 wells in Burscough and several of the larger farms and inns such as the Bull and Dog also possessed a pump. Many of the smaller households and cottagers also possessed their own wells, but their supply was uncertain in times of drought. The greater number of wells in Burscough were situated along the old turnpike road down Moss Lane and in the Burscough Town areas.

In the 1890s sewage was still being disposed of from the sewage farm at Ormskirk into brooks running through Burscough and it was not until 1902 that a scheme for a sewage disposal plant was undertaken at New Lane. Refuse and the contents of privies were thrown in nearby meadows or the canal. Ashpits could only be emptied at rare intervals. The manure wharfs were often a source of complaint and the Sanitary Authority had to issue stringent regulations governing their construction. Cess pools that stood near houses were also a source of infection.

By the 1880s many of the wells in Burscough had become contaminated and in 1884 application was made to the Ormskirk Rural Sanitary Authority for some definite action to be taken to supply pure drinking water for Burscough. There were whole rows of houses with no water supply at all and from reports written by such men as Mr. R. Tomlinson J.P., of Burscough, it appears that unfiltered rain water was the common beverage, and even in the best houses, where no expense was spared to obtain the best water, it was highly unpalatable and on some occasions was suggestive of sewage percolation in the wells. The manure wharfs did not improve the situation as the following report aptly indicates:

'the drainage of the manure heaps on the banks of the canal - gracefully meandering towards an adjacent well!'

Second only in importance to the effort to get pure water, it seems, was the removal of the manure wharfs to some unpopulated site. Farming as I have said before was of paramount importance in this area, but the well-being of the inhabitants is 'the supreme law'. At this point the following statement given by Mr. Tomlinson J.P., of Burscough, will give the reader some indication of the abhorrence of the manure wharfs in Burscough:

'It is monstrous that such accumulations should be tolerated in the midst of such a populous village. Honest horse and cow manure deserves respect, but the villainous compounds that are positively ennobled by being styled "manure", reek with noxious odours that send one home to Sunday dinner many a time with a sickened appetite. To put a parallel case: Ormskirk is a market town, but if similar deposits were permitted in the centre of it I think the honest burghers would soon - like the Easter buns - be both hot and Cross.'

Therefore, it was little wonder that fevers were rarely absent from the neighbourhood of the canal and, if any serious epidemic developed in the township, it undoubtedly took the form of a miniature plague.

Subsequent to the above reports in September 1884, a deputation consisting of the Rev. W. Wannop and Messrs. James Bromley, T. Peet and J. Sherrington appeared before the local authority with references to verify Mr. Tomlinson's statements. The Rev. W. Wannop and the above represented the ratepayers of Burscough and they presented the Ormskirk Rural Sanitary Board with a memorial which had been signed by all the persons resident in Burscough. Samples of water from the present supply were also presented to the Board which Mr. Wannop said 'he thought they would consider very pernicious stuff and not fit for use'. I cannot quote the entire memorial, but the following extract expressed their desire:

'We believe that the spring which the Ormskirk Local Board draw their supply furnishes the best water obtainable in the neighbourhood, and should, therefore, prefer an arrangement with Ormskirk as mentioned by the Clerk to the Local Board at a recent meeting.'

The Greetby Hill Waterworks had supplied Southport since 1854 and the

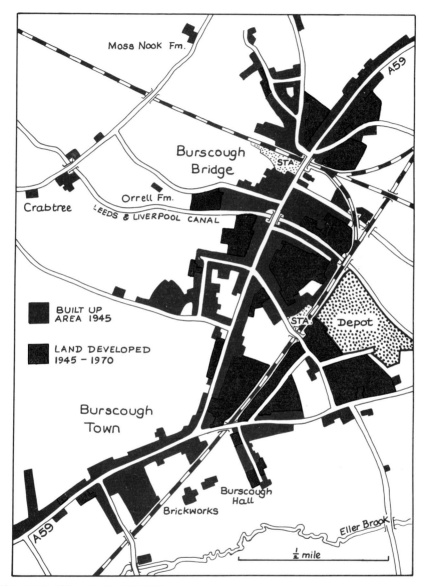

The growth of Burscough 1945-1970

By 1945 the continuing growth of industry and population in the Burscough area had expanded the village so that its two distinct parts — the Town and the Bridge — has coalesced, with housing and other development following the A59 between the two. The major expansion of the Ordnance Depot had had a very striking impact upon the area south of the railway and the canal, and elsewhere the military camps were a new feature of the Burscough landscape. Fingers of new housing were beginning to extend away from the A59 along the side roads.

In the ensuing 25 years the pace of change accelerated, so that in only a quarter of a century Burscough grew from a large village to a small town. Large new housing schemes filled in most of the remaining open land between the main road, the railway and Briars Lane, and the old linear shape of the community disappeared after hundreds of years.

Ormskirk Rural Sanitary Authority approached the Southport Water Works Company in connection with supplying water to Burscough. However, after long and tedious negotiations the company named a figure, but before proceeding any further the Company at the request of the local authority made a survey of the Burscough area. A number of persons were interviewed concerning the scheme to supply Burscough with pure drinking water from Ormskirk, but they met with an indifferent response. From the evidence available the situation was not one of indifference, but expense, for during the interviews it was found that 9 out of ten owners of property refused to take the water, but the majority of the tenants were in favour of the scheme. It also appeared from what Mr. Bromley had to say that a number of people in Burscough did a good trade in water.

The Local Board considered Burscough's application, but would not give an answer one way or the other. It appears that there was some concern over the supplies of water available, but a Mr. Newsham reminded the Board that at one time they supplied the railway company and the Ormskirk workhouse, which were then both large consumers.

Apparently Burscough had not supplied the Local Rural Sanitary Board with sufficient evidence to put before the Local Government Board, and it was considered that some independent evidence would have to be obtained.

Subsequent attempts were made to bring water to Burscough and in 1891 when the Ordnance Stores was established at Burscough Junction the matter was raised again. However, a reply was received to the effect that until it was decided from whom the water was to be obtained the matter would remain closed.

Dark Lane waterworks

In 1894 the work of prospecting for water by boring was commenced in June of that year, the contractors being Messrs. Timmins & Son Ltd. of Runcorn, and on completion of the first bore to a depth of 252 feet, test pumping was resorted to. After a week's continuous pumping at three times the rate per day of the then volume of water required for the total supply, there appeared to be little or no reduction in the water level. However, the pumps were again set in motion for another week at their full power and it was found on that occasion there was a significant reduction in the surface flow through the basin connected with the Bath Spring, which, however, on the pumps being stopped soon resumed its natural flow. A sample of the water was taken and sent by the Clerk to the Council on the 24th August 1894, to Dr. Campbell Brown S.Sc., of the University College, Liverpool and the following were the particulars of his analysis:

'I have analysed the sample of water received from Mr. F. C. Hill on the 24th August 1894, with the following results expressed in parts per 100,000 - Total solid matter in solution 16; organic carbon ·079 and organic nitrogen ·023 (minute traces only); amonia ·000; amonia from organic matter by distillation with alkaline permanganate, ·002; nitrogen as nitrates, ·437; combined chlorine 3; hardness temporary 0; hardness permanent 7; total 7; clear, no iron, no organisms. This is excellent water for domestic use.'

In accordance with the requirement of the Local Government Board, a second borehole was completed to a depth of 152 in October 1894. The two wells in connection with the boreholes were 6 ft. in diameter and 14½ ft. in depth from the engine house floor. As soon as the water was proved so excellent in quality, and sufficient in quantity, instructions were received to provide mains for its distribution to Burscough and neighbourhood and for some time a supply by gravitation from the well was given and this was supplemented for the higher proportion of the district by mains laid and by the fixing of a temporary pumping engine.

Therefore the site, after much controversy and negotiation, was at last secured by the Lathom and Burscough U.D.C. from the Earl of Derby on satisfactory terms and on a long lease.

The tower was completed in 1897 (Messrs. Wood and Brodie were the engineers) and was opened by Lord Lathom in November 1897. Lord Lathom on that occasion was presented with a key supplied by Messrs. Elkington of Liverpool which bore on one side a representation of the Lathom coat of arms and on the other the following inscription:

'Lathom and Burscough Victoria Water Tower opened by the Right Hon. The Earl of Lathom G.C.B., 17th Nov., 1897.'

The Victoria Tower is situated on Greetby Hill and consists of a substantial stone structure supporting two storage tanks at different levels. The lower tank has a capacity of 72,000 gallons, top water level 246 ft., above ordnance datum and the higher tank has a capacity of 25,000 gallons, the top water level being 284 ft., above ordnance datum.

In January 1913 new pumps were installed which were operated by a Campbell suction gas plant. On that occasion Mr. Sephton who was then the chairman of the Lathom and Burscough U.D.C. entertained members and officials of the Council to tea at the Red Lion Inn, Newburgh, to celebrate the installation of the new engines at the water works.

A new well was sunk in 1914 and in 1923 the works were extended in order to increase the yield of water. Subsequently in 1942 it was decided by the Council to remodel the whole of these works. The Lancashire Electric Power Company installed a transformer and electric switch panels at a cost of £466 which meant that the original plant was dismantled and the building was altered to accommodate the new electrical apparatus.

In the 1940s a chlorination plant was installed and a minimum amount of chlorine is added to the water by the Council to both the Greetby Hill and Dark Lane Water Works. Subsequently, due to amalgamation, the Urban District Council's water undertaking was replaced by the West Lancashire Water Board who undertook to supply the Ormskirk U.D.C. from 1st December 1960, and their offices are situated in Portland Street, Southport.

Electricity

The Ormskirk U.D.C. obtained powers to supply electricity within its area in 1900. However, from the evidence available, it would appear that these powers were not put into operation, and the main reason for this course of action appears to have been to prevent the Gas Company - who were at that time aware of competition from electricity - from buying the Council's powers, and thus delaying its installation in this district. Nevertheless the development of electricity in this area remained in a state of inertia until 1915 when the Ormskirk Gas and Electricity Bill received the Royal Assent. From 1915 the Gas Company became known as 'The Ormskirk Gas and Electricity Company' but with the intervention of the 1914-18 War development was slow and in 1925 its electricity powers lapsed and the Company became 'The Ormskirk and District Gas Company'. From 1912 numerous industries and public institutions obtained gas engines for producing their own electricity (e.g. the Stanley Institute) which were sold by the Gas Company on a hire-purchase basis.

H. & R. Ainscough Ltd. were the first to generate their electricity by this means at Burscough in 1885. Brooklands (built c. 1885 and demolished in the 1960s) which was also close to Briars Hall had been owned and occupied by the Ainscough family from 1885 to the 1960s, and appears to have been the first to have received electricity in this area. The date of the installation is not known, but it would probably have been in the late 1880s or early 1890s according to the information available.

Lathom and Burscough electricity supply

The Lathom and Burscough U.D.C. applied to the Electricity Commissioners under the Electricity (Supply) Acts 1882 to 1928 for a special order in January 1930. The objects of this would take too long to go into here, but briefly the special order was divided into seven parts in which the Council asked for permission under the above Acts for powers to authorise the installation of electricity and be given the powers usually conferred on distributors of electrical energy and the like.

Electricity Commissioner's enquiry

On Tuesday 1st April 1930 an enquiry was held at the Stanley Institute, Burscough, under Col. Ekin, an inspector appointed by the Electricity Commissioner to enquire into two applications for orders to supply electricity in the Urban District of Lathom and Burscough. Various representatives of the Council were present and several well known barristers were there on behalf of the Council and the Lancashire Electric Power Company, who proposed to supply electricity to the Lathom and Burscough U.D.C and several other townships in this area.

The case for the Lathom and Burscough U.D.C. was put forward by Mr. R. J. Sutcliffe, barrister-at-law, and he outlined the various advantages that the local Council had in providing electricity in this area. Since 1928 (December) the Council had considered that the time was ripe to apply for an electric supply order. They called in an electrical engineer to advise them and upon his findings they decided to apply for an order. In comparing prices which the L.E.P. Company offered, the Council were confident that they could supply electricity on better terms than the L.E.P. Company. The Council was mainly influenced in their decision by the success of similar undertakings in the adjoining district of West Lancashire and Formby. They also considered because of their knowledge of the district they could meet the demands of the people better than the L.E.P. Company. The Council also contended that if there was any profit from the undertaking that it was better to go back to the Council rather than to a private company. However, the amalgamation had been proposed between the Lathom and Burscough U.D.C. and the Ormskirk U.D.C. and although Ormskirk had been originally opposed to the scheme they were now in agreement with it.

Mr. Gorman, barrister-at-law, put the Lancashire Electric Power Company's application forward, in which he stressed the importance of the whole of the area being under their control. Various concessions could be given to the consumers if they had full control and their knowledge and experience of the cost of implementing a scheme of this nature was far greater than Mr. Scott's (electrical engineer) who had advised the Lathom and Burscough U.D.C. It was made clear at the enquiry that if the L.E.P. Company came into this area they would meet the demands because their prosperity depended not merely upon spending the ratepayers' money, but that they had to satisfy a much more audible class of people - shareholders.

Mr. C. D. Taite, the engineer for the L.E.P. Co., gave an outline of work they had done and were already doing and reported that at the end of December 1929 they were supplying electricity in bulk to 12 local authorities and that they had over 13,201 consumers. He also questioned the Lathom and Burscough scheme, especially the return which Mr. Scott had indicated they would receive. Again he stressed the importance of the L.E.P. Co. obtaining the order for the whole of the district (urban districts of Lathom and Burscough, Skelmersdale, Parbold; Dalton and Mawdesley in the Wigan Rural District and Bispham in the West Lancashire Rural District). Otherwise it would be uneconomical for them to develop any of the district excluding Lathom and Burscough. In the compulsory area (Burscough Bridge and Burscough Town were designated a compulsory area, having been scheduled as an industrial area by the South-West Lancashire Regional Planning Committee) underground cables would be used, but the high tension cables would be placed overhead.

It was further pointed out that it would be better for the whole area including Ormskirk if the scheme was developed under one authority, be it the L.E.P. Co. or the local authority. Further, the L.E.P. Co. had the full rights of supply and the local council could only have the right for domestic supplies. The L.E.P. Co. intimated that, if Lathom and Burscough were successful in their application, they would be glad to get out of Ormskirk where they were already established.

The enquiry continued on the following day, in which matters of building, rateable value and the like were discussed and the importance of having advisers and technical staff not only on the generation side, but also in distribution, was also pointed out. Subsequently Col. Ekin was approached with regard to the legal and other matters that had arisen during the enquiry, after which the proceedings were brought to a close.

The outcome was that the L.E.P. Co. were successful with their application and on and from 16th February 1931 by the Electricity (Supply) Special Order of 1930, gave notice that they would supply electricity for lighting, power, heating and general domestic requirements which would be available to Lathom, Burscough, Newburgh and Parbold. Their local office was situated in Park Road, Ormskirk and after nationalisation in 1948 became known as 'The Electricity Board' and subsequently after the Act of 1957 became known as 'The North Western Electricity Board'.

Communications

MUCH of the history of Burscough has been influenced by the pattern and the development of its communications. Its position on the main road from Preston to Liverpool has been in large measure responsible for its growth as a linear village and for its early expansion after the road was turnpiked and became a nationally important highway in the middle of the 18th century. The canal, which arrived not long afterwards, provided an impetus towards the growth of local industries, some of which retained their importance into recent years. The railway and later the improvement of the main road have played a major part in the expansion of Burscough as a residential area in the period since the First World War, as they put the village within commuting distance of Liverpool and other large towns. Today the road plays another role, that of dividing the community by constant streams of heavy traffic, and a bypass, long planned and equally delayed, is now desparately needed. At the time of publication it is, apparently, moving close to fruition as part of general plans to upgrade the A59 from Ormskirk to the outskirts of Preston.

Roads and the turnpike

The origins of the local road network clearly predate recent growth and expansion, and almost all of the roads in and around Burscough, apart from those constructed as part of new housing schemes in this century, were orginally typical rural tracks and lanes, their winding and seemingly random alignments reflecting this ancient function, the modern urban developments being superimposed on a road network of far greater antiquity.

In the 12th and 13th centuries Burscough Priory and the parish church of Ormskirk were built and Ormskirk subsequently established itself as a market town. In 1286 the Thursday market and the Whit Week Fair were granted to the Priory of Burscough by Edward I and an additional fair which was held in September was granted by Edward IV. Minor markets existed at Formby and at Rufford (which also had a fair). Therefore, in medieval times Ormskirk would attract many merchants, visitors and worshippers from the surrounding areas and this would probably have led to some improvements of the roads. During the development of Burscough Priory in the 13th and 14th centuries there is evidence of draining and at that time no doubt they made small tracks which subsequently would become small roads to their granges and elsewhere. There is no recorded evidence that the large landowners in the district built any roads during the medieval period, but some roads did exist in the 12th century, apart from the ancient 'ridge road' because there is mention of the high road of Wirplesmoss in the Charter of Burscough Priory of 1190.

The only road shown in any detail in this area of Lancashire on some 18th-century maps, especially those of Badestade's (1742) and Bowen's (1767), ran westwards from Bolton through Wigan and Ormskirk to the port at Formby. It is recorded that in 1596 Richard Stones was sent to Formby from Smithells, near Bolton, with three horses, by this route to fetch two barrels of herrings.

The journey took him over two days. In those times Formby was a fishing village and small port. This was the only east-west route in this area of Lancashire and was important to travellers coming from the east who wished to go to Liverpool and thus avoid the marshes and mosses.

Mr. Ashton in his book, *The Evolution of a Coastline,* quotes Mr. John Formby of Formby Hall who informed him that there was a fishing hamlet and pier there in 1711 and that the troops embarked at Formby pier to suppress the rebellion in Scotland in 1715. He also stated that there was a discussion as to whether the docks should be built at Liverpool or Formby about 1700, but by the 1730s this old port at Formby was destroyed by sand. After the destruction of the port in the 1730s and the development of the Liverpool docks from 1719, the importance of the route from Ormskirk to Formby declined. Previously the route was probably used by the Stanleys of Lathom who could have used the port for their journeys to the Isle of Man. It has also been suggested by some writers that the monks from Burscough Priory brought their grain along this route to Formby.

There are many vivid descriptions given about the state of the roads in the 17th and 18th centuries by several writers. Oliver Cromwell described the road from Wigan to Preston as 'twelve miles of such ground as I never rode in all my life'. Richard James, author of *Iter Lancastrenie* in 1636 described the Lancashire roads thus:

'Our ways are gulphs of durt and mire, which none,
Scarce ever passe in summer withoute moane'.

In the 1690s Celia Fiennes in her journey through Lancashire, instead of coming through Ormskirk, went via Prescot, the reason for this being explained as follows:

'Not going through Ormskirk I avoided going by the famous Mer call'd Martin's Mer, that as the proverb sayes has parted many a man and his mare indeed; it being evening and not getting a Guide I was a little afraid to go that way it being very hazardous for Strangers to pass by it.'

Turnpike Acts, 1663-1774

The main object of the Turnpike Acts was to transfer the cost of repairing the main roads from the various parishes through which they passed to the actual users of the roads. The local roads or highways were still looked after by the inhabitants of the parish. Funds were raised by erecting toll houses and gates at which the users had to pay a fee in order to travel upon that stretch of the turnpike road. This subsequently led to gradual improvements in the condition of the main roads.

Throughout Lancashire roads were turnpiked from the 1700s to the 1820s and the Liverpool to Prescot road was one of the first to be turnpiked, the work beginning in 1725. In 1726 the Warrington-Wigan-Preston road was commenced and in 1771 an Act was passed for the repairing and widening of the road from Liverpool to Preston. This was the beginning of the Liverpool and Preston Turnpike Trust road.

Before the introduction of the turnpike road in 1771, Burscough, like many other areas, was responsible for the upkeep of its own local roads. From original documents it appears that a supervisor of the highways of Burscough was chosen annually, the position being held in 1707 by William Culshaw, in 1759 by Oliver Tytterington and in 1769/70 John Travise and a Mr. Bradshaw were joint superintendents. The local inhabitants helped to maintain the roads and certain individual members of the community supplied stones and wooden stubs as follows:

'1707 William Tasker for stones.....................................6d.
'1707 William Culshaw 3 stubs.......................................6d.'

Repairs were also carried out on brooks adjacent to the roads and small areas were paved, but by and large the work was only of a minor nature with no real construction or development being undertaken. The annual expenditure for 1707 and 1759 was only £4 4s. 7d. and £8 1s. 4d. respectively. As I have stated before, in 1662 an Act was passed for the levying of local rates for the upkeep and repair of the roads and in Burscough this appears to have been carried out, for in 1719 the inhabitants of Burscough had to pay a highway tax; about 74 persons contributed, amongst whom was the Right Hon. James, Earl of Derby, who contributed £2.

The inhabitants of any parish were liable to do work on the roads by the law of the realm commonly called statute work (except the inhabitants of Liverpool, Kirkdale and Walton who did much work in paving most parts of the Liverpool-Preston turnpike road from Liverpool to Ormskirk, were exempt from statute work on this road), by the Act of 1771. Each inhabitant of Burscough had in theory to spend three days a year working on the roads in his own parish. No tools were provided and they had to give their services; however, exemptions were made in this area during hay-time or the corn harvest.

It was the duty of the surveyor, churchwarden, overseer of the poor or one of the principal inhabitants of the town or village to make up a list each year of all persons liable for statute work. The list also had to contain all the names of the inhabitants of each township distinguishing those inhabitants who kept a team of horses or occupied plough-lands which were liable to team's duty. All the labourers had to be shown on the list and any other duties that could be done by the inhabitants on the roads together with the names of those who refused to do statute work. If the person who refused was liable to do a team's duty, he was fined 10/– and every person liable to do a labourer's duty was fined 1/6d., for each day respectively. A surveyor, churchwarden, overseer of the poor or principal inhabitant who refused to prepare the list was fined £5. On 16th July 1774 a list was drawn up by the overseer of Burscough in which appeared all the names of persons with teams or single horses and those without horses the result was as follows:

23 inhabitants with three horses)
34 inhabitants with two horses   )   (team's duty)
16 inhabitants with one horse   )
74 inhabitants without a horse   (labourers)

The Liverpool and Preston Turnpike Road 1771-1873

The original Turnpike Act of 1771 was concerned with the repairing and widening of the road from Patrick's Cross in Liverpool to the town of Preston. The length of road controlled by the turnpike trust was about 32 miles. This road was described in the Act as the public high road for carriages and posts. The state of the road in 1771 was described as:

'being too narrow, and from the nature of the soil and many heavy carriages passing thereon, are become very deep and ruinous and almost impassable and cannot be effectively amended and kept in repair by the laws now in being. The amending of the road would greatly facilitate and improve the communication and commerce between Liverpool and the other towns mentioned.'

For road mending, the surveyors of the turnpike trust were allowed to dig gravel, sand, stones and other materials from the waste or common lands in the Burscough district. If a building, bridge, ford or the like was close by, the materials could be taken at a distance of 50 yards from these obstacles.

If the materials could not be obtained from the waste lands, the surveyors were authorised under the Act to obtain the materials from private lands with certain exemptions, e.g. if the land was in use as a yard, garden or avenue to any house, or any enclosed ground planted and set apart as a nursery for trees. They also had to make good any damage done whilst on private land.

It was the duty of the surveyor to remove and prevent annoyances such as filth, dung, ashes, rubbish, straw or turn any watercourse, sinks or drains running into or out of the turnpike and township roads. In some instances the inhabitants would put straw on the roads in order to collect the manure. The surveyor's powers were very wide and he was responsible, not only for the road itself, but for the widening of drains and watercourses that ran alongside the turnpike road. They had the power to remove trees and bushes, and, if the trees overhung the road from an owner occupier's land, he was given notice of 10 days in which to remove the tree or trees.

However, it was the responsibility of the trustees if the road was to be widened; the maximum width allowed being 30 feet. The trustees also had the power to turn or alter the course of the turnpike road. They also contracted with the owners of land for such loss or damage that they may sustain by enlarging the highways. Any differences that arose were settled by a jury at Ormskirk, Wigan or elsewhere within the hundred of West Derby or Leyland.

Before the Act could come into force, £4,000 had to be raised. No fewer than five trustees had to be appointed and they had to qualify as follows: they had to be twenty-one years of age and be in possession of personal estates of the value of £2,000 without reprises and had to be resident in the county of Lancashire. When the sum of £4,000 was raised, then it was the duty of the trustees to see that the respective toll houses, tollgates and turnpikes were erected upon and on the sides of the highways, and kept in repair. Turnpikes and toll houses had to be erected at the following places:

Turnpike and Toll House at Walton
Turnpike and Toll House at Lydiate
Turnpike and Toll House at Burscough
Turnpike and Toll House at Tarleton
Turnpike and Toll House at Penwortham
and side gates and toll houses had also to be erected on the sides of the Turnpike road as preventative stop-gates to prevent payment of tolls granted, being eluded.

On the map reproduced here I have shown the site of the original toll house and gate at Burscough which was used from 1771-1832; this toll house was sold in 1832, together with the toll house at Lydiate, for £34 3s. 0d. A new toll house was erected a short distance away and further north along the road in 1832 and remained there until about 1880 when it was pulled down. The size of toll houses varied throughout Lancashire, but in this area they were about 5 yards in length and four yards in breadth, built either of brick or stone according to cheapness, thatched and with no upper storey.

The tolls were vested in the trustees and it was their duty to demand and take tolls and duties. Briefly the tolls on the Burscough section of the turnpike were as follows in 1771:

> For every horse passing the toll 1d., every cow, bull etc. ½d., every sheep, swine, calf ¼d., every four-wheeled carriage 1s., every coach, post-chaise drawn by six horses 1/6d., by four horses 1s., by two horses 6d., and by one horse 3d. Wagon tolls varied in price depending upon the width of their wheels.

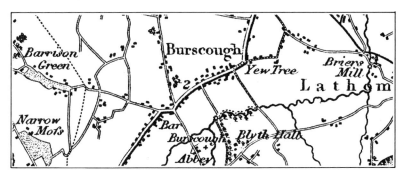

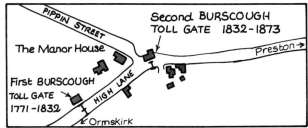

A slightly enlarged section of Greenwood's map of Lancashire, 1818, showing the Preston-Liverpool turnpike and the location of the toll bar at this date. Below is a sketch map showing the locations of the two Burscough toll gates.

On the first Monday of June in 1771, nine or more of the trustees met at the house of Samuel Hanmer, the sign of the Wheat Sheaf (now demolished) in Burscough Street, Ormskirk. At the meetings a clerk or clerks were chosen to write their orders, take minutes and make entries of the proceedings. Subsequent meetings were held alternately at Liverpool, Ormskirk, Tarleton and Preston. The cost for attending these meetings was defrayed out of the trustees own expenses. Orders were made at public meetings, but no fewer than 5 trustees had to be present on these occasions.

Tolls were paid only once a day within certain districts. Items such as coal and cannel which were carried by wagons on their return would not pay the toll again the same day. On the Ormskirk to Preston section of the road, tickets were issued. If a horse, gelding, mare, wagon, wain, cart, or other carriage was carrying stone, gravel, sand or other materials for repairing the turnpike or any road, they were exempt from paying the toll. The clergy visiting a sick person, carriages containing soldiers or crops going to be stored, horses taking milk into Liverpool (in 1804 a Mr. Blundell carried 16 gallons of milk from Burscough to Liverpool daily, at 6d. per day) were also exempt from paying tolls and many more variations existed, but they are too numerous to mention.

The toll collectors were only appointed for a term and in this area they rented the toll house and in many instances the collector was a farmer. At the end of the term the collector had to leave on the appointment of another officer, if he did not leave then the trustees had the right to remove him. The last toll collector at the Burscough toll house was Mr. Thomas Thompson, who was a collector from the 1840s to the 1870s.

The effect of the turnpike trust

In the days before the improvements made by the turnpike trust, in the Burscough area only £4 to £8 was spent on the roads annually; but when the turnpike trust was set up over three times this amount was initially spent on the roads annually. This was not a lot, but improvements were made and by the late 1780s and 1790s statute labour was beginning to be replaced by certain individuals who did most of the road repairs themselves. As early as 1779 Edward Jones of Burscough was doing road repairs himself, such as the following:

'1779 to mending a plat below Dark Lane......................1s. 7d.
      to laying a horse plat Pippin Street........................ 6d.
      to myself 7 days repairing causeways......................9s. 4d.
      to myself 2 days paving and breaking and laying flags.........2s. 8d.'

Materials for the roads in Burscough during the 18th century were obtained from local landowners often numbering up to twenty. The materials were usually sand, gravel, stubs (for the erection of gates, fences etc.) stones and gorse. How the gorse was used I was unable to find out, but from the evidence available it was just laid on to the roads or was used to fill up holes.

The introduction of the stage coach

Stage-coaches were used on the Liverpool-Preston turnpike road for the first time in 1774 and were called 'Liverpool and Preston Machines on Springs'. This name probably originated from the fact that springs had only recently come into use on the majority of stage-coaches; the earliest date that coaches were fitted with springs was about 1754. The stage coach passed through Burscough for the first time in 1774. Prior to this date only a very small number of wagons and wains had used this road and the mail was carried through Burscough on horse-back in the 1750s. Although the Turnpike Act was passed in 1771, it would take at least three years to get the road in good repair in order that the stage-coaches could use it. Since the introduction of the 'flying coach' as it was called in the 1750s, it was necessary to have good hard-surfaced highways upon which they could travel.

At the same time as the roads in Burscough were being widened and repaired, the canal was also being cut, and by 1777 packet boats had been introduced which ran from Liverpool to Newburgh.

The union packets set off from Liverpool every morning except Sunday at seven o'clock from 23rd March to 28th September, and at eight o'clock from 29th September to 24th March. They carried passengers to Burscough and elsewhere and at the time the fare from Liverpool to Burscough was as follows:

1st place 2/–, 2nd place 1/3d.

At Burscough the Packets were met by the stage-coach called the 'Union Machine' which conveyed passengers to Preston and Lancaster. The fare in the 'Union Machine' was as follows:

From Burscough to Preston 4/6d. (inside) 2/6d. (outside)
From Preston to Lancaster 5/– (inside) 3/– (outside)

If a person wanted to travel from Liverpool to Preston by stage-coach he or she would have had to take the coach called the 'Union Diligence' from Liverpool to Burscough (cost 4/ –) where they would have had to change over to the 'Union Machine' which would have taken them either to Preston or Lancaster, the fares being those already quoted above. The Union Diligence set out from the Golden Lion in Liverpool every morning at nine o'clock and arrived in Burscough (at the Packet House Inn which was then known as the Bridge Inn) at about twelve o'clock. The amount of luggage allowed was 14 lbs., but excess weight was charged at a 1d. per 1 lb., but charges on excess weight also varied according to the distance of the journey undertaken.

In 1777 any person in Burscough who had to travel down to London would have had to pay the following:

Burscough to Liverpool by the Union Diligence 4/– (Inside) 2/6d. (Outside)
Liverpool to London by the London Diligence 51/6d. (Inside) 21/– (Outside)

The journey took about 4 days and each evening they would stop at an inn for the night and at other points along the way for a change of horses.

By the late 1790s a post-coach left Ormskirk for Liverpool every evening at 6 o'clock; and to Lancaster at nine every morning, Sundays excepted: Mr. Cooper of Preston was the proprietor. Carriers had also established themselves and were using the Liverpool-Preston turnpike road as early as 1774, amongst whom was Henry Farrington who carried goods for Ormskirk and Preston on Thursdays after travelling as far as Lancaster and Kendal, and many places in Westmorland and Cumberland. Three other carriers also transported goods at Ormskirk in 1774. They were: John Hesketh every Tuesday, Alice Liptrot every Wednesday and John Riding every Wednesday and Saturday. Initially there were only three or four stage-coaches leaving Liverpool in the 18th century and these carriers often transported people in their wagons who did not possess sufficient funds or means to travel by any other method. In the 1820s the number of carriers supplying the Ormskirk district had risen to ten and their sphere of influence spread to Liverpool, Freckleton, Southport and Wigan. There were no fewer than 10 stage-coaches calling at Ormskirk; four called at the Kings Arms (now demolished) five at the George and Dragon (on the site of the present post office) and one at the Wheat Sheaf (now demolished) in Burscough Street. Names of the coaches like the following: 'The Invincible', 'The Umpire' and 'The Eclipse' have no doubt echoed down the streets of Ormskirk and Burscough to the sounds of Tally O! and many a schoolboy would probably prefer Bretherton's coach and others that of Coopers. The coaches travelled as far afield as Carlisle, Glasgow, Edinburgh and Newcastle.

The finance of the Liverpool-Preston Turnpike Trust 1823-1873

In the 1820s the income of the trust was over £4,500 per year and in the 1830s had reached its peak of over £6,000 per year. On only two occasions did the trust borrow money on the security of the tolls during this period, namely in 1823 £500 and in 1826 £1,000. The decline, however, set in with the introduction of the railways in 1849 when the income dropped to £4,000 per year and by 1870 had fallen below £4,000 per year. Over 90% of the income was derived from the tolls, the remainder of the income was made up from fines which ranged from as low as £2 to a maximum of £55 in total, for any one year. Revenue from incidental receipts brought in more revenue than the fines and averaged about £50 per year on top of which was the occasional sale of an old toll house or other equipment.

On the opposite side of the balance sheet was manual or day labour and team labour which averaged respectively over £1,000 and £500 each per year, and the surveyor's, clerk's and treasurer's wages averaged about £300 per year. The largest single item apart from the payment of salaries and wages was the material for the repairs of the road which nearly came to £2,000 per year during the 1830s, but later averaged about £1,000 per year. Other expenses included the repair and maintenance or building of toll houses, gates or bridges. In Burscough during this period the bridges were neither repaired by the county nor the hundred, but were the responsibility of the proprietor, e.g. the Leeds and Liverpool Canal Company were responsible for the canal bridges with one or two minor exceptions, and the railway companies were also responsible for the upkeep and repair of their own crossings and bridges. In Lathom the repair and upkeep of the bridges was the responsibility of Edward Bootle-Wilbraham. It was the duty of the constable of Burscough to see that the bridges were kept in good repair by the proprietors in the 18th and 19th centuries. They were also responsible for the repair of bridges which belonged to the parish. Many other incidental expenses, law fees, printing, advertising, tradesmen's bills, mortgages paid off and the like were also incurred. During the turnpike era in Burscough the Liverpool-Preston turnpike trust road represented 18 acres of the 100 acres of the public roads of this township.

Revenue began to drop - owing to the introduction of the railways in 1849 (Liverpool to Preston) and 1855 (Wigan to Southport) and steamboats on the canal - and the trust began to get into financial difficulties. No doubt increased tolls were asked for, but this is not reflected in the accounts and on this trust no extra gates were erected as was done on so many other turnpike roads. Many trusts were consolidated in an attempt to reduce management expenses, but this did not occur on the Liverpool-Preston trust. In 1864 a House of Commons Turnpike Committee condemned the whole system, and through the efforts of this Committee, between 1,000 and 2,000 miles of road were 'dis-turnpiked' each year.

The creation of highway boards

On 4th April 1864 the Ormskirk Highway Board was formed which resolved in December 1870 that the Liverpool-Preston turnpike road should pass into the hands of the District Highway Boards and that the debt owing by the Trust at the expiration of the Act should be apportioned amongst local boards whose districts it passed through. Burscough came under the Southport District in 1873, when the Liverpool-Preston trust expired. Unfortunately, the early records of the Southport Highway Board are only available from 1893-1899. However, I have been fortunate in obtaining several older accounts which show that the cost of the upkeep and repair of the roads in Burscough fell back upon the parish, thereby increasing the burden of the local taxpayer. Much more was spent on the roads of Burscough during the period 1873-1893, e.g. in 1881, £1,226 was spent on repairing and improving the roads. Manual and team labour were still in force and initially when the Highways Boards were formed paupers and prisoners were employed on the roads. In 1870 Mr. Henry Brighouse said 'that the paupers in the workhouse would be better employed on the road breaking stones than picking oakum'. Subsequently, contract labour was employed and up to twenty tradesmen did paving, made footpaths and pitched and macadamised the roads in the 1880s.

In 1882 Mr. Gladstone's Parliament helped to alleviate the burden of the local taxpayer by granting a contribution to the annual cost of maintaining 'dis-turnpiked' roads. By the Local Government Act of 1888 these grants were discontinued, the maintenance of all the main and dis-turnpiked roads was made the responsibility of the County Councils, thus spreading the cost over a larger area. The roads in Burscough under the Southport Highway Board were classified into main, secondary and district roads and the amount of money allocated to each parish for the roads was assessed according to their rateable value; in 1893 the rateable value of Burscough was £20,577-10/– and the amount debited to the district fund for roads was £988-7-4d. Towards the 1890s the rates on the roads were increased in Burscough to help pay for certain roads in Scarisbrick and because there was only one representative from Burscough on the Southport Highway Board a request was put forward that Burscough might withdraw from Southport Highway Board and join the Lathom Local Board. In January, 1894, the Southport Highway Board's books were audited under the Local Government Act by Mr. George Kay and after an adjustment of the accounts Burscough joined Lathom in March 1894 to form a joint local highway board. The Local Government Act of 1894 abolished these highway boards, and in 1895 the Urban Districts were established and in that year the Lathom and Burscough Urban District Council was formed. This council became part of the Ormskirk Urban District Council in 1931, who then became responsible for the upkeep and repair of the roads in the district.

For a description of the roads in this area during the period of the highway boards, I can do no better than to quote the Rev. W. Wannop who recorded when he first came to Burscough in 1840: 'The bye-roads narrow and unpaved, many farmhouses almost inaccessible to conveyances . . .' In the 1880s he recorded the following: 'Our highways broad and well paved, equal to what our turnpike roads were a few years ago'.

The development of the omnibus services

As the condition of the roads improved, numerous small undertakings began to develop omnibus services in different parts of Lancashire, and one in particular, the Ribble Bus Company, subsequently was to become a large undertaking. This company was formed as early as 1919 to acquire the business of the late Mr. James Hodson who, in 1910, had started a bus service between

Preston and Gregson Lane, Walton-le-Dale. Initially the Ribble began operations on 15th May 1919 with five vehicles and on 6th June the Company, registered with an authorised capital of £20,000, received its certificate of incorporation.

As early as 1925 the Ribble Bus Company was operating a two hourly service between Preston and Liverpool. The Ribble Bus Company has been connected with Ormskirk since 1926 when Bretherton's Motors of Wigan were acquired by the Company. In the following year Webster Bros. of Wigan were also taken over, and by 1930 the Ribble Bus Company had two buses garaged at the Talbot Hotel (now demolished) in Aughton Street, Ormskirk. The bus services of Cadmans of Ormskirk were acquired in 1935. By this time the Ribble Bus Company was expanding and there was a need for more accommodation and in 1937 a new garage, bus station and enquiry office were opened at the corner of Knowsley Road, Ormskirk.

Garages and petrol stations

In connection with the development of road traffic, garages, repair shops and petrol stations evolved along most of the major roads and the first two garages to develop in Burscough were the Central Garage, Victoria Street, and the Burscough Bridge Garage, near the Packet House Hotel. Central Garage (originally known as Piggot's Garage and subsequently as Abrams) appears to have been the first to be designated a garage and was established about 1920 and was owned by Mr. Piggot. A little later Mr. Robert Ritchie, motor engineer, developed the Burscough Bridge Garage. The Burscough Bridge Garage was subsequently acquired by Mr. A. E. Newall in 1930 and it is of interest to note that this was the only garage in this district at that time with a solid tyre press used in connection with vehicles travelling up to 12 mph. Mr. Newall remained there until 1961 when the garage was taken over by Mr. Dennis Finch and subsequent owners have since occupied the site, and today the premises have been replaced by a new building. Before 1920 there were no garages in Burscough as we know them today but small repairs were undertaken by individual owners themselves, and by various other persons, one of whom was a Mr. Foden of Liverpool Road, Burscough. Since the 1930s garages have developed at Burscough Bridge and Burscough Town, and similar to their predecessors, the blacksmiths, they are situated along the Liverpool to Preston main road.

The canals

As the roads were being improved in this area in the 18th century, the canals were also being constructed and rivers were being made navigable. Trade was increasing and it was found that large consignments of raw materials, coal, stone etc., were required by the various industries in Liverpool, which also needed an outlet for their finished products on a larger and cheaper scale than could be provided by the road transport of that time. We have seen that the roads were often impassable in the winter months, and to cater for an industrial centre of any size and importance would have required many wagon loads. Therefore, the answer lay in the use of water transport.

River Douglas

The earliest attempt to develop water transport in this area of Lancashire was the improvement of the River Douglas which was undertaken in the 1720s.

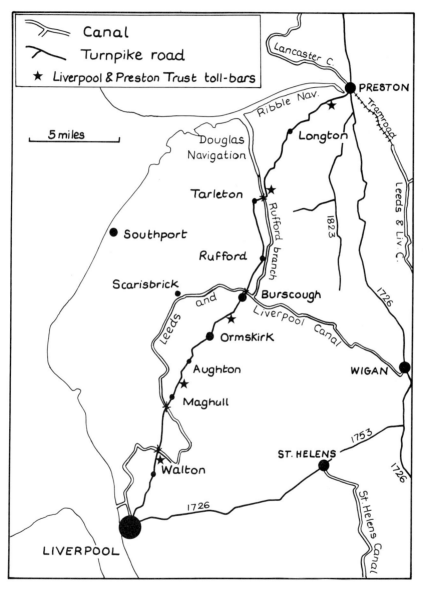

The canals and turnpike roads of South West Lancashire.

The river was surveyed in 1712 by Thomas Steers and William Squire and in 1720 an Act was passed for making the Douglas navigable from the Ribble to Wigan. However, the undertaking was not effectuated until 1717; under the terms of the Act they were given 11 years in which to complete the work.

The principal reason for this undertaking was to facilitate the movement of coal and cannel from the Wigan and Newburgh areas to Liverpool by way of the Ribble and to provide work for watermen and seamen in the adjacent areas. The coal was also transported via the Douglas to the northern parts of Lancashire and Westmorland where very little coal was mined, and in return stone, limestone and slate were brought back in exchange.

The boats using the Douglas were most probably coastal flats with small sails. Subsequently, in 1783 the proprietors of the Leeds and Liverpool Canal Company purchased the Douglas Navigation from the River Ribble to Wigan. By an Act of 1790 they were given the power to raise £200,000 to make a variation in the course of the canal and in 1794 they were permitted to alter the Douglas by substituting an artificial cut in place of the natural channel. They commenced their operations at Top Locks and continued through to Rufford and in the early part of the 19th century further modifications were made to improve the canal. Locally this stretch of the canal is known as the 'Rufford Line', but officially it was designated the Lower Douglas Navigation; the Upper Douglas Navigation running from Newburgh to Wigan on the Leeds and Liverpool Canal.

Locks and bridges

The Rufford branch or the Lower Douglas Navigation runs from Burscough to Tarleton, where it joins the tidal estuary of the River Douglas. The tide flows to the tail of Tarleton Lock where high water is about 2 hours after high water at Liverpool. From the junction with the River Douglas at Tarleton Lock to the estuary of the River Ribble is a distance of about 4 miles. In the 19th century a small trade used to be carried on down the River Douglas on spring tides to Freckleton Mill, on the north shore of the River Ribble's estuary. The distance from the Top Locks to Tarleton Lock is just over 7 miles and has no fewer than 8 locks, viz. Lathom Top and Bottom Locks, Runnel Brow Lock, Moss, German's, Baldwin's, Rufford and Tarleton Locks. The names have been taken from the surrounding land, people's names who farmed the land at the time of the cutting of the canal and from the places through which it passed. The maximum size of vessel that could use this canal was as follows: 2 feet in length, 14′ 3″ in width with a draught of not more than 3′ 6″.

Bridges had to be built over this canal so that the farmers could cultivate their lands and these again were named accordingly, e.g. Prescott's Bridge.

Rates for tonnage

In 1829 clay, brick or stones were transported for ½d. per ton per mile, coal or lime for a 1d. and timber, wares, goods, merchandise or other commodities for a ½d. Soap, ashes, salt, dung, dust; rags and tanner bark and the like to be used for manuring the land was carried for ¼d. per ton per mile. Coal represented by far the greatest commodity carried on this canal but trade started to decline with the introduction of the railways in the 1840s. Today this canal is not used by commercial craft and, to the best of my knowledge, it is also closed to private vessels.

The Leeds and Liverpool Canal

The section of the canal which runs through Burscough is sometimes referred to as the Longbottom line, because in 1767 Mr. John Longbottom surveyed the line and made estimates of the probable expenditure involved. Mr. James Brindley was consulted, after which the survey was approved and at two meetings of gentlemen, merchants and manufacturers held at Bradford on the 5th and Liverpool on 9th December 1768 the plan was adopted.

Work was first commenced in the parish of Halsall on 5th November 1770 and the first turf cut by the Hon. Charles Lewis Mordaunt of Halsall Hall.

The section of the canal from Liverpool to Newburgh was completed as early as 1774 but it took until 1816 before the whole of the canal was completed to Leeds. The total length of the canal was 128 miles and cost just over £1,200,000. There were several variations made from the original plan and opposition was met with from local landowners in the Burscough, Lathom, Ormskirk and Wigan districts. By and large, however, the canal follows the 50 foot contour from Liverpool to Wigan and this obviated the necessity of building a tremendous number of locks. It has been suggested to me that the canal was initially proposed to come through Ormskirk but I have been unable to find any evidence to support this either in the Act of 1770 or the original plans that were drawn up by Mr. Longbottom in 1768. In 1816, when the canal was officially declared open from Liverpool to Leeds, great rejoicing took place throughout Lancashire; in Liverpool a banquet was held and no doubt in Burscough celebrations took place as well.

The main purpose in developing the Leeds and Liverpool Canal was a commercial one and to a considerable degree the canals opened up the Lancashire coalfields. In the past there had been no really good transport facilities between the west coast of Lancashire and Yorkshire to allow the movement of large consignments of raw materials to either area, until the construction of the Leeds and Liverpool canal virtually solved this problem. Coal, limestone, lime and manure, stone and bricks etc. and merchandise were the chief materials carried. Over 250,000 tons of coal was transported annually in the 1820s on the Leeds and Liverpool Canal. This canal also carried large quantities of potatoes but documentary evidence is not yet available to confirm either the volume or the direction of the potato traffic. Nevertheless, it is highly probable that the movement was from west to east, that is, its supplies were directed to Manchester, possibly in barges which having delivered their coal to Liverpool were returning eastwards for fresh supplies.

As I have mentioned before, packet boats carrying passengers also used the canal and as early as 1777 a regular passenger service was in operation from Liverpool to Wigan. The 'Union Packets' as they were called set out every morning except Sundays at seven o'clock from 25th March to 28th September, and at eight o'clock from 29th September to 24th March, and carried passengers on the following terms:

From Liverpool to Gathurst Bridge 32 miles, front cabin 2/8d., after cabin 1/9d.,
- to Newburgh, 27 miles, front cabin 2/3d., after cabin 1/6d., - to Burscough,
24 miles, front cabin 2/ − , after cabin 1/3d.

At Burscough the packet boats were met by the stage-coach called the 'Union Machine' which conveyed passengers to Preston. Even at this date Burscough was an important transport centre because it was a focal point of routes. It had the canal on one hand which connected Burscough with Liverpool and Wigan and the turnpike road on the other, which afforded the most up to date form of communication then known between Preston and Liverpool. In 1790 as more people began to use the service Maghull and Halsall were added to the list of stops and about 1800 the packets began to stop at Scarisbrick Pinfold. By 1812 the Liverpool Canal packets were running two ply between Liverpool and Wigan, one packet leaving Liverpool at 8 o'clock in the morning and the other leaving Wigan at 7 o'clock; they arrived at Burscough as follows:

From Liverpool to Burscough arr. 1-51 pm.
From Wigan to Burscough arr. 10-04 am.

There were 35 stops in all from Liverpool to Wigan and at Burscough they were the following: Martin Hall Ground, Martin Hall Wood, Burscough Bridge (Bridge Inn), Briars Mill and Thomas Rigby's at the Ring O' Bells. Stones were set up at these points to indicate a stop.

Subsequently the packet boats travelled as far as Manchester and with the growing importance of Southport as a holiday and health resort, many persons from Wigan and Manchester travelled down by packet boat to Scarisbrick Bridge (superseding the name Scarisbrick Pinfold). At this point according to Gore's Directory of 1827 and Baines' Lancashire Directory of 1825 they were met by stage-coaches which conveyed them to Southport, a distance of about 5 miles. Owing to the extra stops, the time taken from Liverpool to Wigan could take from 8 to 9 hours, which was an average speed of about 4 mph.

Referring to the Leeds and Liverpool Canal in 1799, a writer of the period in Burscough described the packets as 'elegant' and added that, 'The right bank of the canal at Burscough affords a very pleasant walk; but it is inaccessible from dirt and the parsimony of the proprietors in wet weather. And there is no carriage way.' In 1878 the situation appears to have become worse in Burscough, according to Mr. John Cooke of Mr. Blundell's Canal Office: 'The water was much more liquid in the 1790s than now, and passengers would not now care to be dragged in boats over its sluggish, slimy surface.' By 1840 the canal packets were still in operation but the passenger boats to Wigan only went on Tuesdays, Thursdays and Saturdays. Eventually, owing to the disagreeable surroundings of the canal and the superior facilities of the railways in the 1850s, it ultimately proved too much and the packet boat became one of the things of the past in this neighbourhood.

Even in the 1790s wharves were constructed in Burscough for the storage of coal and there was a small warehouse for the lodgement of grain or merchandise transmitted up and down the canal. However, the full effect of the canal was not felt in Burscough until after 1816 when the canal was completed to Leeds.

Boat-building

It was at this time that boat builders began to appear. The first one on record in Burscough was Henry Mayor in the 1820s who was a timber merchant as well as a boat-builder; he occupied the site which was later to become the offices and warehouse and yard of the Leeds and Liverpool Canal Company in the

1880s. In this area of Lancashire, one of the earliest shipbuilders was Anthony Cartmel, shipwright, of Newburgh, who built the 47 ton *Industry* at Newburgh in 1786. It is recorded that in 1786 a Burscough Bridge wheelwright owned part of a Preston ship which was used on the River Douglas. The number of boat-builders in this area began to increase during the 1840s to the 1860s until in 1870 there were three principal builders in Burscough, namely: William Fletcher, Burscough Bridge, James Hunter, Top Locks and Richard Tyrer, near Glovers Bridge. However, by 1880 Richard Tyrer was the only boat-builder left in this area, both William Fletcher and James Hunter having turned their hands to farming.

Interestingly, the graving dock used by James Hunter is still in existence, but is not used today on a commercial basis. This graving dock was built by the Leeds and Liverpool Canal Company and was used by them until 1849. From 1904 until 1908, Richard Williams & Sons, boat-builders, used the yard at Top Locks formerly belonging to James Hunter.

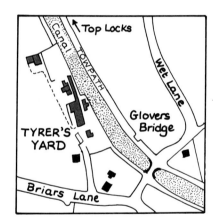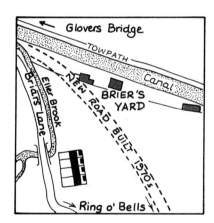

The boatyards of Burscough in 1890.

Richard Tyrer was originally a carpenter before he became a boat-builder in 1860. He was most probably apprenticed and learned the art of boat-building from one of the existing boat-builders in the area of either Burscough or Newburgh. Richard Tyrer as well as other early boat-builders along the Leeds and Liverpool Canal made boats for the Leeds and Liverpool Canal Company initially and subsequently built canal barges for other companies such as Pearson and Knowles of Wigan and Richard Williams (est. 1846), coal and timber merchants of Liverpool. The firm of Richard Williams was connected with Tyrer's boat-building yard from the start and, together, they formed an important trading link which they maintained until the boat-building yard finished about 1933. Richard Williams required canal barges to carry coal from Wigan to Liverpool and he chose, as well as several other boat-builders along the Leeds and Liverpool Canal, Richard Tyrer's boat-building yard, near Glovers Bridge. The timber for the boats was supplied by Richard Williams, whose main supply came from North Wales; oak and pitch-pine and later American Oak was used. Mr. Thomas Tyrer (great-grandson of the founder) informed that his grandfather Thomas Tyrer used to go to North Wales to select the timber, and in doing so would choose those trees which were bent because this facilitated the making of the crooks used in the construction of the beams of the ship, which needed to be curved.

In the 18th and early part of the 19th century it was important to locate boat-building yards near to a good supply of timber. However, it is not easy to account for the supply of timber in the Newburgh area in the 18th century which Anthony Cartmel might have used. Jonathan Binns in his book *Notes on the Agriculture of Lancashire* (1851) recorded that nursery grounds for trees and shrubs were more extensive in the areas of Formby, Scarisbrick and Burscough than anywhere else in England. On the word of Mr. Thomas Tyrer (Great-grandson of Richard Tyrer) I can say that the local timber was of no use in the building of canal barges in this area. I have been unable to find any evidence of boat-building of any note in this area before 1786 but, because of the opening of the Leeds and Liverpool Canal in this area as early as 1774, which connected Newburgh with Liverpool, I am of the opinion that the wood was obtained via Liverpool timber merchants in a similar manner to that which was employed by Richard Tyrer in the 1860s. During 1800-1820, and possibly before, numerous small timber merchants established themselves along the Leeds and Liverpool Canal, e.g. Henry Mayor (Burscough Bridge) and later in the 1830s William Backhouse (Lathom) in close proximity to the area which was to become Tyrer's boat-yard and three timber merchants were also in operation at Wigan during this period. Many of these early timber merchants subsequently became small boat-builders and from the evidence contained in parish registers a large number of these men had previously been carpenters, joiners or shipwrights before they became either timber merchants or boat-builders. Timber could also have been obtained from Preston via the River Douglas, or subsequently from Yorkshire, but initially I still think that the bulk of the timber would be supplied via Liverpool either from North Wales or Delamere Forest, because of the demand for coal and the mutual co-operation and benefit which could be afforded to both boat-builder and timber merchant.

At Tyrer's boat-yard each barge was designed according to the type of merchandise or raw material which it was going to carry and for the conveyance of coal timber boats appear to have been the best, for the firm of Richard Williams continued to use Tyrer's boats until 1933.

It took from 6 to 8 weeks to build a canal barge and it was usual to do most of the repair work in the summer months and leave the building of one or two boats for the winter when trade was not as brisk, and at periods when the canal was frozen. By working in this manner it was possible to provide sufficient work for the boat-building yard without having to lose too many of their workers to other employers during slack times. This was the practice at Tyrer's yard and no doubt the same method was employed by many other boat-builders as well. The number of men employed varied between 20 and 30 at any one time.

Mr. Thomas Tyrer, son of Richard Tyrer the founder of Tyrer's boat-building

A Leeds and Liverpool Canal warehouse as it appears today, 1987.

Top Locks, looking north along the Rufford Line in 1969.

Mr. Thomas Tyrer (centre) with his workmen outside the Bull and Dog Inn, Burscough Town.

A rare photograph of an actual launch of a canal barge from Tyrer's boatyard in 1927.

Workmen posing at the launch of a canal barge from Tyrer's boatyard in 1902. Mr. Thomas Tyrer is at the tiller.

A poor quality but evocative photograph, dating from 1913, of three typical Burscough boatwomen dressed in the traditional costume at the St. John's School procession.

A modern view of Top Locks showing, on the left, part of the old graving dock, which was used by the Canal Company until 1849.

yard was apprenticed to one of the boat-building firms in either the Wigan or Newburgh area and at the age 21 years he became a journeyman and was then sacked along with three of his colleagues, Isaac Shelton, Richard Forshaw and Ellis Lund. The reason why they were sacked appears to have been due to the firm being unable to afford their wages when they were out of their apprenticeship. Thomas, however, subsequently came to work for his father and in 1886 when his father died he took over the business which he enlarged and modified. By 1895 two boat-building yards were in existence but the Briars yard, the oldest, was not employed as much as the newer yard at Glovers Bridge; both of these yards are now in ruins and have almost disappeared. The forge used by Tyrer's was on the site now occupied by Mr. Cheetham (motor mechanic).

Canal barges are usually called 'narrow boats' to distinguish them from 'lighters' which usually carry upwards of 1,000 tons. Each builder had his own style and the boats which were built by Tyrer's for Richard Williams of Liverpool were designed to carry coal and were made in two sizes, a long boat capable of carrying from 70-80 tons and a short boat capable of carrying from 50-60 tons of coal. Initially, the boats were drawn by horses and it is recorded that even teams of men were employed on some occasions. Subsequently, steam-driven craft were used in the late 1870s and in 1889 the Leeds and Liverpool Canal was deepened to 5' 6" for 103 miles so that it could be used by 80 ton flats. At that period Richard Williams of Liverpool started to use a steam-driven tug which pulled from 4 to 6 barges daily from Wigan (loaded with over 200 tons of coal) to Liverpool. Subsequently, this steam-driven tug was replaced by a diesel-driven boat about 1920. Small private barges still continued to use horses until the early 1900s because the steam-driven barges robbed them of much of their living accommodation. However, by the 1910s, very few people in Burscough were living entirely on the canal, but Burscough supplied the large canal companies with most of their labour force.

The 1884 Canal Boat Act precipitated the development of about 90 houses for the canal boat people in Burscough in 1888. Subsequent to the 1884 Act, canal boats had to be registered by the boat-builders who had to conform to certain standards in respect to the living accommodation. It was due to this Act of 1884 that many of the boat people of Burscough were forced to find living accommodation on the land and, by 1890, many families were living on the land and their husbands remained on the canal boats. The men either owned their own boats or worked for the larger companies such as Richard Williams or the Leeds and Liverpool Canal Co., the Wigan Coal and Iron Co., or H. & R. Ainscoughs Ltd., Burscough, and many more. In many cases they were often away for two or three weeks and in some instances took their families with them, as the following log-book entry of St. John's C. of E. School suggests:

'June 19th 1893 — The children of Watkinsons are away at Leeds in the Boat also Langton.'

Before the passing of the 1884 Canal Boat Act, very little could be done about the attendance of canal boat children in this area and they were often employed on the land or on the boats, as the following log-book entry of St. John's C. of E. School confirms:

'Oct 22nd 1880 — The attendance for the past month has been the worst (in proportion to numbers) for the last three years. The Compulsory Powers do not affect irregulars owing to the absence of bye-laws. No attendance officer has visited this village for the past three months and in consequence of this the farmers employ children in farm work and boatmen in boating with impunity.'

However, by the late 1880s the effect of the Canal Boat Act was being felt in the Burscough area and there are several reports extant, such as the following which show that the Act was being enforced:

'May 26th 1887 — Richard Jackson of Burscough was summoned at Wigan on Monday for refusing to produce a certificate of registry of the canal boat "Catherine" to Thomas L. Hughes, inspector of canal boats for the Wigan Corporation on the 13th inst.'

Life on the barges in those early days was not easy and, to add to their discomfort from time to time in the Burscough area and elsewhere, it is on record that several men, women and children met their deaths by falling into a lock, thereby being crushed by the barge or having one of their arms or legs badly damaged. The winter months also proved to be a very hard time for the barges, especially if the canal became frozen. In 1879 the canal was frozen over for many weeks and the following entry in the St. John's C. of E. School log-book shows some of the problems that it presented:

'20th Dec., 1879 — The continued frost having prevented the boat people of the village from working, many children (from 30-40) have been and still are absent as the parents having no wages cannot pay the fees.'

When the frost continued for a long time it was the usual practice to set up soup kitchens in the district, the earliest on record in the Burscough area being in the 1850s. In 1913 when the boatmen in Burscough were out of work because the canal was frozen over, their needs were partly met by the establishment of a soup kitchen at the Stanley Institute. Mrs. Laing of Netherby House, Junction Lane, undertook the work and on average about 90 families were supplied every day.

The boat-builders were also concerned about alleviating the distress caused when the canal was frozen over and on Dec. 13th, 1877 a new ice boat was launched at the Briars Yard, Lathom, called *The Storm*. The boat was built for the Leeds and Liverpool Canal Co. and was launched under the supervision of Mr. William Moss, one of the agents of the Company. Before ice breaking boats were employed on the canal in this area, Mr. Joseph Webster of 'Watkinsons' Farm, Hall Lane, Lathom, supplied the Leeds and Liverpool Canal Co. with men to break the ice on the canal in Lathom and Burscough from the 1840s to the 1860s and when the Canal Company's Yard was built in the 1880s he supplied hay and straw to the Company for a considerable time.

The Briars yard was formerly the dock building yard of the Leeds and Liverpool Canal Co. and at Moss Cottages close by was their workshop and yard. This dock building yard was developed in the 1820s but, owing to the building of the Dock Office etc., at Burscough Bridge, the yard lost its significance and gradually declined.

Launching of boats

The first detailed record of a launch in Burscough that is extant was in October 1861 when the screw steamer *Estella* was launched from the yard of Mr. William

Fletcher, boat-builder, Burscough Bridge. The boat was to ply between Southport and Lytham in the summer months. It was 62 feet overall, 15 foot beam and 6 feet in the hold. The boat was 12 horse-power, the engine being built by Messrs. Bromilow and Rogerson of Bolton. The following was recorded on the day of the launch:

> 'When the boat went into the water, she was christened by Miss Fletcher, the daughter of the builder, in a very admirable manner, breaking in the usual manner a bottle of good old port as she named her 'Estella'. Nothing could excel the splendid manner the boat made her debut.'

After the launch about 30 people sat down to a supper at the Bridge Hotel (now the Packet House).

The next boat on record was the launching of a canal barge by Tyrer's at their boat-building yard at Glovers Bridge in November 1872. The barge was built for Mr. George Fowler and was named *Clara* and was to be used in the coal trade. No complete records exist of an actual launch in this area subsequent to the one of 1861 but the following information supplied by Thomas and John Tyrer (great grandsons of Richard Tyrer) who took part in the launchings in the 1920s provide us with an interesting account of what took place:

> On the day of the launch a flag was hoisted which was an indication to the people in the neighbourhood that Tyrer's were about to launch a boat. On several occasions the minister of St. John's C. of E. church was present, notably the Rev. T. S. Stoney who blessed the boat after which in the usual manner a bottle of port was broken as the boat was named.

It was also customary after the launch to serve hot pot and red cabbage to whomever was present at the launching ceremony and in the 1870s and 80s as many as 50 persons were given a dinner at the Ring O' Bells Inn after the launching of a boat. The day of the launch, therefore, was quite an occasion and reflects something of the spirit of the time which is now a thing of the past. The grandfather of Thomas Tyrer was superstitious when launching a boat and said: 'It must always sway across and back', in other words it must go stern first. Thomas Tyrer's father, John, who took over the business in 1909, to show he was not superstitious launched his boats on a Friday. When a boat hit the canal the water was thrust out of the canal, over the tow path, and into the field opposite and the bottom of the canal could often be seen.

When a boat had been in use for a number of years, it was customary in this area that they would be put up for auction when the owner had decided upon buying a new boat or boats. In October 1889 the following information was exhibited on a handbill:

Glovers Bridge Lathom
Near Burscough Bridge

To be sold by Auction by Mr. William G. Idle on Wednesday Nov 6th 1889 at three o'clock in the Afternoon at Mr. Thomas Tyrer's Boat Yard the Two well-known long boats 'Mary of Lathom' and 'Good Friday', at which yard they now lie, and may be seen up to the sale. The Boats will be sold without reserve to the highest bidder.

Traffic on the canal

From the 1820s to the 1920s the traffic on the canal increased and the materials carried became more varied. Coal remained one of the main items, but subsequently wool, flax and timber from the Baltic ports became increasingly important. The Leeds and Liverpool Canal became a 'highway from Liverpool to the Baltic'. The canal opened up new and cheaper sites for industries, thus enabling manufacturers to choose sites other than take expensive sites in the towns as they had had to do in the past. Road costs and the labour of road maintenance were kept down in this area to a certain extent because the bulky and heavy traffic was being sent by canal.

With the increase in traffic, many wharves and much handling equipment had to be erected alongside the canal and at Burscough in the 1880s the Leeds and Liverpool Canal Company built their offices, warehouse, stables and yard at Burscough Bridge and constructed several wharves in this area. Coal, limestone and manure amongst other things were mainly stored at these wharves. Several wharves were owned by farmers and these were mainly used to store manure which was usually brought from Liverpool; it contained human as well as animal dung and very often contained the entrails of animals. The Rural Sanitary Authority made special regulations concerning these wharves because they were a source of infection and, according to the following, were also a nuisance:

> 1873 — 'Liquid Manure at a Manure Wharf — New Lane, owned by William Forshaw, the liquid manure was running in front of several houses'.
> 'A nuisance caused by James Thorougood by liquid from his manure wharf meandering past certain cottages at Burscough Bridge'.

Employment and investment

The canals in Burscough have provided the people in this area with employment for a long time and in the past have given character to the place. Several of the old boat houses still exist; many had a stable attached but these have subsequently been modified to suit present day needs. The canals brought an economic stimulus to the farms in this area and, together with the turnpike roads, seem to have had an effect of evening out wages. This effect is very noticeable in the townships of Halsall, Burscough, Rufford, Ince Blundell and Ormskirk, which lie on or near the Leeds and Liverpool Canal where the wages by all accounts were the same: two shillings per day in 1833. Wages on the canals appear to have been a little higher than those received by a farm labourer in this area and it appears that there were mutual agreements between the canal companies and certain farmers. For example J. Webster of Lathom supplied farm labourers to the Leeds and Liverpool Canal Co. for various purposes as the need arose. Just how many men were employed on the canals in Burscough throughout the 19th century is difficult to say but, by and large, up to 60% and over of the total working population were employed on the canals directly in the middle of the 19th century, together with an unknown amount of indirect labour which would be concerned in the business of the canal as a whole. However, a more definite figure can be given for 1913 because in that year there was a boatman's strike at Burscough which involved 200 boatmen. Of this number 150 came directly from the Burscough area. It would take too long to record the details here but, briefly, the strike was concerned with payment of Sunday labour and resulted in 30 men being summoned before the Liverpool magistrates for having ceased to work without giving a week's notice in accordance with their contract of service. They were ordered to pay a week's wages as damage for breach of contract.

The canals also afforded security and people in all walks of life invested their money in the Leeds and Liverpool Canal Company, which usually paid about 5% per annum. Nearly all the accounts of the Charity Commissioners show that the money of the charities of Burscough was invested in the Leeds and Liverpool Canal during the 19th century.

Railways

The Liverpool, Ormskirk and Preston Railway was opened between Walton Junction and Lostock Hall near Preston on 2nd April 1849. The original company amalgamated with the East Lancashire Railway and the Blackburn and Preston Railway, well before the opening, to form the East Lancashire Railway. The line between Liverpool and Preston had first been proposed in 1844 but its Bill had been rejected. It was resubmitted in 1845 with the support of the other two companies, which stood to gain considerably from being associated with this important new line, and the union of the three undertakings was always part of the overall plan. The Act received Royal Assent on 18th August 1846 and, by its terms, the amalgamation of the three companies was effected.

The Liverpool terminus was originally at Tithebarn Street, after a brief temporary station at Great Howard Street, in use by trains from Preston for less than a year. Subsequently Exchange Station was built close to the Tithebarn Street Station. Exchange Station was itself closed in the mid-1970s when the new underground link was built across Liverpool to connect the Southport and Ormskirk lines with the southern route to Garston and Hunts Cross.

The line to Preston was very easy to build, with few notable engineering works and little trouble encountered during construction. The route climbed gently out through the suburbs of Liverpool, to the low plateau around Ormskirk, and then closely followed the alignment of the turnpike road through Aughton, Ormskirk and Burscough. Beyond Burscough it ran in a straight line out across the flat mosslands to Farington, where it joined the existing line to Preston.

The station at Burscough was situated south of the main road in an area which was then undeveloped. Only since the 1930s has building gradually filled in the land between the main road and the railway line, as Burscough has grown as a residential area.

In 1859 the East Lancashire Railway was amalgamated with the Lancashire and Yorkshire Railway to become the largest local company, and a fierce rival for the larger and nationally important London and North Western Railway. The route between Preston and Liverpool via Burscough was considerably shorter than the L.N.W.R. route via St. Helens Shaw Street and Wigan, but the latter was generally used for the major through trains to Glasgow and Edinburgh and the north because it was not in the interests of the L.N.W.R. to use the line of its great rival. The Lancashire and Yorkshire, however, did use the Burscough line for trains on the route to Yorkshire, via Blackburn, Colne and the Midland Railway to Leeds.

The life of the railway was largely uneventful; locally, the most dramatic event was a major accident at Burscough Junction station on 15th January 1880, in

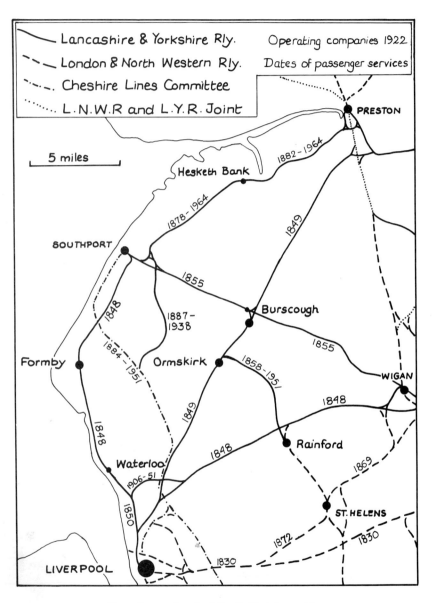

The railway network of South West Lancashire.

The physical layout of the railway network in the Burscough area has meant that the railways and their related buildings are prominent features of the town from which you are never very far away.

which nine people were killed and more than 50 injured. The accident was caused by a combination of human error, a defective and outdated signalling system and an inadequate track layout which could not cope with complex train movements. The opening of the line from Wigan to Southport in 1855 had brought major changes, since spur lines were built to link the Preston line and the Southport line at Burscough Station, which was renamed Burscough Junction. The changes meant far more, and more complicated train movements, but the signalling and track layouts were not modernised sufficiently to cater for these.

Owing to the Burscough collision of 1880, the Lancashire and Yorkshire Railway Company promised to carry out improvements to Burscough Junction Railway Station to prevent a similar disaster occurring again. By January 1882, the following improvements had been carried out. The Burscough Station and Burscough Junction signal boxes were done away with, and new cabins were erected, one on the south side of the canal bridge and the other on the south side of the station (since taken down in the 1960s), and the entire points system for the main line and sidings was operated from these cabins. The local trains from Southport to Burscough, instead of running on the main line as formerly and doing all shunting work on the main line, were subsequently to cross from the main line into a bay siding provided at the north end of the station (most of the sidings have been removed in the late 1960s). The engine then ran round in a siding provided, and backed up to the train, which was ready to load and return to Southport. This work was all done independently of the main line. At this end of the station a new platform of over 200 yards in length was erected to give ample accommodation for excursion trains. On the Ormskirk side of the station a new platform was erected which was over 100 yds long. The local trains from Liverpool, Ormskirk and Burscough Junction entered the station as formerly but, after unloading passengers, were shunted into a bay siding from Ormskirk and Liverpool. Various other operations were undertaken at the time, e.g. the platforms were raised up to their present level and waiting room accommodation was provided on the Ormskirk side of the station (demolished in September 1970), the platforms were covered in and a bridge was provided for passengers to cross from one side of the station to another. (This bridge is no longer in use since the introduction of single line working from Ormskirk to Lostock Hall in 1970).

The opening of the Southport-Wigan Line, 1855

The Manchester and Southport Railway was authorised by Parliament in 1847 but, because Parliament sanctioned the Liverpool to Wigan, Bolton and Bury Line, the promoters withdrew their support. For a time the scheme was dropped but, because of the fear that Southport would be cut off from Wigan, support for the project was again renewed and, on 12th January 1852, the public demanded that something must be done. After a relatively short time the Court of Queen's Bench (August 1852) issued a mandamus to the directors who were then compelled to construct a line from Wigan to Southport.

During the construction of the line, no less than seven acres of sandhills, some of them seven feet in height, were removed from near Southport to Burscough Bridge for the new railway in August 1854. There were very few outstanding engineering works undertaken along this section of the line and, apart from the various bridges over the Leeds and Liverpool Canal and the River Douglas, there were only two short cuttings between Gathurst and Parbold that presented any problems. The stone obtained from these cuttings was used to build the stations along the line. However, the opening of line was delayed on 26th January 1855, when Captain Tyler of the railway department of the Board of Trade, refused to sanction the opening of the Wigan and Southport Railway until a second line of rails was laid between Burscough and Southport. On 4th April 1855, Captain Tyler sanctioned the opening of the line from Burscough to Southport, but the line from Burscough Bridge to Wigan remained a single line until 1st November 1861, when it was opened as a double line (except for the bridge over the canal at Burscough). A new bridge was constructed over the canal at Burscough which was tested on 6th December 1862.

On Saturday 7th April 1855, the opening ceremony took place. The train was gaily-decorated and was full of directors and railway officials, and at Southport detonating signals were placed along the line (and no doubt elsewhere through which the train passed) and as the train drew into Southport it was met by the sound of the Churchtown Band. Over 400 guests were also invited and these arrived half an hour later in a second train.

Initially, only six stations were built along this line from Wigan to Southport, Gathurst, Appley Bridge, Newburgh (for Parbold), Burscough Bridge, New Lane and Bescar Lane, and the station houses at each of these stations built of stone in the 'Elizabethan Style'. Subsequently, three other stations were opened along this line, at Ash Street, Blowick and, in this area, Hoscar Moss Station which was opened on November 1st 1870 and on 1st January 1900 it was renamed Hoscar Station.

The trains from Burscough Junction to Southport used the Burscough South Fork (closed 30th August 1964) and the Burscough North Fork was used in the early days by trains coming from Croston and Rufford to Southport. This railway, similar to the canals, was built by navvies and on April 26th 1854 a serious riot took place in Burscough and seven persons were hurt.

Road alterations

Before the railway was constructed from Wigan through Burscough Bridge to Southport in 1855, Red Cat Lane joined the present Liverpool Road nearly opposite the parish church, the site now being partly occupied by the Cambridge Hotel. A small house licensed to sell beer was situated on the corner of the then Red Cat Lane in the 1840s and 1850s, and was occupied and run by Jane Rylance. Various alterations were made to the roads and two access roads were made to connect the railway station with Red Cat Lane and Liverpool Road. The present Cambridge Hotel was built in the 1860s and from the records of the Highway Board it appears that the bridge over the railway was built soon after the completion of the railway line in 1855. The railway companies were responsible for the upkeep of the bridges which went over their lines and from time to time the Highway Boards would prefer an indictment upon them if they were not kept in good repair.

Railway fares

In the early years of the railway in this area railway fares were competitive, but as amalgamations took place a more uniform system of charging began to be enforced. A good example of this occurred in 1855 when the Lancashire and Yorkshire Railway competed with the East Lancashire Railway as a result of the opening of the new lines which connected Liverpool and Southport via Crosby and Burscough respectively. After the fares had been reduced several times, they dropped to as low as 6d. single and 9d. return, but in 1856 the two companies came to an agreement and a common fare between Liverpool and Southport was established at 1/6d. single, and 2/6d. return. Railway fares from Burscough to Ormskirk, Southport and Liverpool are not known, except for the odd record which is not indicative of the general pattern of charges at the time. The approximate fares in operation from Burscough to Ormskirk in the 1850s would be as follows:

1st Class 6d. return
2nd Class 4d. return
3rd Class 2½d. return

By 1860 a market train left Burscough for Liverpool every Saturday morning at 5 o'clock and subsequently market trains ran on Thursdays and Saturdays to Ormskirk when they carried passengers at reduced rates. Subsequent innovations were tried by the railway companies in order to attract passenger traffic and, at the same time to try to control the use of their rolling stock, so from time to time special trains and excursions were introduced in an attempt to overcome this problem.

Railway employment during the 19th and early part of the 20th century

Initially the railway not only provided regular and permanent work for its staff and workpeople but there were many other advantages which, although not in every case expressible in monetary terms, were nevertheless substantial privileges peculiar to their enjoyment. During the 19th and early part of the 20th century, there were very few industries or trades which guaranteed steady and permanent employment and there were still fewer who gave added advantages to their employees. Therefore, in the early days of the railway and on into the greater part of the 20th century, the employees of the railway companies enjoyed a privileged position.

Not surprisingly, therefore, the railway companies found it easy to attract people into their ranks at Burscough, Ormskirk and elsewhere in Lancashire through which the railways passed. It also meant that the working population of Burscough became more flexible and, to a few, new opportunities for advancement and learning were to be given for the first time. In the early years the railway companies at both stations in Burscough employed in total about 40 men, but during their peak probably reached about 70 to 80. At Ormskirk in 1900 the station staff excluding the permanent way staff numbered 35. These figures do not represent the total numbers of men employed by the railway in this area, for many railway employees who were living in the Burscough and Ormskirk area worked in Liverpool and adjacent areas.

Railway traffic

In the 1850s, 60s and 70s, the movement of passengers was not very significant because most people found work locally, and by and large only used the railway for holidays, with the possible exception of farmers and businessmen. By the 1870s small industries were beginning to emerge which were either directly or indirectly connected with agriculture, and they needed, as an outlet and in some cases as a supplier, the services of the railway. It will be noticed that the industries or firms in the Burscough area established during the 1850s to 1870s occupied positions near to the railway (e.g. James Martlands Ltd., Peet's Mill, H. & R. Ainscough Ltd., Bridge's Saw Mill, and the Brick and Tile Works) and subsequently had their own private sidings built. Because of the transport facilities and proximity to Liverpool and other industrial areas, the Ordnance Depot was established at Burscough, and this again was sited adjacent to the railway and was equipped with its own private sidings. The Ordnance Depot provided much work for the people of Burscough and the surrounding districts and during both World Wars used the railway services to the full, both for the movement of men and equipment. I shall have more to say about the Ordnance Depot when I discuss the development of industry in the Burscough area.

The goods traffic carried by the railway in this area consisted mainly of the following: bricks, timber, grain, agricultural produce, especially potatoes etc., and military equipment. Subsequently, small coal depots were set up at both stations, notably the Wigan Coal and Iron Company at Burscough Junction, which was established there about 1910, the coal being brought by railway from the Wigan, Skelmersdale and St. Helens coal fields. James Martland was one of the early coal merchants in Burscough who utilised the railway services as early as 1890 and it is interesting to note that he also undertook in 1896 to deliver coal at special prices to farmers and others for wagon loads. (The best Atherton coal sold at 12/6d. per ton in 1896).

This Company, along with many others was taken over by the National Coal Board in 1948. The Company's office still remains at Burscough Junction, but is now closed and the sidings and storage accommodation has now gone. At the time of writing, a new warehouse was being erected for F. & N. Motor Supply Co. (the firm has occupied a site on the airfield for a number of years, but will subsequently move to their new premises at Burscough Junction) on the site of the former sidings adjacent to Burscough Junction Station.

During the 1930s in Burscough the pattern of transport was beginning to change and this was reflected by the number of firms who were either using their own road-motor transport or were conveying their goods by means of road hauliers such as Sykes of Preston. Subsequently, such firms as Messrs. Price, Guy, Hague and Barker have developed their own road haulier business, and the traffic which they are carrying today would in the past have been sent by rail. With the gradual reduction in the use of coal and with the change over to electricity and gas by domestic and industrial users, a vast amount of revenue was lost to the railways and, by the end of the 1960s, the small coal depots at Burscough Junction and Burscough Bridge had become a thing of the past. However, with the introduction of several new industries in Burscough, namely Outrams Ltd., (later known as Southport Cakes and now in the premises of Brocklebank Plastics Ltd.), Lavery's Ltd., (premises now occupied by

Westbrooks Ltd.) and Elkes and Fox Ltd., the railway began to handle large consignments of cake traffic which was despatched to many areas in the U.K. and the republic of Ireland. The agreed flat rate charges which were introduced by the railways, helped to secure still more of the traffic, especially between Southport Cakes and Lavery's but, when these two firms closed in 1967 and 1965 respectively, the goods and passenger parcels traffic being handled by Burscough Bridge fell appreciably and resulted in staff redundancies and transfers.

Passenger traffic has also declined appreciably in the past 20 years and since the Beeching Plan of 1962 the services have been much reduced, economies in staff have taken place, signal boxes have been taken down and station sidings and handling facilities have also been largely removed. Steam trains were withdrawn in the 1960s in this area and superseded by diesel units and in 1962 the only remnant of the East Lancashire Railway, the Liverpool to Southport service, was withdrawn on 5th March of that year, though the curve or fork from Burscough Junction to Burscough Bridge remained in use for summer passenger trains until 30th August 1964. The curve or fork to Burscough Junction North was retained for summer passenger services until 4th September 1965. In 1969, through passenger services from Preston to Liverpool were discontinued, and in 1970 single line working was implemented between Lostock Hall and Ormskirk and on 24th May 1971 a 'conductor' service was introduced on the diesel units between Ormskirk and Preston, on which the fares are collected and tickets issued by the guard. Thus Burscough Junction, Rufford and Croston booking offices have been closed and have now become halts only.

The importance of the railway passenger service in the past can be gauged from the number of trains calling at Burscough Junction: in 1914 there were no fewer than 102 trains per day and in the 1969 the number had been reduced to less than 30 trains per day.

The electric train service from Ormskirk to Liverpool was first opened on 7th April 1913 and consisted of two stopping trains from Liverpool to Ormskirk and vice versa. Subsequently, a ten minute service of quick trains was provided within the Liverpool conurbation to and from the centre and, to more outlying places, a twenty minute service with additional expresses during rush hours was provided. The object of the electric services was to provide a cheap and efficient service into Liverpool where the labour was required. In 1930, for example, to do the double journey of some 38 miles between Southport and Liverpool (electric service), which took 32 minutes each way, the cost of a workman's ticket was 1/3d. It was also proposed at that time to electrify the railway to Southport via Burscough, but the extension was never undertaken.

Canal and railway transport has, therefore, been very important in the growth and development of Burscough in the past and, because it was and still is, a focal point of routes, it became an important military centre during the Second World War, as evidenced by the airfield, various military camps and the Ordnance Depot. When both the canals and railways were being constructed in this area, much opposition was shown by many of the landowners and inhabitants to these projects and, if they could be sited as far away as was practicable from the better class districts, this was done. This latter problem mainly arose when railways were being constructed; thus, as in many places, railway stations existed on the periphery or at the far end of the town. On several occasions, Lady Wilbraham of Blythe Hall tried to persuade the L. & Y. Railway Co., to have a halt built at the Abbey for the people of Burscough Town, but permission was never granted.

Both the canals and the railways brought the people of Burscough into contact with inhabitants of other towns, which in the early days of canal transport resulted in persons marrying further afield than they had done before, and in some cases meant that either they came to live in Burscough and introduced new blood into the area, or they left Burscough altogether. Many persons moved to Blackburn, Bradford and Nelson from Burscough and, similarly, numbers of people moved into the Burscough area during the 1820s to 1840s from Yorkshire. This last aspect probably accounts for the high numbers of Wesleyans amongst the community of boat-people by the 1870s in this area. With the introduction of the railways, as we have seen, movement became easier and when the Ordnance Depot was established here in 1891 the people of Burscough came into contact with persons who were widely travelled and, subsequently, when soldiers married local girls when they moved or were transferred elsewhere, they invariably took their families with them.

Postal services

At the beginning of the 18th century and before, a postal service as such does not appear to have existed in this area of Lancashire. Letters and other forms of correspondence, papers etc. were mainly the concern of the gentry and upper classes who usually delegated a servant to deliver their letters on horseback, as the following extract from Blundell's Diary and Letter Book confirms:

'March 3rd, 1703 — I writ to my Lady Webb and sent Walter Thelwall with it the next day to Haythorp'.

The expenses incurred by Thelwall amounted to £1-7s.-4d. and, therefore, although the method was simple, it was none the less expensive.

The only supply of newspapers to Ormskirk and the neighbourhood of Lathom during the period 1805 to about the 1840s was brought by a man referred to as 'Little John Day' who used to walk from Liverpool once a week (every Saturday), with about twenty newspapers under his arm, and 'the supply was rather more than the demand'. Therefore, it is indicative that until the general public was educated in the art of reading and writing there was little demand in this area for the postal service, with the possible exception of the gentry, merchants and farmers, even in the early part of the 19th century. According to Richard Berry, it also appears to have been customary during the beginning of the 19th century and probably before in Ormskirk to have the news told by the village blacksmith or other worthy, who perched himself on a tombstone on a Sunday morning at Ormskirk parish church. Mr. Richard Berry of Burscough also appears to have carried on the tradition because his superior education came in very useful in retelling the news to his less fortunate friends in the late 1820s who used to crowd round him to listen to the then stirring events of the time, read from a Liverpool newspaper which cost threepence.

In the early part of the 18th century, letters were conveyed through Ormskirk on horseback, and the first post which passed through Ormskirk en route from Liverpool to Preston was in the year 1757. Subsequently, with the development of the turnpike road from Liverpool to Preston stage-coaches began to use this road in 1774 but, unfortunately, all letters for Preston had to circulate through Liverpool and were carried by the long circuit, Liverpool-Warrington-Chorley. As a result, the postage on a single letter was often as much as 4d., and it took 4 days to get a reply. The town of Ormskirk and the neighbourhood petitioned for the improvement of the postal arrangements in 1793 and 1797, but they were unsuccessful. What they required was a direct communication with Preston (at this time the stage-coach which plyed between Preston and Liverpool through Burscough and Ormskirk conveyed correspondence from Ormskirk to Liverpool, but not from Ormskirk and district to Preston!).

By 1822, mails from Ormskirk were being conveyed to and from Liverpool by horse-post, but this method of transit was discontinued in favour of the new mail coach from Liverpool. The London mail was sent via Preston for the first time in November 1825 but, for this convenience, postage was increased from 11d. to 1/− per letter.

However, with the introduction of the railways at Ormskirk in 1849, the stage-coach service gradually faded out and the mails were conveyed by train. The railways facilitated the movement of mails and also the delivery of national newspapers from London which were received in Ormskirk the day after despatch.

The postal service in Burscough

About the year 1860 the first sub-post office was established in Burscough on Mr. William Peet's premises (his building is now occupied by Vitax Ltd.) in Liverpool Road near the Burscough Bridge railway station. Letters arrived from Ormskirk at 7.30 a.m. and were despatched at 5.30 p.m. However, money orders could only be obtained at Ormskirk. During the 1870s and 1880s there were no postmen in Burscough, and the letters were delivered by boys who were still at school, similar to the boys delivering newspapers today. The following appears in the St. John's C. of E. School log-book which throws some light on the problem:

'Jan. 1875 — I wish to call attention to the following James Seddon (2nd Class Register) delivers letters from the post every morning, and consequently seldom gets to school before 10 o'clock, the time for closing the registers and then loses a morning's attendance. I have told him this, but I believe he tries his best. It could be called Government employment and allow the lad a few minutes longer.'

On February 3rd 1870, it is recorded that 'the Government commenced its new duties as telegrapher-general'. Messages were sent through the Ormskirk post-office for the first time in 1870 and in 1873 permission was given to erect a line of telegraph poles (under the Telegraph Acts of 1868/9) from Preston to Liverpool.

In 1861 the Post Office Savings Banks were established and this facility was available at Ormskirk in the 1860s, but does not appear to have been introduced at the Burscough sub-post office until about 1875.

As the postal services were developing and the facilities it provided were being used by a greater number of people, it was found necessary to erect wall boxes to receive letters for despatch in country areas. Three of these wall boxes were initially erected in the Burscough and Lathom areas, namely in Junction Lane,

Square Lane and one near the Ring O' Bells, in the late 1870s.

In 1874 the numbering of houses was introduced into the Ormskirk and surrounding districts of Lathom and Burscough to facilitate the work of delivering letters.

By 1881 the sub-post office at Burscough Bridge was handling letters, parcels and money orders and had established a Post Office Savings Bank and telegraph office, but in that year Mr. William Martland became the sub-postmaster. (In 1904 the premises of Peet's Mill was taken over by Messrs. Martland & Co., at which time Mr. Thomas Peet, son of William Peet had removed to Milnthorpe, Westmorland) About the year 1885, the sub-post office at Burscough Bridge was removed from William Peet's premises to where the wine stores of Ashe & Nephew are today. In that year Miss H. Rimmer was appointed sub-postmistress and an insurance agent (Mr. Mayson) for the London Assurance Corporation was also based at the post office.

In 1887 a sub-post office was established at the Three Oaks and Mr. James Seddon was appointed receiver. Only letters were handled at this office and these passed through Ormskirk. Later, postal orders and money orders were issued at this office, but not paid.

The third sub-post office to be established in this area was in 1890 when the Burscough Town Office was opened along Liverpool Road (Now William C. Duttons, grocers) in the premises of Mr. William Carridge, grocer, he being the first sub-postmaster. Letters arrived from Ormskirk at 7 a.m. and 6 p.m., and were despatched at 9.45 a.m. and 6 p.m. Postal orders were issued here, but not paid.

In 1894 Grace Rimmer became sub-postmistress at Burscough Bridge post office and in 1898 an Express Delivery & Annuity & Insurance Office was also added to the facilities then available. Miss Rimmer was also a stationer and bookseller.

Telephones were introduced into Burscough in 1899, Thorougood's Breweries Ltd. being one of the first, if not the first, subscriber in that year; their phone number was 4. A small exchange was also set up about the same time in a house in Mart Lane (No. 4 in the row between W. Ramage's Shop and Martlands Ltd.) which was run by Mrs. Smith from its inception until about 1944. About the year 1939 the building of a new exchange was undertaken but, owing to the Second World War, was not completed until 1944. (This exchange is situated along Liverpool Road a short distance from the war memorial). An idea of the cost of installing a telephone connection in 1901 by the National Telephone Co. Ltd., was given when they were going to connect the Waterworks pumping station with the Ormskirk Exchange, they stated that it would be £10 per annum, but the cost of the connection from the Surveyor's office to the Burscough Bridge Exchange would cost £16-16s.-0d. per annum.

In 1908 Miss Margery Rimmer took over the position of sub-postmistress at the Burscough Bridge post office and continued the business of stationer and bookseller as well. A telephone call-box had been established in Ormskirk in 1905 and was open from 7 a.m. to 9 p.m. week days only. In 1910 a Telephone Call Office was established at the Burscough Bridge sub-post office by the National Telephone Co. Ltd., and by 1918 a telegraph office was set up at Burscough Junction Railway Station, with delivery on station premises only, and was open from 8 a.m. to 8 p.m. on weekdays only. This was the age of the telegraph boys who were paid a penny for local telegrams and 2d. if they had to deliver them to Rufford.

In 1918, however, the post office was moved again to where Walton's shop is today and about 1917 Mr. James Henry Holding was appointed sub-postmaster and he remained there until 1924.

It was in 1924 that the post office was to be moved for the fourth time to what became known as 'Post Office Place' near the parish church, the site being occupied today by Ruth's the Hairdressers. Mr. Samuel Hall became the sub-postmaster in 1924 and in June 1933 when it was decided that the post-office should occupy a more central position on the Liverpool Road (where it is today) he moved everything in two night sittings to get matters in order, so that the public would not be inconvenienced by the change, for the new building was ready before the old one was vacated.

Agriculture and Industry

Agriculture

VERY little is known about the early forms of agriculture in the Burscough area and about the field patterns and organisation of cultivation which the system of farming employed. In the *Cartulary* of Burscough Priory (see Chapter 1) there are some hints about the agricultural activities of the monks who, as in every other religious house, were significant large-scale farmers and estate managers. There is, for example, reference to the use of ditches as boundaries, and it is quite reasonable to postulate that the monks of Burscough Priory were responsible for the first substantial attempts to drain the lowlying marshes and mosses to the west and north of the village and to reclaim the land for agricultural use. Their work probably began soon after the foundation of the Priory in the late 12th century, although it is likely that small-scale piecemeal reclamation was attempted privately before that time, if the examples of the Fens and the Somerset Levels, both rather similar in character to the coastal mosslands of South Lancashire, are any guide. The *Cartulary* also gives some evidence for the way in which the monastic estate was operated: there may have been an open field system in the township, but scarcely anything is known of this. Instead, there is some record of the field names, crops and labour force on the Priory lands.

As many as seven windmills are recorded in the *Cartulary* within the Parish of Ormskirk in 1228, which is to some degree indicative that a fairly large area of land was under cultivation. The Priory would also be the largest employer in this area apart from the great houses from the 12th to the early part of the 16th century, and it was recorded in the 'Brief Certificate' of the Commissioners in 1536, that there were 22 waiting servants of the household and 18 men employed to work the monastic demesnes.

In the 1530s a survey was carried out after the suppression of Burscough Priory in which a detailed statement of the demesne lands, and crops and stock upon them, was given. There were meadows and pastures called Cow Hey, Battleholme, Bradshaw, Marsh, Highfield, Gorse Hey, Crooked Acres and Aspenshoute. The Rushy field was sown with oats, Sandycroft with rye and Bankfield with oats and barley. Wheat was only mentioned growing in the Mill Field of eight acres, of which only 4 acres were actually sown, the other 4 acres remaining as pasture. Common pasture existed at Tarlscough moss, alias 'Wirpulles' moss, and in Hitchcock moss. From the information available it appears that an open-field system of cultivation was operated by the monks, there being no evidence to suggest a two or three field system involving the use of one fallow field for pasture.

There was also a deer park at Lathom owned by the de Lathom family and latterly the Earls of Derby. A park was a tract of land enclosed with a pale or fence for the better preservation of deer (and the surrounding agricultural land!). Unlike the forest or chase, its owner could not enjoy rights over the land of others. In the reign of Edward III a grant of free warren was made to 'Thomas de Lathom' over the manors of Lathom, Knowsley, Roby and Childwall. This free warren was a franchise granted by the Crown to a subject for the preservation or custody on his own land of beasts or fowls of warren, i.e. hare, coney, roe, partridge, quail, pheasant, woodcock, mallard, heron and animals of a like kind. It did not extend to deer or other beasts of chase.

Tithes

The tithe was the compulsory tenth part of the produce of the land levied upon all for the support of the Church. Tithes were either 'great' or 'small'. The great tithes were those levied on such as corn, hay and wood. The small tithes were those levied on inferior crops, such as hops and potatoes; and also there were mixed tithes arising from the produce and increase of animals fed on the land; and on personal tithes (the last named were rare and not important). The rector had the great tithes, whether he was a clerical or lay rector, and the vicar usually had the small tithes.

Before 1836 payments were made 'in kind' to the clergy, of corn, fodder etc., and were stored in large medieval barns known as tithe-barns. The tithe-barn at Burscough was situated near to the old Priory (it is probable that the original building belonged to the Priory) and lay a little to the south of the present Abbey Farm. Its size was approximately 90 feet long by 30 feet wide and was owned and occupied by the Tasker family. Unfortunately, the tithe-barn was pulled down about 1860, this probably being due to the fact that after the Tithe Commutation Act of 1836 by which a sum of money was payable every year in place of the tithe, the function of the tithe-barn would become obsolete. The only description that I could glean from the records was that it was a building with a fine timbered roof.

The tithe-barn, together with the possession of the rectorial tithes, had been held by the Tasker family for over 200 years. The Tasker family eventually went to live at Billinge but held the rectorial tithe until 1891. However, the tithe-barn and Tithe-Barn Yard originally belonged to the vicar of Ormskirk and was referred to in the tithe awards as the 'Glebe'.

The earliest documents of the advowson (the right of presentation to a church benifice) of Ormskirk parish is dated Aug. 25th 1663, the following being an extract from the 'Third Register':

> 'A true and perfect terrier of all the glebe lands and barning and a shippon with gardin and two closses of ground Containinge by Estmacon betwix three and foore acars or there abouts valued at five or six poundes per annum:
>   An Estate in Bursco.
>   Do Mossland in Lathom.'

After 1836, as I have mentioned, money was payable every year in place of the tithe. The amount was based on the average price of corn for the past seven years. The parishioners paid the amount which would have purchased the same number of bushels of wheat, barley and oats in equal proportions, at the prices of 1836 (Wheat 7s.-0¼d; barley 3s.-11½d.; oats 2s.-9d. per bushel). The tithe award of 1849 for Burscough was the following:

Henry White Valuer 1849
Gross Rent Charge.
The Township of Burscough in the Parish of Ormskirk in the County of Lancaster, £827-19-0d.

	£.	s.	d.
The Earl of Derby	30	0	0
Charles Scarisbrick Esq	50	0	0
William Leyland	10	0	0
Robert Reynolds and Alice wife of James Sumner	8	15	0
Alice Vose's Representatives	3	16	0
Alice Harrison		8	0
The trustees under the Will of Thomas Tasker	725	0	0
	827	19	0

18th-century agriculture

Before the draining of Martin Mere was undertaken, a large area of land in Burscough would remain uncultivated. Initially, when the Mere was being drained in the 18th century, the land that was reclaimed during this period was mainly used as pasture and it was not until the 1860s that cultivation of the soil could take place on a fairly large scale with any success. However, as early as 1784, many areas of reclaimed land were sown with spring corn and in the following year crops of barley and oats were sold for £11 the Cheshire acre whereas, only a few years before, the land had been let for about four shillings per acre. Unfortunately, due to the sea breaching the barriers and floodgates from time to time, the land was successively inundated with water, with the result that land prices tended to fluctuate very quickly during this period, and were only arrested when the Mere was effectively drained in the 1850s.

It was during the 18th century that large portions of land in the Burscough and Lathom area were brought into an efficient state of cultivation. The farming was mainly of a mixed character and the breeding of poultry, and especially geese, was very important. Even in the 17th century and before, the breeding of wild fowl had formed an important part of the economy and by 1700 the 'cross breeds' between wild and tame ducks were regarded as a delicacy by Epicureans. During the 1700s eggs, geese and poultry were sold in quantity at the Ormskirk and Liverpool markets, where the demand was often greater than the supply.

Although Lancashire is famed for the growing of potatoes, I could find no evidence to suggest that large quantities of them were grown in this area until the draining of the Mere, i.e. after 1850. Prior to this time potatoes were grown here by the majority of the farmers, but mainly for their own use. Blundell's diary does not give any indication that this area of Lancashire was becoming one of the main potato-growing districts of England. The diary confirms to a degree what I have found in the Burscough area that potatoes were chiefly grown as garden crops. During the 18th century various kinds of seed potatoes were in use — the ox-noble and cluster potato were planted for cattle, the pink-eye was very popular and a variety of others, together with different kinds of kidney-potatoes for the table were also grown. Many experiments were carried out with potatoes and several varieties of early potatoes were developed. During the agricultural survey of 1793, the surveyor had the opportunity of seeing some of the cluster potatoes of Colonel Mordaunt of Halsall being taken up. Colonel Mordaunt and another farmer were of the opinion 'that they never saw so large a crop; and yet, as they were informed, raised without dung.' This was only one farm but, as we shall see later, even in the 1840s and still later the use of manure was not widespread.

Manuring of the land did not take place during the 18th century and marl, ash from burned moss, lime and animal manure were used. Marl was probably the most extensively used and marl pits could be found on many of the farms in Burscough during the 18th century.

The storing of potatoes in clamps, which is still done by some farmers today, especially in the Scarisbrick area, was in use during the 18th century in Burscough. In the 18th century it appears that any method which improved the quality or increased the yield of any vegetable was a closely guarded secret by the farmer concerned. The cutting of potato sets and placing them in spritting boxes (covered with shells or saw-dust) and being kept in a dry room with a good circulation of air was, before 1793, only known to a few farmers, amongst whom was Mr. James Blundell of Ormskirk.

During the 18th century the principal grain was oats, which, when ground to meal, formed the staple diet of the labouring classes in this area. The meal was made into several kinds of bread cakes either by using sour leaven or no leaven at all and rolled very thin. Porridge was also made by boiling water and thickening it with meal, and this was eaten with sweet milk or butter milk. Treacle was very widely used at this time and was employed to sweeten many things. Tea was becoming more popular during the 18th century and was starting to reduce the consumption of meal at breakfast.

Turnips were not cultivated on a large scale in the Burscough area in the 18th century, but were first used as a garden crop. The nearness of a ready market such as a large town appears to have been the controlling factor before the crop was grown on a large scale.

Clover and vetches were grown and carrots were successfully cultivated at Scarisbrick, Burscough and Rufford chiefly for the supply of the Liverpool market. Horses were also fed on carrots that had been damaged or were not suitable for the market. The selling price of carrots in the 1790s at the Liverpool market ranged from 2/6 to 3/– per hundredweight.

Very few peas were grown, but beans were grown for the Ormskirk and Liverpool markets. Onions were grown as a garden crop and several farmers exported them. Barley was not grown on a large scale in Burscough, but several large areas of wheat were sown. Buck wheat was grown in small quantities, chiefly for poultry and, during this period, it was usual to sow the buck wheat on poor land which was also used in some instances for manuring the land and this probably explains why the turnip was not widely grown here.

During the 18th century, large numbers of cattle were not kept in this area and only the main landowners such as the Derbys, Bootle-Wilbrahams, Scarisbricks, Blundells and Mordaunts kept more than they required for their own use. The average farmer in the 18th century kept sufficient cows and horses for his own use and probably had a few pigs, but these were never kept in large numbers until the 19th century. Sheep have been bred in this area for a long time and records exist of their presence here in the 12th century.

In 1706 Nicholas Blundell, the diarist, paid £20 for '83 good sheep'. Just how many farm animals were kept by these landowners is not known, but from reports in diaries, markets etc., it appears that by today's standards, the number was relatively small.

The greater majority of farms in Burscough during the 18th century were small, the average size being from 25-35 acres. There were 41 farms which were not less than 30 acres in size, two of which were 445 acres and 360 acres each and six farms ranged from 100-195 acres each. The total acreage for Burscough was 4,887 statute acres and, although I do not have exact figures for this period, approximately 66½% of the land was used as meadow pasture, 30% was used as arable land, and the remaining 3½% was made up of woodlands, navigable canals, roads and waste. In total there were about 95 farms in Burscough during the latter half of the 18th century.

It was during the 18th century that Liverpool began to grow and about the year 1780 a regular cattle market was established. On the day that this market was opened, the following was stated:

'. . . there was a most pleasing and numerous show of fat oxen and other cattle, together with an incredible number of sheep and lambs.'

During the 19th century with the continued growth of Liverpool and the flood of Irish immigrants into the city during the Irish potato famine of 1845-7, the demand for agricultural produce, especially potatoes, eggs, poultry, butter and cheese, rose appreciably and, with the development of the railways in the late 1840s and 50s, the farms in the Burscough and Lathom area were provided with the facilities to supply the Liverpool market.

Since the beginning of the 17th century the greater part of Burscough belonged to the Lathom, Derby and Scarisbrick families who subsequently let their lands to tenant farmers. In time, certain yeomen purchased their lands from the Derby, Lathom and Scarisbrick families, notably the Tasker family who then leased their lands to tenant farmers who in turn in certain instances sub-let their holdings to another person. Eventually, by the end of the 19th century, with the increase in wages and the gradual improvement in conditions, which were being brought about by the local authorities such as the Local Board of Health, Sanitary Board, etc. upon these large landowners, they began to break up their estates. During the 20th century the process gained momentum and the estates of the Lathoms and Scarisbricks have now gone, and much of the land belonging to the Derbys has been sold.

Enclosures took place at Lathom and Skelmersdale during the period 1779-1781 and in June 1813 an Act was passed for the enclosing of lands in the township of Aughton and this subsequently closed the racecourse there in 1815. From the information contained in Blundell's Diary and Letter Book, the enclosing of land in the Crosby area was not done in a ruthless manner. The small farmers, landowners, cottagers and tenants and yeomen were represented by a village jury who authorised and supervised the enclosures and those who already occupied the land had access to 'ye waste'. In Burscough the enclosures most probably were undertaken at a similar time to the Lathom and Skelmersdale enclosures because most of the field patterns since the late 1780s remained very much the same in the 1840s with minor modifications here and there.

The 19th century

During the first half of the 19th century, new farming methods were slowly introduced but, according to the report of 1849, there was very little change in land utilisation. In that year the total land use for Burscough was as follows:

Acres
1,575 as arable land, (32%)
3,141 as meadow pasture land, (64%)
  20 as woodlands, (0.5%)
  25 as navigable canal, (0.5%)
 126 as roads and waste, (2.6%)

Nevertheless, the agrarian revolution, although it arrived later here than in most areas, appears to have gained impetus in the 1850s and 1860s in Burscough and the surrounding districts of south-west Lancashire. After the effective draining of the Mere in 1850, land prices became more stable, and with the second drainage loan of £2,000,000 (the first was in 1846, £2,000,000) and the Drainage and Improvement Acts provided Government supervision and, as I have already stated, stimulated the development of the tiling (for drainage) industry here. Each farmer, therefore, began to try to improve his own land, developing his own field drains which improved his pasture lands and thus enabled him to keep more cattle instead of just grain crops.

During the 18th century, many of the so- called farms were less than 15 acres and by today's standards would be classified as small-holdings. There were many more leaseholders who had less than 1 acre of land, but during the early 1800s small potato gardens were developed in Burscough, ranging from between five to ten roods. The reason for their growth would most probably be associated with the Napoleonic Wars (1793-1815), during which period, especially the years 1809 and 1810 when the English harvest was deficient, and the price of grain rose to 160/- per quarter in 1812. Ironically, famine was prevented by the import of wheat from France under licence. At the same time a substantial increase in food was sought at home and a large area of land was brought under cultivation. As a result of the continued increase in the acreage under cultivation during the Napoleonic Wars, there was a corresponding increase in the price of corn and the rise in prices resulted in a rise in rents.

With the reclamation of the Mere lands, great quantities of peat, locally called turf, was largely cut for fuel, and the surface was burnt, (in many leases burning was prohibited, no doubt because of the danger to thatched cottages and the like, which were more numerous at that time) which, accompanied by draining, produced rich, valuable soil. The main product of this new land by the 1860s was potatoes, which were exported by tons from Ormskirk (by railway) for the London, Manchester and Liverpool markets.

The railway enabled greater quantities of perishable goods to be transported from the country to the towns and milk appears to have been one item that was exported from the Burscough and Lathom area to Liverpool in fairly large quantities. Even before the introduction of the railway, several farmers in the

A photograph showing the threshing machine in Martland's Yard, Mart Lane, in about 1897. Notice the railway wagon at the extreme left of the picture. Note also that, despite the machinery, some 15 men can be seen at work here.

Burscough and Lathom area journeyed to Liverpool on horseback with sweet and butter milk which was sold at the old St. James's market and elsewhere. Some farmers went two or three times a week and some daily as Mr. Blundell who in 1804 carried 16 gallons of milk from Burscough to Liverpool at 6d. per day. Therefore, during the 19th century in Burscough, dairy farming began to develop and with the advent of the railway their markets were widened till eventually some farms became predominantly concerned with the production of milk. Butter and cheese were other products which were made at most farms in Burscough, during the 19th century and before, and it was the custom for the farmers' wives to attend the Ormskirk market and sell the butter, cheese and eggs.

Many cottagers apart from farmers had either a cow or several pigs and a few hens. These were often bought from drovers who came from Liverpool bringing their animals along the road. Geese were also brought in this way and it was usual for the cottager to barter with the drover for either a cow or a pig, whichever was required. Cottagers could also buy pigs and cattle at the Ormskirk market. The variety of food eaten increased in the Ormskirk and Burscough areas and this was reflected in the variety of foods obtained both in the market and in the shops, which continued to increase throughout the 19th century. By the 1870s depending on the time of year, the variety of food was quite wide, there being no fewer than 50 different items available at the Ormskirk market which included the following: beef, mutton, veal, lamb, pheasants, hares, cucumbers, peas, damsons, strawberries, rhubarb, duck eggs and hen eggs.

In 1850 the staple diet of the farm labourer in Burscough was jannock (made of oat-meal in the form of a loaf), but by the 1880s had largely been replaced by wheaten bread, and barley bread, eggs, 'resty' bacon (bacon which had been salted and hung in thick slices), potatoes, porridge and various fruit pies, meat and white bread were still usually reserved for Sundays and a dish of buttermilk with various other ingredients together with treacle was also eaten and it was not uncommon to serve a dish of tea and bread. There is very little information regarding fruit but, since the 18th century, apples and pears have been grown here and were usually stored in barrels which contained very dry sand during the summer for use during the winter months. Tea was becoming more popular and by the 1830s there was a tea-dealer in Burscough called John Rigby.

The development of local agricultural societies

The period from 1850 to 1874 is usually referred to as the era of High Farming, when the application of science to farming was becoming more widespread and experimentation with new methods was beginning to show results.

The Royal Agricultural Society, which was founded in 1838, helped to promote scientific knowledge as applied to farming and in August 1854 public attention was drawn to the need for an agricultural society for the district of Ormskirk. On October 9th 1856 the Ormskirk and Southport Agricultural, Floral and Horticultural Society was formed.

Burscough Bridge Show

Although formed much later than the above, Burscough did establish a society in 1890 known as the Burscough Bridge Horticultural, Poultry, Pigeon &c., Society, the first meeting of which was held on 4th and 5th of September 1891 in St. John's C. of E. Schoolrooms. The formation of the Society was instigated by a number of gentlemen who considered that there was in the neighbourhood a sufficient number of breeders of poultry and growers of flowers and vegetables to make up a show equal to any in the district. The Society appears to have lasted for only a few years and only two more shows were held by this society on the same scale as that of 1891.

The interest taken in these local shows can be gauged from the numerous exhibits; for example at the Rufford Show (founded 1864) in the 1920s there were as many as 2,000 exhibits. The Rufford Show was very popular and was probably one of the reasons why the Burscough Show did not develop into a major event.

Ploughing matches

From the 1840s to the 1890s ploughing matches were very popular and these were mainly held on the land belonging to Mr. Edge of the Bull and Dog Inn. It was usually an annual event which took place either in January or February (depending on the frost) of each year and the contests were well supported by competitors and spectators alike. The Burscough ploughing matches were established about 1844. Competitions took place in other areas, notably at Bickerstaffe and, by the 1890s, other events such as the 'Neatest and Cleanest Turnout', and the 'Most Valuable Pair of Horses' were added. A small space of land was usually reserved for agricultural implement makers or their agents for exhibition purposes. Money prizes were given ranging from £1 to £7 and gold and silver medals were also awarded. The ploughing competition was arranged in four classes. It is of interest to note that classes 3 and 4 were confined to farmers, their sons and workmen; professionals were excluded. One of the judges for many years at Burscough was Mr. Henry Banks, and one of the great promoters in this area of Lancashire was Mr. S. T. Rosbotham of Bickerstaffe. Subscribers to the Burscough Ploughing Society held their annual dinner at the Bull and Dog Inn.

Potato digging contests

During the 1890s potato digging contests were established and these took place in September of each year on land belonging to James Martland Ltd.

The Burscough Bridge Cattle Show and Sports

This show was established in 1897 and took place on Mr. James Walker's recreation ground (where the piggery is now situated at the rear of Fletcher's farm). The show was so successful in 1897 that the following year the occasion was made a holiday in the Burscough Bridge district. A long stream of canal barges lined the Leeds and Liverpool canal and the streets were decorated with flying banners bearing the inscriptions, 'Long may the House of Lathom and Knowsley Flourish', 'Success to the Lathom and Burscough Show and Sports', and 'Prosperity to the trade of Burscough and Lathom'. The Lathom Brass

Band paraded through the streets on this occasion and the show was attended by a large crowd. The founder of the show was Mr. W. Reynolds, the horse superintendent of the Leeds and Liverpool Canal Company. Competitions were held between canal boat horses and field horses, the major prize being a silver Challenge Cup, valued then at 5 guineas, which was offered by the Canal Company and, if won three times it became the property of the individual concerned.

This show, similar to several others that had started in this area, did not last many years and as I have stated before the influence of the Rufford Show was very great and most probably was the reason why the Burscough shows only had a limited success.

Problems and improvements

Potato disease

From the 1850s to the 1890s potato diseases harrassed the farmer and on many occasions resulted in complete loss of his crop. In 1857, the potato disease was rampant in this district during the month of August; the same occurred on several other occasions, and in 1871 there was another serious outbreak of the disease. In Burscough during August 1878 the following was recorded:

'In this township the corn crops are all that could be expected. Potatoes, however, are not so; for disease is visible in many fields in different parts of the district. One farmer believes that in a very short time the tops will be completely gone.'

On one farm in the locality, 3 acres of land which had been sown with early potatoes about the year 1872, realised £120; and the mangolds that followed, which were planted out of a bed, paid the whole expenses. The same field in 1882 only realised £56-10s-1d., and this with a better crop, but not early enough to command the best prices. The three worst years were 1877/8/9 in which the losses on this one farm alone amounted to £1,200. In the 1880s it was considered that the gross produce per acre should realise £15 in order to allow a fair profit. It was also customary at this time to grow swedes in between the potatoes in order to realise as much from an acre as possible.

Manure

Various contracts were entered into with the Liverpool Corporation in the 1880s to take several boat-loads of their ashes and manure every working day of the year. The Corporation delivered the manure into the contractor's carts and paid him £2 a boat-load, and as he carried up to 40 tons or more per boat, he obtained on average one shilling per ton for all he took. Several manure wharves were established at Burscough, principally for the receiving of this manure. Wharves were built at New Lane, Crabtree, Gobbins Bridge (this bridge was removed over 80 years ago) just off Orrell Lane, the Canal Company's Yard, the Ring O' Bells and a private wharf which was owned by the tenant of Martin Hall, at New Lane.

The manure chiefly came from ash pits and therefore contained a quantity of stones and other debris. If wharves were not readily available, the contractor could hire the farm labourers to deliver the manure to adjacent fields for about one half the above allowance. The manure was applied at the rate of a load in a yard, 6 to 9 inches thick and, when mixed with the soil, was said to produce the most beneficial results. Sometimes if the cinder content was very great, the farmer would employ local labour to remove the cinders and other debris after the land had been manured.

Therefore, by the 1880s, the lands in Burscough had received a wide variety of manures which not only included natural manures such as animal dung and marl, but artificial manures such as lime, soot, ashes and rags. The land was also further improved by 'paring' and 'burning' commonly called breast-ploughing and burning, which was a practice that had been carried out in the 18th century and before in this area.

Use of machines

During the 19th century new methods were still being introduced and the use of the steam engine was becoming more widespread. In August 1870, the introduction of steam cultivation into this district was advocated on the grounds that some lands in this neighbourhood were very hard to work and steam power would enable farmers to work their land in all weathers and would therefore be a great advantage. In the 1860s, information about farming methods and their application was becoming more widely known and literature on the subject was being made accessible to the small farmer. Agricultural implement depots were established in this area of Lancashire in the 1860s.

In connection with this development, blacksmiths played an important part from 1870 to the early part of the 20th century. One example was Thomas Myers of Burscough Bridge, who was a blacksmith, machinist and agricultural implement maker. During the 1880s and 1890s (and on into the 20th century) several of the larger farmers and merchants such as James Martland Ltd., Burscough, and Dickinsons Ltd., of Ormskirk, owned threshing machines which they supplied to farmers together with men to work these machines throughout the year. A threshing machine was too expensive an item for the average farmer to own, and as it was only used for a short period during the year it would also have proved uneconomical for the work it would have to do.

Farming in this area towards the latter part of the 19th century

Land during the latter half of the 19th century was very highly farmed in this district and the main reason for this was that the expenses were so great that good crops were a necessity if the farmer was to exist. The average size of farms in the Burscough district altered slightly, there being several amalgamations of land, but nothing more. The tenants were at liberty both as to the growth of crops and sale of produce. The potato crops principally consisted of second-early and keeping sorts. During this period, there were many evidences to suggest that the farmer's capital had been very seriously reduced.

To give an indication of the situation, the following example of a farm in this district during the 19th century may help the reader to understand the problem a little better. The farm in question was 175 acres in size and the farmer in 1882 paid for rent, tithes and rates £631 (= 72 shillings per acre). From 1868 to 1882 the rates increased from £50 to £70 per year. Correspondingly, labour which was formerly 10 shillings to 12 shillings had risen to 15 shillings for Irishmen and £1 a week during the harvest by 1880. Nearly all the work on this farm was done during the day, except pulling turnips and lifting potatoes.

On this particular farm no livestock was bred, except for his own use and he had a good market for his produce and kept the land in good trim with large supplies of manure. One of the main complaints during the 19th century in this area was that the suburban farmer was severely affected by competition, not only from abroad, but from farmers who were farther from the market. Most farmers in this district lost large sums of money during the 1870s and the local view as to the cause of the depression was attributed to bad seasons and low prices owing to American competition. Many farmers doubted that farming would ever again be as good as formerly, because deficiency at home did not, as formerly, result in high prices. Early potatoes that were grown on this farm were formerly more certain and remunerative than in the 1880s. His rotation of crops comprised: potatoes, wheat, barley, seeds, seed mown. He top dressed the seeds and also grew very heavy crops of hay.

This one farm reflects to a certain degree what the situation was on most farms in this area and indeed throughout the greater part of Lancashire at that time. However, during the 1890s and early part of the 20th century, there was a drive towards mixed farming, but specialisation in the growing of potatoes as a monoculture in this area has continued on into recent times.

Potato merchants

As we have seen, the population of Liverpool grew very rapidly between 1821 and 1856 and, as a result, the demand for food, especially potatoes, vegetables and milk went up accordingly. This demand for food had to be met to a large degree by the farms in south-west Lancashire and several farmers in this district saw the opportunity of promoting various crops, especially potatoes, not only in Lancashire, but elsewhere. One of these men was Mr. James Martland of Burscough.

James Martland Ltd.

Mr. Martland was a native of Burscough and was the son of Mr. William Martland, a farmer of Moss Lane, Burscough. However, James Martland had other ideas about what he was going to do and by the time he had reached his 20th year, he had decided that there were quicker roads to fortune than through farming alone. In 1861, he struck out for himself, becoming what was then generally known as a 'badger' or produce dealer, himself taking a load to Bolton, Liverpool and other markets. He continued doing this work for a number of years, but all the time he was on the look out for betterment. At length with a little capital he was enabled to launch out in the direction he had long desired.

Either by purchase or tenantry, Mr. Martland acquired several farms in the Burscough district until he had over 600 acreas under cultivation, and he was as thorough in this as in his general dealings. His motto was: 'You must put something in the land if you want to get something out'; he spared neither expense nor labour, with the result that his crops were seldom failures and frequently were above the average in the worst seasons.

He saw great possibilities in the potato trade and he developed it. He opened markets before unheard of and he revolutionised much of the farming industry in this district, the potato taking the place of corn. Without doubt Mr. Martland's business in this vegetable alone was so extensive during the 19th century that he could have claimed to be the 'Potato King of the World'. In Jersey he was the leading man both as a grower and a buyer. He was also the founder and chairman of the Potato Merchants' Steamship Company whose boats ran from Jersey to Holyhead, Fleetwood, Preston etc., ports to which in the season there were as many as 13 sailings a week.

Mr. Martland had offices in Jersey as well as in St. Malo, France, Gunness, Lincolnshire, Dundee and at Great Nelson Street, Liverpool, the latter dealing largely with the fruit trade. However, his sphere of influence grew until his operations were world wide. He dealt extensively in Belgium, Germany and other parts of the continent, and shipped to America and several of our colonies, while he was represented in every important agricultural district in the kingdom.

Mr. Martland was equally successful in the manufacture of oatmeal. He commenced in a small way at the old watermill near the Priory and, eventually, as business grew he found himself cramped for room and during 1885-87 built a mill in Mart Lane near his offices and warehouses, fitted it with what was then the most up-to-date machinery and had made such progress by this time that he was regarded as one of the leading producers of oatmeal in England.

It is of interest to note that Mr. James Martland also carried out experiments for himself from time to time and this particular aspect of the man is not widely known. In the early 1890s he purchased a piece of land known as 'The Bents' in Lathom (a low-lying district off Moss Lane) with a view to carrying out experiments upon it. At that time the land in question was almost completely covered with rushes and other weeds to be found on marshy land. It did not grow any profitable crop and Mr. Martland had an idea that, if he could get rid of all the water, he could turn the land to good use. Accordingly, he put down a centrifugal pump, worked by a portable engine, and pumped the excess water into the canal. To do this he had to dig sluices to get the necessary fall so as to bring the water down to the pump, but he was successful.

The firm of James Martland Ltd. was established in 1875 down Moss Lane, but in 1887 moved to the new premises in Mart Lane. By 1880 the firm was growing at a rapid rate, sales in that year being more than ten times that of 1875. The variety of goods began to expand and in the 1890s the firm even began to supply coal to this district. On the death of Mr. James Martland the firm passed to his son, Mr. Walter Martland, who inherited some of his father's aptitude in business and, under his management, the firm continued to expand and employment was found for many people in Burscough and the surrounding districts. He continued the work of the improvement of draining and maintenance of streams in this area, and he was a member of the Crossens Catchment Board. He was a pioneer like his father and in this respect he did much to promote the Jersey potato trade in this district.

Since the death of Mr. Walter Martland, the firm has passed to his sons. Times change, new innovations are tried to meet the public's demands and requirements (e.g. crisps were made by Martland's Ltd. in the 1950s and their distribution was far and wide), but basically the firm remains geared to the progress of agriculture in this and other areas of the world.

During the 19th century, several other small potato merchants arose in this area, but did not last very long. A Mr. Robert Pilkington established himself as a potato merchant at Burscough Junction in 1880, but by 1898 had discontinued in this line of business; he was also the victualler at the Burscough Junction Inn.

Market gardening and nurseries began to develop in the 1870s, but it was not until the 20th century that they became firmly established in this area. The forerunners in this district were Mr. Thomas Williams who was a nurseryman in 1870 and Thomas Lowe who was a market gardener at that time.

The 20th century

During the first half of this century, several merchants developed who are directly or indirectly connected with agriculture. James Martland Ltd., as we have seen, grew rapidly during this period and other potato merchants and the like have followed in their footsteps. One of the first potato merchants and produce dealers to develop in the 20th century was Mr. John Martland (known locally as 'Cabbage Jack'), farm produce merchant at Burscough Junction. Before road transport had developed to any degree, Mr. John Martland acted as the middleman who purchased farm produce from the farmers who brought their vegetables, especially potatoes and cabbages to him at Burscough Junction station.

As road transport began to gain momentum in the 1920s, potato merchants began to collect and deliver the farm produce direct from the farmer to the buyer or market and thus gradually cut out shipment of goods by the railway. One of the first produce merchants of any note to develop along these lines was Mr. Alfred Price of Moss Lane, Burscough, who started on his own account as a farm produce merchant at Burscough Bridge in 1919. This firm soon developed until today it is one of the most extensive of its kind in Lancashire. In 1938 he took some of his sons into partnership and the firm was formed into a limited company. The firm has business interests in Cheshire, Yorkshire and Lincolnshire and elsewhere.

To mention all the individual merchants would take too long, but briefly in order of development they are as follows. Mr. Harry Hague, who originated from Tarleton and who came from a family of blacksmiths, began in business in a small way down Moss Lane about 1927. He was principally connected with the potato trade and, as the business grew, he moved to larger premises down Briars Lane about 1930 and recently the firm has been sold and is now under new management. Thomas Guy commenced business in a small way in haulage and was established in 1944 at Burscough Town. The firm expanded and in 1965 developed the drome storage on the disused airfield, and they now also occupy part of the premises of the former 'Old Abbey Brick Works'. In recent times other hauliers such as Mr. R. Barker have developed, and are now doing the work of what would in times past have been undertaken to a large degree by the canal and railways.

In recent times various other firms have evolved alongside agriculture which are either supplementary or complementary to its advancement, and in this connection the development of fertilisers have proved of immense value. Vitax Ltd., fertiliser manufacturers, have established themselves in Burscough during recent times and in the course of their development have acquired several properties to enable them to carry on their work. At the present moment their offices are situated in what was formerly Peet's Mill erected in 1863 and subsequently purchased by Messrs. James Martland Ltd. in 1905, who occupied the premises for some time. Subsequently they obtained the premises which had formerly been Thorougoods's Brewery and in 1961 purchased 22,000 square feet of land, which included two Nissen huts which were erected during the Second World War at the rear of the Burscough Bridge Garage, Liverpool Road North. These Nissen huts are used for the storage of fertilisers, one for raw materials and the other for the finished product. Many improvements have taken place over the years, and in 1961 one of the most important advances was the installation of a new and modern laboratory which has enabled the firm to experiment and produce the best quality fertilisers which are so necessary in agriculture today.

Mahood Bros.

Mr. Thomas Sutcliffe started a nursery down Red Cat Lane, Burscough, about 1905 and like many men who commenced in this work, had another job as well; Mr. Sutcliffe was a pork butcher in Mart Lane. In 1910 Mahood brothers, Ronald and Wilfred Mahood obtained this nursery and extended it in 1928 to 15 acres, this being part of what was called the 'old farm'. In 1930 Wilfred Mahood left and commenced in business at Ormskirk, subsequently opening a sports shop there in Beaconsfield buildings (opposite the statue of Benjamin Disraeli) which is today managed by his son. Mr. Stanley Cross, who is connected with the firm at Burscough, joined Mahood brothers in 1920. Today Mahood Brothers are wholesale suppliers of trees, shrubs and hedging plants to county councils, local authorities and government departments.

Adjacent to this area is Moss Nook, in which another nursery was developed by Mr. Ashcroft and this has now been taken over by Messrs. Spencers. In the past there were several smallholdings here and onions were widely grown, and onion drying sheds were a common sight. During the 19th century Rufford became noted for its onions and in the lands bordering Rufford they were also grown in large quantities.

Developments

An old chronicler in Burscough during the 19th century said the following in comparing the state of agriculture in 1830 with that of 1890:

> 'The state of agriculture, with an exception here and there, indicated little or no improvement upon what it had been for generations before. But what a change has taken place! What a contrast is furnished between Burscough past and Burscough present! Our fields shapely and well formed; our hedges neat and trim looking; whilst agriculture has made such rapid strides in advance that our ploughmen are bold enough to compete with all England, and not only compete, sir, but carry off the palm of victory and bring it home in triumph to their own township.'

If the old chronicler had lived on into the 20th century, his exclamations would have been even greater in connection with improved techniques and increased mechanisation. Probably one of the most significant changes that have been brought about in the 20th century in this area and elsewhere is that the output is being achieved with a declining labour force. At the beginning of the 19th century, the number of families engaged in agriculture in Burscough ranged from 170 to 240 out of a total number of from 280 to 340 families which represented between 60 to 75 per cent of the total families in this area. This meant that there were approximately between 140 and 180 persons per 1,000 acres engaged in agriculture at varying times in the Burscough area throughout the 19th century. Towards the end of the 19th century, this number was probably reduced to between 100 and 120. By 1930 the number of agricultural workers in Lathom and Burscough amounted to 900, which represented approximately 70 persons per 1,000 acres engaged in agriculture which indicates how quickly mechanisation had developed in the 20th century and, by 1965 this figure had been reduced to about 35 persons per 1,000 acres engaged in agriculture, which in comparison to some areas still reflects an intensively developed agricultural industry.

In south-west Lancashire, arable farming is by far the most prominent and widespread type of agriculture practised and this is related to the rich alluvial soils and the climate. The annual rainfall for the area of south-west Lancashire is about 30-33 inches and the temperatures vary from a mid-winter mean of 39°-41°F, to a mid-summer mean of 60°-62°F. These figures vary according to aspect, distance from the sea, height above sea level and proximity to hills and the like. Some records do exist in the 18th century concerning climate per year. From the 1870s to the 1880s the mean annual rainfall in this area was about 37 inches and during the period 1915-1950 the mean has been about 35 ins. per annum. My own rainfall records for the Burscough area during the past ten years show a mean of about 38-40 ins. per year. However, averages tend to be deceptive and maximum and minimum figures, together with the incidence of frosts and when they are most likely to occur are necessary if a true picture of the climate of this area is to be given.

The early development of industry in the Burscough area

Milling

Because flour was a staple commodity needed by everyone in every village, one of the oldest industries to develop in this area was milling. Windmills were usually placed on the highest ground and the watermills were situated on fairly low ground. The seven mills alluded to in the *Cartulary* of Burscough Priory were the following:

> Bickerstaffe Windmill, Burscough Watermill (Mill Dam), Burscough Windmill (the site nearly opposite the Bull and Dog Inn), Cross Hall Windmill, Quassum Windmill (site occupied by a disused windmill near Slinger's Farm) and the Scarisbrick Watermill.

The mill in these early days and even until the middle of the 19th century in this area was all important to the economy of the countryside. Before the introduction of steam mills in the 19th century, windmills were governed by the weather and quite often when the mill was not working it was not uncommon for it to be used by the villagers for dancing or a village meeting. The essential machinery for both watermills or windmills was the millstones or burr stones which had to be of good quality and of the right hardness. The Peak District of Derbyshire was noted for its fine millstones, but whether these early mills in Burscough obtained their millstones from that area or locally I cannot say. Millstone is found in the Parbold area and was quarried there over 150 years ago. These mills were usually family concerns and they would no doubt employ extra people after the harvest when the work was heavy and the autumn winds would provide the necessary power required to do the grinding of the corn. A millwright had an important position which again appears to have run in families who also worked in teams. During very windy weather the sails would often be broken and these were usually repaired by the village tailor, who would use local material.

The Burscough Mill (Mill Dam)

The original mills have long since disappeared, but on the site of the Burscough watermill subsequent mills have been built and the one in existence today was rebuilt in 1856 by Mr. Robert Fletcher. Today the mill race together with the dam has been filled in and the building now houses poultry and agricultural equipment. It is built of brick with a slate roof and rises to a height of about 30 feet. This old watermill is now disused, but remained in working order until the 1890s and was supplying grain (mainly crushed oats) up to the early 1920s, the last time that the wheels were set in motion being during the flood of 1927. The original old watermill on this site had been run by the monks, who also fished trout in the Ellerbrook and, on the authority of several local inhabitants, trout were still to be found in this stream at the early part of this century. After the dissolution of the monastery and its destruction by the year 1572, the mill was most probably taken over by John Rutter, known in the time of Henry Earl of Derby (4th Earl of Derby, died in 1593) as the 'Burscough Miller', and on Thursday, October 19th 1589, the following was recorded:

'John Rutter mylner (miller) at Burscough mylnes (mills) had meate from New Park by my Lo. (Lord's) commandment.'

According to Peter Draper in his book *The House of Stanley* (pub. 1864), this John Rutter was the grandfather of Samuel Rutter who was chaplain and confidential friend of the Earl of Derby and he was also tutor to Lord Strange, the eighth Earl and biographer of the family. Samuel Rutter was chaplain of Lathom Chapel during the siege in 1644 and subsequently he was appointed prebendary of Lichfield in 1660, archdeacon and afterwards Bishop of Sodor and Man. He died on the Isle of Man in 1663.

The Fletcher family appear to have been millers at the Burscough Mill since the latter part of the 17th century and from all accounts had been connected with milling since the 16th century. According to the *Victoria County History* Vol. III a Robert Fletcher in 1591 'had erected a horse-mill of his own and withdrew his custom, the reason he gave for this action was that the existing mills were inadequate for the needs of the people and that some of them were even using hand mills, while others took their corn to watermills up to 8 miles off.

In the 1780s Widow Fletcher occupied the watermill at Burscough and also possessed the windmill and croft nearly opposite the Bull and Dog Inn, the field being known as Mill Hey. From the 1740s, and for a long time before, the Fletchers' had held both the watermill and windmill. The windmill was taken down between 1830 and 1845 and it is stated locally that the late Mr. James Lyon (wheelwright) at Burscough Town had in his possession a small portion of the sails. This windmill would probably have been constructed mainly of wood with a brick or stone foundation but, as details are not available and the site has since been disturbed, a true picture cannot be formed.

The remains of Burscough Corn Mill (Mill Dam) and, below, the remains of the dam itself.

Briars Mill, now disused, photographed in 1969.

An early photograph of Whimbrick Mill or Aughton Moss Mill taken about 1905.

As I have already stated, Mr. Robert Fletcher rebuilt the watermill in 1856 and he also re-equipped the mill with new machinery throughout. At that time it was a thriving little industry and he catered for farmers and flour dealers of the several townships of Burscough, Lathom and Scarisbrick. The mill was reopened on February 5th 1857. Robert Fletcher was also a farmer and tilled part of the lands formerly belonging to the Priory. The Legh family during the 17th and for part of the 18th century had occupied the land formerly belonging to the Priory before the Fletchers' held it, and subsequently the land passed to the Rothwell family in the 20th century. In 1880, Robert Fletcher was joined by his brother James and about the year 1890 the mill went over to steam in an attempt to compete with the newer and larger steam mills of Ainscough's and Peet's. Subsequently, the mill was taken over by Mr. James Martland who manufactured oatmeal here, but by the late 1920s had fallen into disuse. Today the mill is used partly for storage and partly for housing various machines which belong to Mr. and Mrs. Charnley, the present occupiers of the mill and farm.

Quassum or Whassum Mill

In ancient times when Martin Mere was undrained, several islands existed in the Mere, one of them being called Whassum, which was formerly accredited as the centre of the Mere. Walter Whassum in the year 1300 gave this island to Gilbert Scarisbrick, who built a mill there in 1312. The site of this mill was near to the present Windmill Farm (now occupied by Mr. M. Slinger) and is today occupied by a disused windmill. The original windmill would most probably have been made of timber obtained from the Tarlscough Wood which contained oak saplings, as mention is made of this wood in the survey which was made in 1536. However, the present disused mill, which consists of one large tower, is said by some never to have been completed. It is reputed to have been built in competition with the 'Factory Mills', by two brothers about the end of the 19th century, one of whom was killed during the building of the tower. Whether this account is true or not, I have not as yet been able to confirm, but I do know that a mill was working on this site in the 18th century and continued to do so up to about the 1870s. In the 1840s the mill was occupied by a Mr. Henry Ashcroft, and at that time there was also a mill-house, outbuilding and yard adjacent to the windmill.

In addition, there were three smaller mills: Briars Watermill, Lathom Windmill and the Ring O' Bells Mill. All these mills were built at a later date than those which I have already discussed; two of these have now gone and only the Briars Watermill now remains. The development of these mills indicate an increase in the amount of land under cultivation during the 19th century in this area and was no doubt precipitated by the draining of Martin Mere. Both the Lathom Windmill and the Ring O' Bells Mill were built of brick, but the Briars Mill is mainly constructed of stone with sections of brickwork here and there which appears to have been repairs or possibly extensions.

Briars Mill

The Briars Watermill (corn) is again situated on the Ellerbrook, just over a mile further down stream from the Burscough Mill, and is constructed of trimmed and untrimmed stone and rises to a height of about 35 to 40 feet.

However, unlike the Burscough Mill, it did not possess the mill dam which had a diameter of approximately 300 feet (now filled in, but part of the Dam Wall still remains); very often in the winter the dam was frozen over (one of the hazards which stopped the mill from working) and skating was enjoyed by the villagers on numerous occasions. In close proximity to the Abbey railway crossing was an area known as the Damstead and at this point the Bath Brook occasionally used to flood in times past (before the railway was constructed in 1849), and no doubt skating was indulged in here as well in the winter months. Briars Mill still possesses its mill race for driving the mill wheel and up stream there used to be some flood gates, but these have now gone. The mill was probably built about the middle of the 18th century and was in operation two hundred years ago. At the beginning of the 19th century, John Hewitt occupied the mill and about 1852 he was followed by Abraham Hewitt who only remained at the mill until the year 1869. Abraham Hewitt then became the victualler of the Ring O' Bells Inn, a position formerly held by James Hewitt. In the 1870s the mill was taken over by John Fletcher (a relation of James Fletcher of Burscough Mill) who remained there until the mill closed in 1891. William Farrimond lived near the mill at Vine Cottage from 1870 until 1890 when it was sold for £485 to a Mr. Joseph Webster. This mill was never converted to steam and in 1891 it closed down and, although it has been used for other purposes since, it has remained in a disused state as a corn mill until the present time. Today the mill is used by Mr. Pepper, but originally it belonged to Briars Hall and in the 1840s was owned by Mr. Riddle. This mill has been used for the storage of grain and other produce since it was disused in 1891.

Lathom Mill (Causeway End)

This mill was pulled down in 1966 and all that remains is the base of the brick tower. The old millstone is situated at the rear of Hawthorn House and forms part of the path. It appears to have been built during the latter part of the 18th century, and in the 1840s was leased by Jane Martland from Lord Skelmersdale and was occupied by Richard Halliwell. The windmill was built of brick and during its working life does not appear to have been converted to steam. In July 1870 a fire broke out in one of the outbuildings and the windmill was also badly damaged, after which it does not appear to have been used. At the time of the fire the mill and farm were occupied by Mr. Thomas Lowe.

Ring O' Bells Mill

This mill was built about the year 1825 and was mainly a corn and provender mill. For many years the mill had belonged to the Coxhead family, the last of the line being Thomas Coxhead who was a grocer and corn dealer in 1890, but by 1898 he was just a grocer. Again, competition from the 'factory mills' appears to have been responsible for the gradual running down of these small concerns. In 1927 the mill was finally demolished, although it had remained closed and practically abandoned for trade purposes since about 1909.

Peet's Mill

Mr. William Peet was the founder of this mill which is situated close to Burscough Bridge railway station. Before the railway came to Burscough, the founder had a grocery and provisions dealing business which he carried on in a little stone house which stood on the side of the railway opposite to the present site. In 1855 newer premises were built specially for the business, and in 1863 the mill was built, and at that time contained all the latest appliances for grinding. The buildings included a bakery and shop which, apart from the mill, was run by William Peet who was also the first sub-postmaster for Burscough, a position which he held until 1880. In 1881, the bakery and shop was let to Mr. William Martland who also became the sub-postmaster. Dealings in corn and in provender for horses and cattle were the main feature of Mr. Peet's business. There were horses and stables suitable for the needs of the business.

Mr. Thomas Peet succeeded his father and continued in the business until about 1904, when he sold the business to Messrs Martland & Company. He was very interested in the welfare of Burscough and in 1892 was one of the first to start the agitation for the secession of Burscough from the Ormskirk Rural Sanitary Authority and, in 1894, the township of Burscough became amalgamated with Lathom to become the Lathom and Burscough Urban District Council. Mr. Peet had to fight very hard for the amalgamation, because he had a strong opponent in the late Archdeacon Fletcher, then the Rector of Tarleton and chairman of the Rural Sanitary Authority. He became one of the first representatives for Burscough on the joint Council and it was Thomas Peet who initiated the water scheme for Burscough and Lathom.

Shortly after the mill at Burscough had been taken over by Messrs. Martland, Mr. Peet moved to Milnthorpe in Westmorland. Today the mill is occupied by Vitax Ltd.

H. & R. Ainscough's Flour Mills

The founder of Ainscough's Flour Mills at Burscough was Hugh Ainscough. He was born on a 60 acre farm at Ulnes Walton in 1816, but about 1820 the family moved to Parbold where his father Richard Ainscough commenced in business as a grocer. In 1825 the old windmill (flour) adjoining the canal was occupied by Richard Charnock, but subsequently this was taken over about 1826 by Richard Ainscough who ran the mill in conjunction with his grocery business. This windmill is still in existence (shorn of its sails) and is now a private residence. Hugh Ainscough in his early life spent about 4 years in Spain, and was some time with Dr. Hawett of Wigan with a view to entering the medical profession. On the death of his father, however, he, in conjunction with his brother Richard Ainscough, began to build the mill at Parbold which was completed in 1851, and afterwards about 1858 he erected still larger mills at Burscough. Before this date there was no Mill Lane, but subsequently after the erection of the Mill the lane was established.

By 1872 the mills were described as 'extensive' by Worral and he also pointed out the fact that the mills were conveniently situated near the railway and canal, an important point in connection with both mills. It was owing to the transport facilities and nearness to the corn growing area that Mr. Ainscough decided upon the site at Burscough. He could also see the direct connection between Burscough and Liverpool being linked both by rail (they had their own private railway sidings at Burscough Junction) on the one hand and the canal with the Mersey on the other. This latter advantage meant that Ainscough's barges could be loaded directly with wheat brought by ship from America as she lay at her moorings, which thus facilitated the transporting of the wheat to the mills at

Burscough and Parbold, where it was transferred to the giant hoppers to await grinding.

By the late 1850s when the Burscough Mill had been built, Richard Ainscough, Hugh's brother, became a full time partner in the business and the name of the firm was then changed to 'H. & R. Ainscough, Millers, Burscough Bridge and Newburgh'.

Initially the number of men employed in the Burscough Mill in the 1850s and 1860s was about 30, by the 1870s the number had risen to 50 and by the 1880s over 70 people were engaged in work at the mill, until in 1900 over 100 persons were employed there. Today about 200 people are engaged in various aspects of the business.

Relationships between management and men in the 19th century at Ainscough's Mills appears to have been fairly good and it was the custom at the beginning of each year for Messrs. Ainscough to give a treat to their workmen; for example in 1859 at a local inn (usually the Red Lion and subsequently the Royal Hotel) it was recorded as follows:

> 'Messrs. Ainscough's gave a treat to their workmen, good English fare of roast beef and plum pudding. The proceedings were kept up until 12 o'clock.

In the 1880s wives and lady friends attended these treats and dancing was often kept up to a late hour. During the depression in the 1860s, Mr. Richard Ainscough in 1861, the year in which he had moved to Burscough to live, gave £5 for the relief of the poor of the town. Subsequently the Ainscoughs came to live at Brooklands and at a later date occupied Briars Hall.

In 1885 the mills were enlarged at Burscough and a new building was erected to accommodate the roller plant. This new mill formed part of the main building. At this particular period millers, especially in the north of England, were determined to resist the growing influx of American flour and this new roller mill at Burscough was fresh evidence in support of their cause.

At the same time that this new factory was built, electricity was installed throughout the mill. They generated their own electricity by means of a gas engine and subsequently supplied electricity to Mr. Ainscough's residence at Brooklands and Mr. James Rigby's residence in Junction Lane by means of overhead wires. Therefore, these two houses were the first to receive electricity in Burscough.

The new mill building was 5 storeys in height and was erected according to the plans of Messrs. Hind and Lund, who also supplied the whole of the machinery in the mill at that time. There was also a uniformity about the placing of the machines on the various floors; the elevators were on a line and the roller mills and dressing and purifying machines were also placed with a due regard for precision. The roller mills are, doubtless, too well-known to require description here.

In 1894, Messrs. H. & R. Ainscough submitted plans to the Lathom and Burscough Local Board in connection with a proposed extension of the mill on the canal bank area; because the walls were not of the required thickness according to the bye-laws, however, their approval was not given initially. By August 1894, the plans were passed and the extension was built. This was the last major building programme to be undertaken in the 19th century and by and large the mill has not grown appreciably in size or altered very much externally since that time.

Originally, Ainscough's Mill was a steam mill and the coal was brought until the 1960s by canal barge from Wigan to feed the large furnaces which in turn provided the power to drive the massive wheel in the engine room to which connections were made by ropes to ever decreasing wheels which were further connected to nearly every room throughout the mill. By means of adaptations, wheels and pulleys, therefore, this one wheel drove the mill machinery in every room connected with the processing of flour. Today the power is obtained from the main electricity supply.

In 1933 the whole mill was completely modernised and further improvements were made just before the Second World War to bring its capacity up to a 30 sack flour mill. Recently further modifications and improvements have taken place both in the storing and handling of the flour and with the improvements in the roads and the development of a fleet of road bulk-carriers since the decline of the canals and the railways, the amount of handling has been much reduced, and the despatching of flour has been made easier. Until recent times the firm had a fleet of diesel-engined barges.

The house adjacent to Messrs. H. & R. Ainscough's Mills, now converted into offices, was once occupied by the Ainscough family and subsequently by Mr. A. G. Verity in the 1920s. The original offices were in the small building facing the mill, but when trade was developing they were found to be too small and were subsequently converted into a canteen.

Trade expanded during the 1880s and Ainscough's flour was being distributed throughout the Burscough, Lathom, Newburgh and Ormskirk district and a wholesale depot was developed during this period in Burscough Street, Ormskirk, where the flour was sold at mill prices. In the late 1890s (instituted Sept. 16th, 1896) the development of the Corn Exchange in Moor Street, Ormskirk, reflected the growing importance of the trade and it is most probable that Messrs. H. & R. Ainscough were associated with this market, as it was a local rendezvous of farmers, traders and businessmen on market days.

As trade grew, the market became wider and by 1907 offices were opened in Liverpool for the wholesale grain trade and retail business. Today, contacts are also maintained with agents in Liverpool and abroad who are in touch with world markets and production belts.

Mr. Hugh Ainscough (the founder) also interested himself in agriculture and by 1850 had acquired 300 acres of farm land in Parbold and in 1878 he bought Fairhurst Hall, previously the house of the Nelson family. By 1955 the firm had acquired four farms: Fairhurst, Damswood, Giants and Priorswood Hall. The founder also spread his net wider for he was a director of the Palace Hotel Company and the Victoria Hotel Company, Southport, and from 1879-1883 he was a director of the firm of R. Johnson & Co. Ltd. In other companies he was also interested, but beyond this he had no connections with Southport.

When Mr. Hugh Ainscough died, the management of the business fell to his sons (Mr. Richard Ainscough died without issue) and has subsequently passed to his grandsons.

Throughout the history of the mill in its early days, there are no doubt some important events which have taken place but, by and large, from my researches covering the period of its development, they have not been very significant. Numerous incidents such as small fires have been recorded from time to time, the first incident being in 1866 when the Ormskirk Fire Brigade was sent for about 2 a.m. The fire brigade only arrived at 3.55 a.m. drawn not by horses, but by a number of men, and the fire engine from Southport arrived at 4.35 a.m. It was stated in a publication called the 'Gingerbread', published by Thomas Hutton, proprietors of the Ormskirk Advertiser, that the fire engines at Liverpool, Ormskirk and Southport were telephoned for, but in fact the telephone as such was not introduced until 1876 and the telegraph was only established from Ormskirk to Burscough in 1873. However, it is most probable that the railway telegraph was used at the time of the incident. Unfortunately, the Newburgh Mill at Parbold has not been so lucky, for in recent times a disastrous fire occurred which resulted in a large section of the mill being destroyed in 1953. During the rebuilding of the mill, the whole of the cattle, pig and poultry feed production had to be accommodated at Burscough Mill, which produced congestion in every department. Nevertheless, when the mill at Parbold was rebuilt, the congestion was relieved at the Burscough Mill and the Newburgh Mill was at this time made fireproof.

Times change and of the once numerous small mills that surrounded this parish in the past, now only Ainscough's Mill remains in working order. The days of the picturesque windmill and quaint, squat little watermills are now over and their work done, but they are not forgotten and I hope they never will disappear from this area altogether.

Subsequent development of other industries during and since the 18th century

Cabinet works

In the latter part of the 17th century, as I have stated before, the draining of Martin Mere began and in due course a large proportion of the Mere and the surrounding area was transformed, firstly being used as pasture land and eventually giving way to the plough. During the draining of the area and subsequent cultivation of the land, great quantities of oak and yew trees were found (and still are found to this day) embedded in the soil at depths varying from one to six feet. These trees, some of huge dimensions (some were over 40 feet), were a hazard to ploughing and periodically the farmers devoted themselves to uprooting the 'stocks', as they are called. Prior to the draining in the 17th century and afterwards, and throughout the 18th century, numbers of poor people obtained a subsistence by digging out the oak trees from the soil, which they split up into firewood, unless the wood was sound and good, and then it was employed in the construction of agricultural implements, the roofing of barns, and in some cases was even employed in making ornamental furniture. In the 18th century a cabinet works was situated at Burscough Town which gave employment to a fairly large number of workpeople in its day, but even ninety years ago the works had long been closed and its exact location and owner had long been forgotten.

Ainscough's Mill near the canal, above in 1902, and, below, in 1955.

Ainscough's Mill at Newburgh in 1955.

The Ormskirk Corn Exchange in about 1905.

An old woodyard existed at Burscough Town in the 18th century and was situated between the road that leads up to the house called 'The Poplars' and Platts Lane. The premises were then occupied by a Mr. William Prescott. It is possible that the old cabinet works existed there or was connected with it in some way.

In the 18th century two cabinet workers did exist in this area, John Davis and John Fletcher, the latter being an old and well-established family in the neighbourhood, together with numerous joiners, wheelwrights and the like, too numerous to mention, all of whom could have been associated with the cabinet works in Burscough Town. During the 18th century it was not uncommon for trees to be felled for the use of the tenants of the Burscough Manor as the following record confirms:

'1775 — Thomas Barton for the Bark of Oaks fallen for the use of the Tenants in this Manor. £3-12s.-0d.'

Old wooden chests, furniture and several wall presses were made from the hard bog oak and an example of some of this work could be seen at the 'Hermitage' in Rufford. It is interesting to note that in 1692, when Mr. T. Fleetwood of Bank Hall began to drain the marsh, he employed up to 2,000 men at various times.

This old cabinet works at Burscough Town would most probably have obtained a large supply of its timber from the drained area of the Mere, but the supply would be limited and, therefore, as demand rose during the latter part of the 18th century, the firm declined (many workers would probably be attracted to the work on the canals which were developing at that time) and eventually closed. The roads, as I have stated before, were in a deplorable state during this period and, although the skilled labour would be in the Burscough area, there was no means of transporting the timber from outside the area in bulk until the development of the Leeds and Liverpool Canal in the 1770s. However, from the number of joiners (including cabinet makers and the like) who subsequently became boat-builders in this area during the latter part of the 18th century and the early part of the 19th century, it is probable that they were some of the redundant workers from the old cabinet works at Burscough Town.

Silk weaving and linen

Apart from agriculture in this area of Lancashire, industries as such were very small and were carried on in the homes of the people during the 18th century and early part of the 19th century. The cotton industry, which is always associated with Lancashire, did not get a firm foothold here, but silk weaving was a thriving industry in Ormskirk in the 18th century. Owing mainly to foreign competition, however, the industry declined in the 1870s and is now extinct. The silk came in its raw state to the Ormskirk factory (pulled down at the end of the 19th century) from the manufacturers in Macclesfield. A good number of hands, chiefly young women and girls, were found employment before the silk passed into the hands of the weavers. The weaving was chiefly done in the houses of the people and everybody from the young children to grandmothers appears to have been busy in the work. The lower or ground-floor rooms of the factory were let off at 'fair' times to small manufacturers of woollen cloths and other material who came from the manufacturing parts of the county, and who did good business in these fabrics amongst the surrounding country people of Burscough and Lathom.

Silk weaving was carried on in several homes of Burscough people in the 18th century, notably at Burscough Town in two cottages which used to be situated at the rear of Mr. T. Leyland's (confectioner) house (just over 100 yards away) and were connected to the main Liverpool-Preston thoroughfare by means of an occupation road or outlet. In the 1840s these cottages were the property of a Mr. Richard Parr of Aughton. It is also interesting to note that middle-class people of this district also engaged themselves in the silk industry and in Ormskirk it was not uncommon to hear the rattle of the shuttle as it sped its way along the 'looms' used in their houses.

In November 1857 trade was not very good in Ormskirk and district and large numbers of men were unemployed, especially amongst the silk weavers and the twine spinners. At the time, a public meeting was held and a relief committee was established. Again, in 1862, there was great distress amongst the silk weavers and ropers of Ormskirk, no doubt as a result of the 'Cotton Famine' of 1861-63. In 1863, the situation does not appear to have altered because about 400 one shilling tickets were distributed amongst the distressed weavers and ropers in Ormskirk (trade being greatly depressed at the time); and there was also a distribution of good soup to all poor persons who applied for it.

The following which I quote from the book *Lancashire Textile Industry in the 16th Century,* published by the Chetham Society, is also of interest:

'There seems to have been a regular connection between linen drapers of the Ormskirk area and the town of Denbigh. Two of the men who supplied linen to Denbigh were Thomas Smolte who in 1576 was owed £7-6s.-0d. by a Denbigh man for linen cloth, and John Withington of Burscough, whose will of 1594 mentions three Denbigh men who owed him a total of £11-6s.-0d. for linens.'

Basket makers or osiers

Another small domestic industry which is associated with Burscough was basket making. This small industry was the forerunner of the textile industries and no doubt the art of basket making has been known for centuries in the Burscough area. However, it was not until the 18th and 19th centuries that they began to increase in numbers until in 1870 there were about 10 families carrying on this work in the Burscough area. Schoolboys were often employed by the osiers to pick the willows and the largest osier bed was adjacent to Martin Hall. Other osier beds existed in Moss Lane and together with the Martin Hall osier bed constituted the main areas in which the trade was developed and carried out. The art of basket making was handed down from father to son and therefore the trade and skill usually tended to run in families such as the Arnolds, Aughtons, Benthams, Deans, Duttons, Hunters, Roughleys and Skillands in the 19th century. Nevertheless, a term of apprenticeship had to be served which usually ran from 5½ to 7 years and an indenture had to be drawn up between the master and the apprentice. The indentures that were drawn up at this time contained the ordinary prohibitions against playing cards and dice, frequenting ale houses, and still more dangerous conduct which should be avoided, and the indenture did not leave anything to chance. In 1876 an indenture was drawn up between William Arnold, basket maker of Burscough Bridge, and Thomas Baybutt, apprentice. The term of apprenticeship was 5½ years and during this time Thomas Baybutt was to receive four shillings a week in the first year and an advancement of 1/– per year in the 5½ years and his wage was to end with ten shillings for the half year following the purchasing of his tools. The indenture was signed by his father, Mr. Fairhurst Baybutt, William Arnold the basket maker and witnessed by Richard Rigby.

During the 1870s and 1880s the basket makers of Burscough were at their peak and it appears that they were not growing sufficient willows to meet the demand, because in the 1870s David W. Dean, basket maker of Burscough, obtained his willows from a Mr. Hugh Sharrock of Wrightington. The willows were sold and delivered by Sharrock at £4 a ton. Mr. Dean would probably be regarded as a master basket maker in his day because he had several basket makers working for him, his foreman was Henry Bentham and one of his workmen was named Mark Bickerstaffe. The basket makers continued on into the 20th century but, with the introduction of new materials such as plastic and factory production, their numbers declined and this industry has now gone.

Peat cutting

During the 19th century in south-west Lancashire, peat was cut in very large quantities for fuel, especially between the mosses of Liverpool and Burscough and in all the mosses lying east of Southport. In 1872 the use of peat as a fuel was given a fresh impetus because in that year there was industrial unrest, especially amongst the coal miners, and at Skelmersdale and Rainford in 1872 the miners demanded an increase of 10% in wages. The price of local coal rose to 20/– a ton (in the 1890s the very best coal was only 12/6d. per ton), and thus alternative means of fuel were sought by the householders in this area of Lancashire and elsewhere. During this period of the 'Coal Famine' peat began to be used from the Lancashire mosses but, by and large, the greater quantities came from Ireland. It seems ironic that in that year the Irish Peat Commission visited various peat manufacturers of Europe, including England, explaining the best methods of drying peat and the various types of compressed peat that were being produced. The coal miners' dispute was eventually settled, but even in the late 1870s and early 1880s peat was still being cut in very large quantities in south-west Lancashire, the price being about 10/– per ton, but by the late 1880s coal prices became competitive and the use of peat as a fuel in this area declined, and has since almost disappeared.

In the 'Geological Memoir of England and Wales' of 1877, C. E. Rance F.G.S., wrote the following:

'Peat — very large quantities of peat are cut for fuel in Halsall and other mosses between Liverpool and Burscough, and in all the mosses lying east of Southport, in Rufford, Croston and Farrington mosses, and north of the Ribble, in Lytham, Rawcliffe and Pilling mosses. The usual selling price in Preston is 10/– a load which would probably weigh about a ton.'

Mr. Rance went on to describe the method of cutting, stacking and drying the peat, in which, when the peat was partly dry, the pieces which had been cut in squares of a foot were placed one upon the other in a circular manner with spaces every so far, until an elongated dome-like structure was produced, to enable the air to circulate.

The Burscough turf stack

In the old court books of Burscough for 1800 appears the signature of James Scarisbrick of Burscough, whose father Thomas Scarisbrick was killed by lightning while building a turf stack in March 1779. The son completed the stack as a memorial to his father and had it maintained for nearly 50 years as an act of filial affection perpetuated for all time by Wordsworth in a sonnet. The memorial stood between two trees on the land now occupied by Mr. Pilkington of Sycamore Farm, High Lane, Burscough. This unique monument was represented on goblets and a decanter which were left to the grandchildren of Thomas Scarisbrick, and on one of the goblets the monogram of James Scarisbrick appeared. Both Thomas and his son James were buried at Ormskirk parish church, on 19th March 1779 and 21st April 1824 respectively.

Amongst the 'Miscellaneous Sonnets' in the 1832 edition of 'Wordsworth's Poetical Works', No. XLVI, is a work entitled 'Filial Piety'; and in Professor Knight's edition of Wordsworth, 1882, and others, this sonnet has the sub-title 'On the Wayside between Preston and Liverpool', and was written by Wordsworth either in 1824 or 1828 when he passed through Burscough on his way to Liverpool.

Filial Piety
by William Wordsworth

Untouched through all severity of cold;
Inviolate, what'er the cottage hearth
Might need for comfort, or for festal mirth;
That Pile of Turf is half a century old:
Yes, Traveller! fifty winters have been told.
Since suddenly the dart of death went forth
'Gainst him who raised it, — his last work on earth:
Thence has it, with the Son, so strong a hold
Upon his Father's memory, that his hands,
Through reverence, touch it only to repair
Its waste — Though crumbling with each breath of air,
In annual renovation thus it stands —
Rude Mausoleum! but wrens nestle there,
And red-breasts warble when sweet sounds are rare.

In the 18th and 19th centuries the villagers usually cut the peat for fuel in the winter months, but in summer when the lanes were dry and could be used, they obtained their supply of coal from Burscough Bridge. The coal came from Newburgh in the latter part of the 18th century and subsequently from the Wigan coalfields by canal barge to Burscough Bridge where it was carted by tenant farmers to the local gentry as legally arranged in their leases.

Employment and population

During the 17th, 18th and 19th centuries, agriculture had been the main occupation of the people of Burscough and by and large up to the early part of the 19th century industry was basically on the lines of the 'domestic system'. Until the 1850s the greatest employers had been the great houses, i.e. Lathom House, Blythe Hall and several other gentlemen's residences in the district. The cutting of the Leeds and Liverpool Canal in the 1770s and the draining of Martin

Mere brought an economic stimulus to the surrounding farming districts and provided much work for many people. During the winter periods in the 18th and 19th centuries, unemployment was often very high in agricultural areas whether they were pasture or arable districts and, therefore, pay was irregular for many farm labourers. At the beginning of the 19th century and up till the 1870s, a farm labourer's pay varied from about 1/6d. to 2/– per day, and from 1880 to 1900 their pay varied from about 2/– to 3/– per day, but the rate of pay tended to be higher on the canal boats and their work was often more regular. Those townships through which the canal passed paid similar wages, i.e. about 2/– per day, to farm labourers in the 1830s and thus had the effect of evening out the wages in this part of south-west Lancashire and elsewhere.

Mass unemployment does not appear to have occurred in this area during the 19th century, with the exception of the year 1831 when, according to the census of that year, out of a total of 198 agricultural families in Burscough, 50 farm labourers and their families were unemployed.

Many children were employed by their parents at this time, and it was not uncommon for families to take in washing to supplement their income. At Burscough in 1831 small potato gardens were kept, where the inhabitants grew vegetables and it is recorded that 'those who have the best gardens keep off the parish'. Friendly Societies also started to develop at this time and in Burscough there was about one friendly society for every family.

The Irish 'Potato Famine' of 1845-47 forced thousands of Irish immigrants into Lancashire, which resulted in increased populations occurring in many townships and, during this period, the population of Burscough rose slightly, but competition from Irish labour was not a serious threat. In 1821 the population of Burscough was 1,755 and by 1831 had risen to 2,244, an increase of 489 persons in ten years; this represented about a 60% increase in the average yearly population figures over the previous 20 years' average, i.e. from 1801-1821. During the period 1821-1831, Burscough's population increased more rapidly than that of any of the surrounding townships, namely: Bickerstaffe, Lathom, Ormskirk, Scarisbrick and Skelmersdale. The increase was probably owing to the influx of canal boat people into this area after 1816 who by the year 1831 would no doubt have formed a substantial proportion of the population, some of whom would settle in Burscough and bring up their families here.

From the statistics available, therefore, it does not appear that many persons moved from the surrounding townships to Burscough at this time. Movement of persons from Burscough to other areas to find employment (with the exception of Skelmersdale) does not appear to have taken place on any scale before the introduction of the railways in the 1850s and even then the movement was only minimal. After 1850, this movement became more important. During the development of coal mining in the Skelmersdale area in the 1850s to 1870s, the population of Burscough declined, probably due to families leaving Burscough to take up employment in the coalmining industry there.

It was not until the 20th century that people from the Burscough area began to seek employment in other districts, such as Liverpool, Wigan, Southport and Manchester and, initially, the majority of these persons were businessmen or professional people. By 1910, however, the occupations of the people of

Burscough were becoming more diverse and a larger proportion of the population began to move further afield in the course of their employment.

Industries which developed in the 19th century

Industries which developed in the early part of the 19th century in this area were very few and very small compared with today's standards and even after prolonged research I have been able to find out very little concerning these early industries, many of which have now disappeared and their sites have subsequently undergone much alteration.

The greater concentration of industry in the first half of the 19th century was situated in the Lathom area between Top Locks and the Ring O'Bells, in close proximity to the Leeds and Liverpool Canal. The industries were the following:

Forges and blacksmiths

Associated with the boat-building industry were the village blacksmith, carpenter, wheelwright and joiner. The boat-builder himself was invariably a joiner or wheelwright but, with the introduction of the canal and boat-building to this area, there was a corresponding increase in the number of blacksmiths and nail makers. In many instances the blacksmith was also a nail maker. The widening use of coal, mainly brought about by the aid of canal transport and proximity to the mining areas, facilitated the growth of many forms of metal industry. When coal replaced wood as a fuel it also enabled the blacksmith or nail maker to build a forge near to his home or workshop.

Prior to the 1820s there appears to have been very few, if any, nail makers in this area but, by 1850, Thomas Gaskell of Burscough Town and Thomas Thompson of Burscough Bridge were established nail manufacturers. Nail making on a commercial basis, however, disappeared in the late 1880s. By 1850 there were six blacksmiths established in Burscough and Lathom. Initially they grew up along the turnpike road where their services would be required mainly by the stage-coaches and other users of the road and, at a similar period, when the canals were developed several smithies sprang up along its banks.

The oldest smithy was probably the one at Sheep Cote Hill which was run by the Charnock family for a long period (Thomas Charnock was the blacksmith in 1830), but today only the ruins remain and the site is in danger of disappearing altogether. Three smithies existed down Moss Lane. A smithy which existed up to recent times was situated at Burscough Town, close to the Red Lion Inn and in the 1840s was occupied by Anne Watkinson who in the 1850s became victualler of the Red Lion. This smithy passed into the hands of the Fields family in the 20th century and Mr. John Fields was the last blacksmith. A smithy also existed on the premises belonging to the late Mr. James Lyon of Burscough Town in the 19th century. Finally there was a smithy at the Top Locks which was established by the Myers family about the late 1820s; at that time a Mr. William Myers was the blacksmith and subsequently in the 1880s his grandson Thomas Myers built the old smithy down Mart Lane where he also manufactured agricultural equipment (he was also a machinist). About the year 1899 Thomas Myers left Burscough to take up the position of engineer-in-charge to the Leyland Council, but the smithy remained in his name until 1901. Another smithy was established about 1914 by Mr. Harry Martland in Victoria Street, Burscough, but like all the other blacksmiths' shops has now gone.

It is of interest to note the following which was recorded in the log-book of St. John's School:

'Dec. 22 1891 — Henry James Suffel accidentally got burned at Myer's Furnace during the dinner hour and accordingly was absent.'

The Myers family appear to have been very versatile for two contemporaries of William Myers carried on the following trades in the 1850s: Thomas Myers had a beer house and Margaret Myers was a milliner and dressmaker. In the late 1870s a Mrs. Jane Myers was an ironmonger in Burscough Bridge, the business remaining in the Myers family until 1907. Mrs. Jane Myers was followed in the business by Mr. Richard Myers (brother of Thomas Myers the blacksmith in Mart Lane) about 1890, but by 1898 a Mrs. Mary Myers was in charge of the business and remained so until the premises were taken over by Mr. Frank Eastwood about 1907. The Eastwood family retained the business until the 1960s when the premises were taken over by Mr. W. Ramage who now deals in hardware, do-it-yourself and gardening equipment.

Lathom Saw Mill

This was situated between Top Locks and Glovers Bridge and occupied part of the site which subsequently became Tyrer's boat-building yard. The business was established about the late 1820s and was owned by Mr. William Backhouse, timber merchant and builder. The business was subsequently taken over by Mr. James Backhouse and for unknown reasons closed about the year 1870. No details exist of this mill and there is no local information available as yet which would enable me to explore any further.

The Mordant Works (pyroligneous acid) and Wainwright's or Wareing's Cottage near the Ring O'Bells Inn

Part of the chemical works and the remains of two kilns, together with several other outbuildings which may have been connected with the mordant works, still exist. All the buildings are constructed of brick with flag slates on the roofs. The adjacent farm called 'Wainwright's Cottage' was thatched up to about 20 years ago and was formerly the home of William Farrimond, who was the manufacturing chemist at the mordant works in the 1830s. The works were established about 1830. Locally the chemical works has been forgotten, but Mrs. Webster who has lived practically on the site all her life can remember the farm being referred to as 'Stink Farm', no doubt because of the smell from the chemical works. Mrs. Webster also remembered seeing the name William Farrimond scratched on a pane of glass in the window of Wainwright's Cottage (now owned by Mr. Weymouth) when she was a young girl. In 1880 Mr. Farrimond moved to Vine Cottage near Briars Mill and a Mr. Joseph Glover became the manufacturing chemist as well as being the registrar of births and deaths (Lathom sub-district of the Ormskirk Union). In 1899 the mordant works closed and Mr. Glover became a wheelwright, but by 1901 the business of wheelwright was taken over by Thomas Glover, but Joseph still remained the registrar of births and deaths up to the 1920s. Wainwright's Cottage was later taken over by a Mr. Webster and in 1924 the property was owned by the Earl of Lathom who put it up for sale in that year. However, the property was subsequently sold privately to Mr. Webster and was in consequence withdrawn from the sale. In recent years the property has been acquired by Mr. Weymouth, the present owner.

The small factory was primarily a dye works; pyroligneous acid was impure acetic acid obtained by distillation of wood and was and still is used in medicines and as a fixing agent in dyeing leather and textiles. Acetic acid can be made from almost any type of wood and according to Binns in his 'Notes on the Agriculture of Lancashire', (pub. 1851) he reported that the nursery grounds for trees and shrubs from Formby to Scarisbrick to Burscough were the most extensive in England, therefore the supply of wood was near at hand. It was no doubt situated near to the canal so that the supply and despatch of materials would be facilitated. Across the road from Wainwright's Cottage was a weighbridge which was shown on the 1845 Ordnance Survey map and, according to Mrs. Webster, was removed about 40 years ago; nothing now remains of the weighbridge.

Brickmaking

Burscough and surrounding townships have extensive supplies of clay and from the early 17th century bricks have been manufactured locally. Building material was never transported more than a few miles, unless the circumstances were exceptional, and until the middle of the 18th century most local buildings were constructed of timber, clay, wattle and daub and thatch. Bricks were still expensive and costly to move, and so were not used by ordinary people. By the 1770s, however, they were becoming more common. The earliest reference to their use in Burscough is in the constable's accounts for the township, dated 30 April 1771:

'for carting two hundred of brick from Martin Mere to school, 1 shilling'.

Nothing is known of the brickworks which supplied this load but the school referred to is the old Burscough Town school.

One or two examples still exist locally of the old type of building, with timber and thatch, but they are (1970) fast disappearing. Only recently a small cottage of wattle and daub was pulled down at Moss Bridge. Bricks have almost entirely replaced the old materials and brick houses have been built where older ones were torn down.

Over the last 250 years the clay for manufacturing bricks has been quarried in the Burscough area in very many places and large numbers of the old pits remain. By the end of the 18th century there were already 19 brickfields or clay fields, belonging to 12 different farmers and covering in total more than 12 acres of land. In this area the bricks were made from the boulder clay and were dried over a period of six weeks so that they were 'well seasoned'. They were hand made and about 9 inches long, 4½ inches wide and between 1¾ and 2½ inches in depth. At the beginning of the 19th century, moves towards a greater standardisation of size were made, and the thickness of locally made bricks increased.

During the first decades of the 19th century, commercial brickmaking on a larger scale began in the area, and the gradual urban growth of neighbouring towns provided a continuing and developing market. Once the railway came, transport, already improved by the canal, became considerably easier.

A damaged, yet splendid, early photograph taken about 1896 showing the Old Smithy in Mart Lane with Thomas Myers at the drill.

An aerial view of Shepherd and Sons Ltd., Burscough.

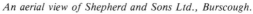

In the 1860s Southport began to expand very rapidly and in 1861 no fewer than 20,000,000 bricks were required in Southport. This was no doubt proof of the rising prosperity of the place when £20,000 worth of bricks were required for the building of 100 more houses. From March 1861 to March 1862, 50,000 bricks were sent daily to Southport which worked out at the rate of a new house every day. This gave impetus to the brickworks at Burscough and also provided the railways with much work for in June 1863 it is recorded that '500 wagons containing 600,000 bricks, lately arrived at the Southport Station in one day'.

Burscough Tile Works (Higgins Lane)

It was not until the 1840s that bricks started to be made on a commercial basis in Burscough and the first undertaking of any note was established in Higgins Lane. The area once formed part of Travis's Farm and the site is now occupied by a garage and store shed belonging to Mr. R. Barker.

The brick and tile yard was commenced in 1849. Previously the land had been used for growing potatoes, the farmer being a Mr. John Bullock in the 1840s.

The first brickmaker appears to have been John Davis who remained there until about 1855 when the business was taken over by John Staniforth. During the late 1850s the name of the undertaking was the 'Burscough Tile Works' and the making of draining tiles seems to have been the main item of manufacture. Mr. Staniforth appears to have left the business about 1864 for by that time the draining tiles etc. were being sold through Mr. Joseph Crook of Ormskirk. The works closed down in 1873 when Mr. Crook was killed at the Aughton Sand Delf in that year.

Isherwood's Brickfield (Burscough Junction)

In the 1860s Robert Isherwood started as a brick and tile maker in this area (he also had a brick and tile works at Formby). The brick works later became known as the Burscough Junction Brick Works and was situated adjacent to the railway. Mr. Isherwood also had a brickfield on part of the area now occupied by Rivington Drive and it was in this area that the erratic block or boulder of Criffel Granite was found. This brickfield was abandoned in the 1870s. From time to time boys still at school used to work at Mr. Isherwood's brickfield, as the following entry in the Roman Catholic School log-book confirms:

'March 1876 — One boy Birrell, has for some weeks been working half-time at Mr. Isherwood's brickfield close by'.

In 1878 Mr. Isherwood gave up the business and for a short period the brickmaking at this works was carried on by Littlewoods Brick and Tile Co. Ltd., who subsequently moved to Croston in about 1881.

John Platt (Burscough Junction) Ltd.

In 1878 Mr. John Platt had also commenced working in this area at the same time that Littlewood Brick and Tile Co. Ltd. had taken over Mr. Isherwood's works. However, Mr. Platt subsequently took over Mr. Isherwood's premises in 1881 and in July 1898 the company of John Platt (Burscough Junction) Ltd. was formed to acquire and carry on the brickmaking business of John Platt of Burscough Junction. The total capital was £10,000 which was divided into 1,200 preference shares of £5 each, carrying a cumulative dividend of 6% and 4,000 ordinary shares of £1 each. At the time 2,000 ordinary shares and one hundred preference shares were allotted to Mr. Platt as part of the purchase money. The firm's books were audited and certified by Messrs. Davies and Crane, chartered accountants of Southport, who stated that the average profit for the last three years had been £1,000 per annum. The value of the business that was acquired by the company — with machines and plant, and including goodwill — was estimated by Mr. G. J. Healey, licensed valuer of Wigan, at £8,080. It was also stated that the quality of the bricks turned out at the works was of a high character, and that demand exceeded the supply. Mr. Platt during the 1880s had a railway siding built to connect with the Lancashire and Yorkshire Railway and at the time of the transfer was regarded as a valuable asset. Mr. Platt undertook to act as managing director for 10 years, and the Board included other gentlemen (one of whom was Mr. James Thorougood) who were well known in the Southport district. At the time it was calculated that the profits, even if they were not increased beyond what it was at the time of the transfer (1898), would suffice to pay the preference dividend and 8% upon the ordinary share and still leave a handsome surplus for the managing director's salary, reserve fund and contingencies. With the additional capital which the transfer to the company would provide, it was expected that a considerable increase in business, representing increased profits, would be secured.

However, about the year 1902 or 1903 Mr. James Thorougood (see also under Breweries) took over the business and absorbed John Platt into the 'Burscough Brick & Tile Works Ltd.' (locally referred to as Thorougood's Brick Works) and Mr. Thorougood's position was that of Chairman of the Directors on the Company's Board. This works remained in the Thorougood family, passing to Mr. H. Thorougood in 1908 and subsequently to Mr. Walter Thorougood in 1918. The brickworks continued on into the 1960s, but it is now abandoned and the works are closed.

Prior to the land being used as a brick and tile works it had been farmed by James Swift in the 1840s, but the landowner was Edward Riddle of Briars Hall. It is of interest to note that there was (and still is) a rent-charge of £2-10/– per annum on this land and in times past £2 of this sum was given to the poor and the remaining 10 shillings was retained by the two constables for their trouble in attending to the collection of the money.

Bridge's Brick & Tile Works (Old Abbey Brick & Tile Works)

This firm was established by Thomas Bridge in 1875 and was the last brick and tile works to exist in Burscough. A large variety of bricks were made here to suit different tastes and to meet specific requirements, such as engineering bricks, fire bricks and the like. The firm was known as the 'Old Abbey Brick and Tile Works', no doubt because it was situated close to the old Priory (referred to locally as the Abbey), being separated only by the railway. Bricks from this quarry have been used to build many houses and the like in Burscough and district, especially during the 1930s and since but, initially, when the firm commenced in business most of the work was centred on Southport. Brickmaking ceased in August 1970 and the works were closed in December 1970 and the premises have now been acquired by Drome Storage.

The Lathom Flax Mill (Flax Lane)

This was established about 1858 and was situated down what is today called Flax Lane (formerly called Speakman's Lane up to the early 1930s). In 1936 several street and road names were altered in Burscough because similar names existed in Ormskirk and this caused some confusion with the postal arrangements at that time. No records exist of this mill and at one period I along with others began to doubt that a flax mill had existed in this district. Mr. George Thierens (grandson of Cornelius Thierens) does not possess any documentary evidence about the mill, but he supplied me with what information he had available. Officially the mill did not exist and there was no reference to a flax mill or even a ruined site indicated on any Ordnance Survey map produced in the 19th century. After several months of prolonged research covering many official and unofficial sources, I eventually found sufficient information to verify the existence of this mill.

Cornelius Thierens (Thierens is a Flemish name) came over from Belgium about the year 1850 and lived in Hedon, near Hull, up to the year 1858, when he came to manage the flax mill which had just been established in Lathom. However, Mr. Thierens' position as manager of the flax mill was not to last very long, for on January 30th 1868 the flax mill was completely destroyed by fire; he tried to extinguish it but, owing to the inflammable nature of the material, he was unable to control the fire and in a very short period of time the mill was razed to the ground. The fire occurred about 6 p.m. and, according to a local report at the time, the night was very stormy and the strong wind fanned the flames until the whole building was on fire and the flames could be seen for miles around. The building was insured for £1,200 and between thirty to forty persons were employed at the mill.

Considering how quickly it was destroyed, the mill appears to have been mainly constructed of wood. Today no remains exist although large stones (possibly foundations) have been found over the years when the land has been ploughed and some of these have subsequently found their way into the Ellerbrook. The site of the mill was a short distance away from the road and was adjacent to the footpath which leads up to the Roman Catholic chapel. However, about the year 1910, the Ellerbrook was straightened at this point and a large bend or meander was removed so as to facilitate the flow of water and thus prevent silting and flooding from occurring. When this was undertaken, no doubt, much of the foundations of the old flax mill were removed. The mill as far as I can ascertain was driven by water power. It was essential in the processing of flax that a good supply of water was available because after the flax had been harvested, dried and the seeds separated (usually by means of an iron comb called a rippler) the flax was then 'retted' or soaked by various methods and in this case the Ellerbrook would be used. The soaking continued until the action of the bacteria loosened the decaying woody part of the stalk, after which the flax would be spread out in one of the surrounding fields to bleach and dry. The pure fibre would then be freed from the stem by two operations — first, by 'breaking', in which the woody part of the stem was cracked by rollers and a scraping mechanism, working in conjunction with these rollers, removed the bulk of the weedy centre of the stem from the fibre; secondly the remainder would be separated from the fibre by 'scutching', in which the

flax would either have been beaten by hand or machinery. Finally the flax would
be heckled, or combed with an iron comb and the short coarse fibres would
furnish the 'tow' that would be used for various purposes.

Scutching was a very dusty and dry job and at the junction of Flax Lane
and Blythe Lane there is a little stone house now occupied by Mr. and Mrs.
Lund (Qualco Bulldog Kennels), which from 1860 to 1908 had been a beer shop
known as the 'Scutchers Arms'. It was quite common to name and attribute
arms to inns and beer houses associated with a local trade, e.g. The Bricklayers
Arms, Miners Arms, Mechanics Arms and the like. This beer house no doubt
owes its name to the Lathom Flax Mill and the process of scutching that was
carried on there. However, some people say that it derived its name from the
fact that when carriages stopped there, they put scotches under the wheels to
prevent them from moving backwards down Flax Lane. Scotches would be used
here in the way described, but the name Scutchers Arms was not derived from
the use of scotches. Before the little cottage was used as a beer house it was
a small farm which was owned by Edward Riddle of Briars Hall and tenanted
by the Swift family in the 1840s and 1850s. Mr. William Dutton (grandfather
of Mr. Alan Dutton of W. C. Dutton's, grocers, Burscough Town) was the
beer-retailer at the Scutchers Arms from 1890 to 1902 and was followed by Mr.
John Garner who remained there until 1908.

The flax was grown in this area but there is evidence to suggest that the main
supply came from northern Ireland and was conveyed from Liverpool to Lathom
by means of canal barge. No doubt a number of Irishmen came over to work
at this mill, amongst whom were some by the names of Birrell. Belgium was
one of the chief flax-growing countries of the world and northern Ireland was
the only large area in the British Isles that had cultivated flax on a large scale;
these countries, therefore, would have the skilled labour available and in the
case of the Lathom Flax Mill they obtained their skilled labour and know-how
from a Belgian in the person of Cornelius Thierens.

After the flax mill was destroyed, Mr. Thierens became a shopkeeper in 1870,
first starting as a grocer and then as a grocer and baker in 1890 and on his death
in 1899 the business was taken over by his son Francis Thierens who, as I have
already stated, subsequently took over from Mr. Carriage as the sub-postmaster
at Burscough Town in 1902. Mr. Francis Thierens was apprenticed to Thomas
Bridge the builder to learn the trade of joiner at the age of 14 and after having
served his time he remained in the same employ for four years. In 1880 he
commenced business on his own account before taking over his father's business
in 1899.

Saw Mill (Burscough Junction)

The original saw mill (this was destroyed and subsequently rebuilt and
improved in the 1920s) was built by Thomas Bridge who established his timber
and contracting business there in 1864. Mr. Thomas Bridge was practically the
founder of Wesleyan Methodism in Burscough, but he was also a timber
merchant and builder and many Wesleyan chapels in the neighbourhood of
Burscough, Lathom, Maghull, Southport and elsewhere were built by Thomas
Bridge.

Mr. Bridge was born at Rufford in 1819 and came of a well-known stock
of yeomen, his ancestors tracing their descent from a family which took part

in the Crusades, and an old coat-of-arms used to be possessed by the Bridge family. He served his apprenticeship with a Mr. Kenyon of Scarisbrick and initially commenced in business at Bispham, opposite the Eagle and Child Inn, afterwards moving to Mawdesley. In 1863 he moved to Burscough where he established his timber and contracting business. When Mr. Bridge came to Burscough there were no houses from the Junction to the Bridge except Messrs. Wells and Ainscough, the Junction Hotel and a few cottages. Over the years, however, Mr. Bridge erected building after building, business grew and the township of Burscough began to develop. Mr. Bridge was also instrumental in bringing pressure to bear on the railway companies to increase the facilities for traders and the travelling public.

Mr. Bridge was a friend of Dr. James Wood of Southport and Mr. Edward Holden and, together, they were responsible for the building of property in Southport and the surrounding districts. Some of the most important undertakings that Mr. Bridge carried out in Southport and district as a contractor were the following: he built a new market in East Bank Street, Southport, the Liverpool District Bank, Kew Gardens, the Leyland Road Wesleyan Chapel and the 'Glaciarium', which was claimed to be the first permanent ice skating rink in the kingdom. In 1875 Mr. Bridge started the old Abbey Brick Works, Burscough, and in connection with his contracting work at Southport had a railway siding constructed so that he could load bricks directly into the wagons for transport to Southport and elsewhere. Trade developed and by 1884 Mr. Bridge was engaged in building the following: Mornington Road Schools, Southport, Walton Prison, Canal Warehouses, a Mr. Parr's House and about February 1884 had become a sub-contractor under Mr. Walton Smith for work in connection with the Cheshire Lines Extension Railway. In connection with the last named venture, however, which was an undertaking of some considerable size, Mr. Walton Smith omitted to pay Mr. Bridge for work carried out in August and September of 1884 and in consequence this threw Mr. Bridge into financial difficulties. Mr. Bridge was prevented from carrying on his business as a contractor for a while until the matter was resolved and it resulted in his having to sell the saw mill in 1887 to Mr. Henry Augustus Robinson. His son Thomas Bridge handled the business affairs and continued to develop the Old Abbey Brick Works which prospered. The business remained in the Bridge family until 1970, Edward Bridge taking charge in 1902 and subsequently being followed by his sons.

The saw mills at Burscough Junction was carried on by Mr. H. A. Robinson until the year 1921 when the business and premises were taken over by Messrs. Bamber and Calder.

Shepherd & Son Ltd.

Mr. Thomas Bamber (born 1874) was originally a boat-builder at Fleetwood who for a short time made inshore or shrimping boats. Subsequently, on seeing an advertisement in a local paper regarding employment at William Shepherd & Sons of Kendal, he decided to apply for a position with the firm; he did so, was accepted, and eventually became a manager. He became the wood buyer for the firm, which involved travelling down to Liverpool by train to inspect the imported timber, and in doing so he noticed Mr. Robinson's saw mill at Burscough Junction. Mr. Bamber was very interested in this saw mill, and on one of his trips to Liverpool he decided to stop at Burscough Junction and see Mr. Robinson with a view to buying the saw mill. After a discussion, Mr. Robinson decided to sell, but before Mr. Bamber took any further action he went back to Kendal to confer with Mr. Calder (as foreman at William Shepherd & Sons, Kendal), to ask if he wanted to join him in his venture; he agreed and they came to Burscough about the year 1921. In that year they established the business under the name of Bamber & Calder, timber merchants, Burscough Junction.

By the year 1925 the Shepherd family at Kendal retired from the business and the Company was re-formed under the name of Shepherd & Sons (1925) Ltd., and shortly afterwards the assets of the Kendal Handle Company were purchased. Over the years Mr. Bamber kept in close touch with the Shepherd family and on their retirement from business became one of the principal managers of the firm which was re-formed in 1925. About the same year the works at Burscough were improved. In 1933 Mr. Bamber came to live in Burscough, residing at 'Halsemere', Junction Lane.

Mr. Bamber was a far sighted man and quickly recognised the importance of developing the Burscough factory because of its proximity to the port of Liverpool, from which by this time the greater proportion of the timber was being obtained as home supplies were becoming depleted. Therefore, the firm of Bamber & Calder was absorbed into the firm of Shepherd & Sons (1925) Ltd., and later the mill at Kendal was closed and the premises at Burscough were enlarged and rebuilt. They now cover more than two acres.

The name of Shepherd & Sons (1925) Ltd., was maintained, largely because of the goodwill and experience which was associated with the firm, but in 1951 the year 1925 (the year of incorporation) was deleted from the name as it was felt that its inclusion was misleading, because the original company had been established since 1861.

Times change and methods of production advance and sometimes it is difficult to maintain a balance between the new methods and production and the employment of one's labour. However, the policy of Shepherd & Sons Ltd. has been to install new machinery whenever possible and to try to combine up-to-date methods with the skill of the old craftsmen. By and large this has meant that production could be increased without sacrificing the quality of workmanship. This factory (at the time of writing) gives employment to about 100 persons in this district.

Today Shepherd & Sons Ltd., as in times past, have always maintained a high standard and rank among the foremost producers of tool handles in the world.

Kew Jam Works (Burscough Junction)

This small works was established in 1895 by John Smith and Son, preserve manufacturers, and was situated adjacent to the saw mill at Burscough Junction. The works were approached by the small road leading off Junction Lane, close to the Junction Hotel. The building in which the jam was made still exists, but there are no details concerning the numbers of people employed and the like. In 1902 shares were issued by the company and a second and first dividend of 1/7d. in the £ was declared. The jam works was the first undertaking in

Burscough to be granted the permission to make a connection for piped water. By 1905 the works closed down but, as we shall see, the premises were again occupied by two more firms. (See Candle Works and Krunch Crisps).

Thorougood's Breweries Ltd. (Near the Packet House)

Mr. James Thorougood was a native of Ware, in Herefordshire, and he first came to Lancashire as a gardener when he was only 19 years of age, where he was engaged at Duxbury Park, near Chorley, for a couple of years, after which he was employed at Cuerden Hall. With remarkable aptitude for his calling, Mr. Thorougood was appointed head gardener at Lathom House by the first Baron Skelmersdale, when he was only twenty four years of age. He occupied this position for thirteen years, when he left to take over the proprietorship of the Packet House Inn, Burscough Bridge, to which a small brewery was attached. Under his directorship the brewery business was developed to such an extent that ultimately the concern was floated as Thorougood's Breweries Ltd. in 1896 with a capital of £50,000 in £10 shares, 'to enter into a certain agreement and to carry on the business of brewers, malsters, hop merchants and growers, wine and spirit merchants and importers, licensed victuallers, tobacconists etc.'. The number of directors had not to be less than three or more than seven and the first directors were Mr. T. W. Thorougood (Chairman and Managing Director), J. Hetherington and C. G. Houghton.

Mr. James Thorougood was also a director of the Company, but in April 1898 the businesses of Mr. T. W. Thorougood Ltd., of Waterloo and Sephton and James Thorougood of Burscough were amalgamated and after this date the firm was carried on under the above name. It was in 1898 that the company purchased the Junction Hotel, Burscough, by private treaty. During the years several more hotels were acquired, including the Britannic Hotel, Blackpool, and the Albert Hotel, London Road, Southport, which was bought for £20,000 in 1899. By 1900 Thorougood's Breweries became associated with other larger companies and syndicates, but in 1904 due to the financial failure of one of the directors associated with these companies it was decided that Thorougood's Breweries should discontinue their connection with them. Eventually, due to competition from the larger breweries and further amalgamations, Thorougood's Breweries closed down in the 1920s. Today the premises are occupied by Vitax Ltd.

Prior to acquiring a large number of licensed houses Mr. James Thorougood built the Royal Hotel, Burscough Bridge, of which he was the first licensee, his term extending over 14 years when he was succeeded by his son-in-law Mr. James Walker in 1891. Prior to the Royal Hotel being built in the 1870s the site was occupied by four cottages which were tenanted as follows: Adam Law, James Forshaw, Peter Abraham and John Banks.

James Thorougood, apart from being a successful businessman, also took a great interest in local affairs. He was a member of the old Lathom and Burscough Urban District Council for over eighteen years and he gave a lot of help and encouragement to the development of the water scheme for Burscough and Lathom. For some years Mr. Thorougood took an active part in the educational matters in Burscough and was a manager of both St. John's C. of E. school and Lord's Gate School.

Thorougood's Brewery at Burscough remained in the family until it was closed in the 1920s, the running of the firm being carried on by Mr. Thorougood's sons when he retired. Mr. James Hewitt Thorougood took over the business when his father retired and for a time lived at 'Clayton House', Burscough, with his father. This house was built by James Thorougood who had lived there since 1890. Mr. J. H. Thorougood continued in the brewery business at Burscough, but later became proprietor of the 'Swan Bank Brewery', Congleton, Cheshire. Subsequently he returned to Burscough (about 1908) and took a small farm, at the same time becoming manager of the Burscough Brick and Tile Works Co. on the death of his father. When Mr. Thorougood came back to Burscough he had an up-to-date workshop built at Clayton House — engineering being his main interest. In 1918 the business passed to Charles and Walter Thorougood. The Burscough Brick and Tile Co. Ltd. was carried on after the Brewery was closed and Mr. Walter Thorougood (who was the last surviving son of James Thorougood) continued as manager until his death in 1948. Mr. W. Thorougood had lived for a time in rooms at the Packet House, but subsequently he had occupied a suite of rooms at the Red Lion for many years. Clayton House, his father's residence, became the property of Mr. Walter Martland about the year 1910.

Williamson's Table Baize Works, Junction Lane (Site now occupied by the Ordnance Depot)

In 1879 Mr. Thomas Williamson of Lancaster decided to establish part of his manufacturing business at Burscough. He purchased the land adjacent to the railway and canal at Burscough Junction from Lord Skelmersdale and in August 1879 laid out the area chosen and began to erect the buildings. The works were quite extensive for the period, and the main item of manufacture was to be table baize. This was the first introduction of an entirely new branch of business into this district and it was mainly due to the enterprise of Mr. Thomas Williamson. Mr. Williamson was the son of James Williamson of Lancaster, a man, a narrative of whose life might worthily occupy a place in Smiles's volume on 'Self-made Men'. Mr. Williamson the elder commenced in business as an operative painter and decorator. By hard work, skill and business acumen, he became one of the greatest and certainly the wealthiest employer of labour in Lancaster in the 19th century, and when he died in 1878 his son James (created 1st Baron Ashton in 1895) carried on the business and his brother's son Thomas came to Burscough, where he established his own manufacturing business.

The erection of the works at Burscough gave rise to much speculation as to the probable influence that it would have on the future of Burscough. Mr. Williamson though that the area was well adapted for a trade of this description, being in immediate communication with the principal towns by means of the canal and railway and as the number of manufacturers were too few to employ the redundant population in Burscough at that time, an acceptable opening for their engagement would be made by the industry in question. A certain amount of labour would have to be imported as necessary, but this difficulty was overcome by introducing some of his workers from Lancaster and elsewhere who subsequently came to live in Burscough. The number of persons to be employed at this factory was rumoured to be 1,000. But in fact the number envisaged was in the region of 250 and even this number of employees at the time would result in their joint earnings reaching several thousands of pounds per annum, a large proportion of which would be spent in Burscough and the surrounding districts, especially Ormskirk. It was thought that the manufacture of table baize would contribute no little to the prosperity of Burscough and similar to its contribution to the well-being of the county town the table baize industry would ultimately raise Burscough into a place of considerable importance. The enterprise and project received the approval of all persons interested in this locality.

Unfortunately, for reasons unknown, the works did not develop into the giant concern which had been envisaged initially and this might have been due to several factors, such as insufficient numbers of skilled or trained men, the demand for the product might have not have been sufficient and increased competition from other sources might also have been instrumental in preventing its growth. However, during the 1880s there was the growing threat of the Boer War in South Africa and during this time the military authorities had been looking for a place which had good communications by river or canal and railway, which was situated near to the River Mersey. After many months, the site at Burscough which was occupied by Mr. Williamson's factory was chosen.

The Ordnance Depot

Mr. Wlliamson was approached by the military authorities and the land and buildings of the table baize factory were eventually acquired in 1890 and were taken over by 1891.

The suggestion that the Ordnance Stores should be located at Burscough was first put forward in April, 1890 when it was announced that the military authorities had decided to remove the ordnance stores from Chester Castle to Burscough Junction. The stores, which had annually supplied the numerous camps in Cheshire and North Wales, had for the past 20 years provided employment for between 40 and 50 men in Chester. The supplies to the various camps in the district were sent out from Chester as before, but by 1891 they were being returned to the new centre at Burscough. In June 1890 the Mersey Infantry Volunteer Brigade, which then consisted of sixteen battalions, was re-organised in connection with a scheme which was under consideration for the defence of the Mersey — of which, it was believed, that the Ship Canal formed a very important item — as well as for the protection of the new ordnance stores at Burscough.

1891-1914

When the site was taken over by the military authorities, many of the existing buildings were converted and some still remain in use today. The C.O.S.D. at Burscough was developed to perform two main functions, the holding of tentage and camp stores and certain wares. In the initial stages between 40 to 50 persons were employed and its development continued until the outbreak of the War in 1914. One of the first, if not the first, officers in charge, during the 1890s was Captain Henry Augustus Anley who lived at Ordnance House.

The 1914-1918 War necessitated the expansion of the Depot to hold clothing and gun stores for regimental army units. Additional buildings were erected both during and after the War, some of which, although of a temporary construction, are still in use.

During the period 1918-1939 the Depot assumed its peacetime role of providing tentage and clothing necessaries and accommodation stores for units stationed in Western Command. In 1926 a detachment of the newly-formed War Department Constabulary took over responsibility for Depot security from the Metropolitan Police.

During the Second World War (1939-1945) Burscough continued to perform its role of maintaining units stationed in Western Command, but on a greatly increased scale. The civilian staff was augmented by a Company of R.A.O.C. and an A.T.S. detachment. A Command Workshop R.A.O.C. was formed to repair vehicles and equipment. This workshop became a R.E.M.E. Workshop on the formation of that Corps as 21 Command Workshops, R.E.M.E. After the War, both units remained in being, but with reduced military complements. The department retained its military officers, but no other ranks. In 1961-1962 the numbers of personnel were further reduced and many civilians were transferred to Deysbrook near Liverpool.

On several occasions, various firms have intimated their interest in the Depot site, but nothing has ever been developed from the enquiries or proposals to date.

From the First World War until the 1950s the Ordnance Depot employed in peacetime some 300-400 persons, but today only a fraction of this number now remain. Therefore, the Depot was for the greater part of the first half of the 20th century the biggest employer of labour in Burscough and Lathom and indirectly provided work for many other people.

Industries developed during the 20th century

Several of the industries which I have mentioned in the 19th century still exist today and by and large have been improved, extended and in many instances the methods of production have been modified to meet the ever increasing changes and demands made upon them in this day and age. Therefore, I have left out those industries in this section which had their origins in the 19th century and before in the Burscough area, except where certain earlier information will help to clarify or elucidate its establishment.

Industries 1900-1950

Coop & Co. Ltd., Victoria Street

The first industry to emerge in the 20th century was a small factory erected in 1901 for Messrs. Coop & Co. of Wigan (clothing manufacturers). This building is still standing today (now occupied by Brook Victor) and is situated in Victoria Street facing the road and lying with its axis approximately north-south between Orrell Lane and Victoria Street. Mr. J. Riding was the architect and Mr. J. R. Bissett was the builder. At the time, labour was cheaply obtained in Burscough and because of the good transport facilities and other improvements that were taking place such as the extensive work at New Lane in connection with sanitation, it was hoped that the new factory was a step towards the construction of large works in the district.

The number of persons employed in this factory would only be very small, varying from about 15 to 20. However, for reasons unknown, the business closed down in 1906 and the premises were taken over by Mr. William H. Isaac in that year.

Isaac's Laundry, Victoria Works

Coming back to the factory at Burscough, I mentioned that Coop & Co. Ltd. left in 1906 and the premises were taken over by Mr. William H. Isaac. This building was then converted into a laundry and initially employed 10 persons, and during 1912-1913, owing to increased business, Mr. Isaac built larger premises adjacent to the former clothing factory, but nearer the canal (part of the building is now used as offices of Brocklebank Plastics Ltd.). The old clothing factory was then taken over by Messrs. J. Martland Ltd., who used it as a warehouse for a time, but in 1929 the premises were purchased by Victor Electrics Ltd. By 1913 up to 40 people were working at the new laundry and the business was thriving; during the 1914-1918 War, however, business declined and about 1919 the premises were taken over by Outram's Southport Cakes Ltd.

Outram's Southport Cakes Ltd.

The above firm was established on 24th April 1914, the object of the Company being to acquire and take over as a going concern and carry on the Cake and Trumalt Bread business of H. N. Outram Ltd. of 97 Tithebarn Road, Southport.

Mr. Henry Outram was the founder of the Company and the other directors were the following: Mr. Ernest Outram, Mr. Herbert Outram and Mr. Alfred Wilson. The factory at Burscough was built in 1914 by Messrs. Buck and Hodson of Southport and the architects were Messrs. J. E. Sanders & Son.

The main products of the Company were slab cake, Swiss rolls, Eccles cakes and trumalt bread and Christmas puddings. In connection with the making of the above products, the number of employees engaged by the Company varied according to the season of the year, but by and large remained at between 50 and 100, of which about 75% were women.

The premises that were originally built in 1914 for Outrams occupy a central position today and stand three storeys high and bear the foundation stone dated 1914. The premises lying adjacent to this building (that is to the left or nearer to Victoria Street) were formerly used as a laundry (Isaac's Laundry) and, after the First World War, Outram's purchased these premises and subsequently joined the two buildings together by means of a single storey building. The name of the Company was changed to Southport Cakes Ltd. about 1930. Further extensions were made as the Company expanded and in 1948 a new Public Limited Company known as Outram Bakeries Ltd. was formed to acquire all the companies controlled by the Outram family, viz: H. N. Outram Ltd., Southport Cakes Ltd., Wigan Wholesale Ltd. and Victor Electrics Ltd. In 1952 and 1956 further large extensions were added to the cake factory at Burscough and, with the installation of new and modern machinery, the Southport capacity was further increased.

The Company closed down in the autumn of 1967 due to a complete change over in consumer requirements. The premises are now occupied by Brocklebank Plastics Ltd.

A photograph of Mr. Wareing with his lorry, which was a product of Victor Electrics.

One of the vans used by Outrams in the 1920s, which was also built by Victor Electrics.

Victor Electrics Ltd.

This Company was formed in 1921 by Mr. H. N. Outram with the object of investigating and experimenting with the use of battery propelled vehicles for the hygienic delivery of foodstuffs, particularly bread and confectionery for the associated companies.

After considerable testing and use in actual house to house delivery, a standard type was put into production in 1926 and within a very short period other bakery companies were enquiring for this new form of transport. Apart from the bakery trade, dairies, laundries, coal merchants and other with daily urban delivery became interested and new types and capacities were designed to meet the ever increasing market. A new factory and offices were built in 1929 and an adjacent works, originally built as a clothing factory (formerly Coop & Co. Ltd.) was purchased and the two buildings were connected to give a substantial floor area. In 1948 a new welding and repair shop was added to cope with increased business. During the Second World War, production was changed to include a wider range of industrial trucks and tractors, all battery propelled and with hauling capacities of two to ten tons and a considerable number were supplied to the War Department for use in Ordnance factories, dockyards and the like. The firm is now known as Brook Victor Electric Vehicles Ltd., and is associated with the Hawker Siddely Group.

Candle factory off Junction Lane

When the Kew Jam factory closed down in 1905 the premises were taken over by Hayes & Finch Ltd., candlemakers. The candleworks were established about 1906. It appears that the demand for candles was still strong even in the early part of the 20th century and the small candle factory off Junction Lane is evidence of this. The principal function of this factory was the production of candles for the domestic trade and coal mines and the outlets were grocers shops, e.g. Irwins, hardware shops and Government departments. The number of persons employed at this factory varied from between 8 and 12.

As the use of gas became more widespread and the development of electricity was gaining momentum in the 1920s throughout Lancashire and elsewhere, the demand for candles declined and the candle works at Burscough closed down in 1929.

Today the firm of Hayes & Finch Ltd. (who owned the Burscough works) still carry on the work of making candles, amongst other things, at their Liverpool factory.

Krunch Potato Crisps Ltd.

When the candle works closed down the factory was abandoned for some months and in December 1929 it was mooted that a potato crisps works was to be established there. The Company reserved a considerable proportion of the share capital for farmers, and undertook to purchase from each farmer who had £100 invested (in 7% participating preference shares) the whole (or any) of his potatoes (according to grade) at 10% more than market prices ruling at Ormskirk at that time. In addition, they would participate in what promised to be a very profitable business.

The Company not only intended to make potato crisps, but also Lancashire hot-pots and potato cakes. At the time several of the leading brewery firms and restauranteurs placed large orders for the Company's product, but it was hoped that the majority interest in the concern would be held by farmers.

The aim of the Company was to make the Burscough factory into a co-operative marketing 'pool' for potatoes, as well as a factory for the manufacture of foodstuffs, and the Company undertook to give the grower, who was an investor, 10% above the market price for his produce.

The originator of the scheme was well known to many farmers and his co-operative marketing plan was considered by the Ministry of Agriculture and the Horace Plunkett Foundation at the time. A Mr. Rawlinson of Maghull had also developed a plan on similar lines to the Burscough factory, the idea being that the factory would be a clearing house or commission agency and it was claimed that it would effectively regulate supplies, secure an equitable price, prevent glut and improve the grading of potatoes. The plan also depended to a certain degree upon the lifting of the ban on Lancashire potatoes, because foreign markets (these were already opened up by the Company) would be available, and would no doubt materially assist in making potato growing a profitable industry.

The Company was incorporated on February 5th 1930, and the manufacturing part of the concern was commenced on 25th April of that year.Until the late 1920s, potato crisps were not available to the general public and were principally sold in hotels and inns. It was only during 1929 that potato crisps were obtainable at grocers' shops in this district and elsewhere and, therefore, the development of 'Krunch' potato crisps was an innovation in this area.

Making Krunch Crisps

Fortunately, unlike so many of these smaller industries for which hardly any records exist, I have been able to piece together the processes that went into the making of Krunch Potato Crisps during the 1930s.

The potatoes were first prepared in a wash-house. Initially, the potatoes were placed in a machine with revolving tub in which they were automatically washed, peeled and had their eyes removed. New potatoes used to pass through very quickly, but the old ones of course took a little longer. The peeled potatoes dropped through into a wire basket and then they were conveyed to a cutting machine where they were fed into a hopper and emerged ingeniously sliced into crinkled snowy flakes. These flakes were then put into a drier, which was a sort of large basin which revolved rapidly, a current of air drying off the superfluous moisture. After drying, the raw crisps were conveyed straight into the factory itself. This building resembled a huge kitchen, with a number of stoves along one side, and a white deal trough-table running down the middle. At this point mostly female labour was employed. One girl was in charge of each stove. Each of these stoves had two large pans of the fish frying type sunk in the flat top. The pans were filled with pure vegetable oil and in this the raw potato slices were cooked, and from which they emerged as golden brown crisps. All that they lost in the process was their water-content and the nutritive value was unimpaired.

On being taken from the pans by means of wire sieves, the crisps were transferred on wire trays to a centre table, where they were at once placed in grease-proof packets. At no time were they touched by hand, the girls using perforated scoops which only allowed the largest crisps to be placed in the packets. Each filled packet was placed on a large tray and a little packet of salt was popped inside. The packets were then carried into the packing room where they were quickly sealed and packed in tins ready for despatch to customers. The cooking was done by gas and the washing apparatus was powered by a diesel oil engine.

Only the ground floor was used at first, but whether or not the top floor was utilised I am not sure. It was suggested initially that the ground floor would be used for preparing and cooking only and that subsequently conveyor belts would be installed to take the crisps up to the top floor, where they would undergo trimming and packing. This would have meant that the factory would have been on the 'endless chain' system.

Working it at its full capacity the factory was handling over 3 tons of potatoes per day, but it was hoped that production would be raised to 10 tons per day.

'Krunch' crisps had a wide sale amongst leading hotels, grocers shops and restaurants in Lancashire, Cheshire and the Isle of Man.

There was a staff of about 40 employed at the factory, of whom about 70% were women. All the cooking and packing were done by girls under the supervision of the chef, Mr. G. McLellen. Adjacent to the factory was a small house and this was taken over along with the factory and was converted into offices. The employees also had rest-rooms, kitchen, dining-room in the house and they had the use of the garden at lunch-time. The girls were allowed time for refreshment, morning and afternoon, and their work was so arranged that they spent an hour alternately cooking and packing.

Unfortunately, the firm did not continue for long and subsequently the premises were acquired by Mr. Bamber of Shepherd & Sons Ltd., and now forms part of the saw mill.

I. H. Lavery & Co. Ltd., and Elkes Biscuits Ltd.

This cake firm was established in 1924 by Mr. I. H. Lavery who formerly had been a manager at Outram's Southport Cakes Ltd. During 1925 the building was enlarged and extended and, similar to Outram's, specialised in the making of slab cake, Eccles cakes, Christmas puddings and was especially well known for their famous Swiss rolls. Over 2,000 people were employed at this factory and again over 70% of these were women. Business increased and in the early 1930s Lavery's built the factory which now belongs to Elkes Biscuits Ltd. and for a short period they made biscuits there, but about 1935 the factory was acquired by Elkes and Fox. This firm specialises in the making of a large variety of biscuits and by and large provides employment for several hundred people, the number fluctuating no doubt according to the season of the year. In recent times (1961) the firm changed its title to Elkes Biscuits Ltd., and the firm's headquarters are at Uttoxeter, Staffordshire. This firm is still in operation and during the 1960s, expansion took place within the firm and is now one of the largest employers of female labour in Burscough.

During the 1940s and 1950s Lavery's business grew and trade developed on a national basis. However, in 1963 the number of workers was reduced from 180 employees who were mainly women to about 45. This was the first time that the firm had reorganised its business on such a scale. At the same time three quarters of their factory premises was up for sale. It was during this period that their retail and catering business on a national basis was cut down to just the catering trade. However, by 1964, the firm closed down and the premises were later taken over by Westbrooks Ltd.

Wilfred Edge & Sons Ltd.

The site of the present works was formerly the Earl of Derby's building premises and estate office and the work carried out there was mainly repairs to houses which were the property of the Derby estate. Mr. Eccles had occupied the house and site for a number of years and the agent for the Earl of Derby during the early part of the 20th century was Mr. Wyndham E. Hale. It is also supposed that, prior to the premises being used as repair workshops, a small brewery had occupied the site. Evidence of small breweries attached to public houses and inns was not uncommon in the 18th and early part of the 19th century (and even into the 20th century) and as I have already stated when discussing Thorougood's Brewery, a small brewery existed at the Packet House in the early part of the 19th century. The Red Lion Inn is adjacent to the site in question and in the 1860s and 1870s (and probably before) there was a small brewery there which was run by Mr. Norris the victualler of the inn. Most of these breweries were very small by today's standards and to a large degree were governed by the supply of water, and although numerous wells existed in Burscough, from time to time they became polluted and during the summer months some of these wells dried up.

The present firm of William Edge took over the premises in 1928, but previously Mr. Edge had commenced in business at Ormskirk before coming to Burscough. The main products of the firm are box clips and various metal fittings for box making and the furniture industry and the number of employees varies between 15 and 20. In 1945 the firm was formed into a Limited Company.

Superwood Products Ltd.

This firm was founded in 1930 by Mr. Bruce Smith who started the business in a very small way. His father Mr. William Smith was a manager for James Walker of Burscough Bridge for a number of years, but after the First World War commenced in business on his own account as a cattle dealer and later as a farmer, and it was in his former capacity that he became a well-known figure in West Lancashire agricultural circles. Mr. William Smith lived at Yew Tree House which is almost opposite to the factory of Superwood Products Ltd., Platts Lane.

Mr. Bruce Smith did not follow in his father's footsteps as a cattle dealer. He commenced business in a small way, first by making sprit (or seed) boxes for farmers at a workshop in Platts Lane; it eventually grew and subsequently he founded the firm of Superwood Products Ltd. in 1930 which is now known throughout the country.

During the Second World War he erected temporary restaurants in Liverpool and, since that time, his interests grew and they included the Abbey Timber

Kiln Drying Company, near to the Old Abbey Brick Works at Burscough Town, the ARI Sawmills in Burscough Road, which is adjacent to the railway and was founded in 1957, and also the Smithfield Modern Homes, a building company with offices in Platts Lane.

Today the factory employs about 250 persons and its success and remarkable growth is attributable to a great degree to the late Mr. Bruce Smith.

James and Edward Davis (brothers of Harry Davis) patented and made a 'bin carrier' (still in use today) for the Lathom and Burscough U.D.C., which facilitated the movement of dustbins and reduced to a certain degree the amount of labour and effort involved in their collection. The smithy in Victoria Street which had belonged to Mr. Harry Martland was acquired by Edward Davis about 1940 who remained there until he retired in 1965. The premises are now occupied by Forge Engineering, a small concern which specialises in the making of gates, railings and ornamental ironwork and the like.

During the 1930s and 1940s there was very little change in the pattern of industry in Burscough and the introduction of new industries which were envisaged in the 1930s did not materialise due to the intervention of the War. During the 1940s, however, several firms did emerge, the principal ones being the saw mill in Victoria Street, Stove Equipment in Mart Lane and Lathom Fabrications in Briars Lane.

The Saw Mill, Victoria Street

Mr. Ashcroft founded this firm in 1940, but previously he had been a tailor and had worked for Mr. John Parr Sturgess, whose premises were along Liverpool Road, now a disused 'washing' machine establishment adjacent to Webbs. Only a small staff is employed at this mill, and the work produced there is varied and is ever changing to meet the requirements of both the home and foreign markets. The premises were built in the early part of the 20th century and prior to being used as a saw mill the site was occupied by the Wigan Coal & Iron Company Ltd., coal merchants, the manager being a Mr. Ormerod

Stove Equipment Ltd., Mart Lane

The founder of the firm was Mr. Griffiths and it was established in 1945. The firm's premises were situated in Mart Lane and were originally built by James Martland Ltd., who repaired barrels (coopering) there which were mainly used in their business to carry agricultural produce, especially potatoes. Subsequently, on acquiring the premises, Mr. Griffiths modified and improved the buildings to suit his own requirements and about 1960 he extended the works into Orrell Lane. Over 100 persons were employed at the works mainly engaged in the manufacture of industrial drying equipment. It is of interest to note that the first control panels (containing all the instrumentation) for the Atomic Energy Commission at Windscale, Cumberland, and similar equipment for France, Yugoslavia and Canada, were manufactured at this factory. In 1958 Brocklebank Ltd. occupied part of the premises but, in 1967, when they left Dewarance Controls Ltd., valve manufacturers, followed them and now they have gone and the site is occupied by Messrs. Cooper, Hect and Manning Brothers, manufacturers of light engineering equipment. The factory in Orrell Lane was kept on until 1965 and the premises were then taken over by Universal Steel Boilers and Plant Engineering Co. Ltd.

Lathom Fabrications, Briars Lane

Originally the site had been a brickfield and the land belonged to H. & R. Ainscough Ltd. Subsequently in the 1940s Mr. Harry Davis built the premises (at a cost of £400) and moved from Hall Lane, Lathom, where he had occupied Mr. Farrington's Old Smithy, to Briars Lane, where he built a forge. About 1946 Mr. Davis sold the premises to a Mr. Fry who was a panel beater and in 1947 the firm established as G. R. Pressings and was subsequently taken over by Mr. Restern. From January until November 1959 the firm was known as Lathom Dye Castings, but in December of that year the name was changed and the present name of Lathom Fabrications was adopted. The firm has a small labour force and specialises in the manufacture of motor vehicle silencers, mainly for the commercial market. Modifications and improvements to the existing building have been undertaken over the years and only recently the building has been extended.

ARI Sawmills, Burscough Road

This is a Swedish type sawmill which is capable of handling home-grown softwood logs with a minimum of labour and effort. The design and erection of the new mill was carried out by Mr. Robert H. Buckley of New Hey, Rochdale, and it is of interest to note that the mill was erected and running in a matter of four months. In fact, four months and two days after the first sod was cut in the stubble of an oat-field, the first log travelled up the log-haul into the new mill.

At this stage it would take too long to give a description of this factory but generally the mill follows the ARI (Swedish) design with certain special modifications to enlarge its usefulness.

The main mill is so designed that, at any time, a 23 feet wide extension can be added to house a bandmill installed to handle larger logs. The whole of the present installation is conveyored throughout and there are about five men in the main mill and four in the reclaiming mill. The conveyors were made by Ebor Engineering Co. Ltd., Littleborough from Mr. Buckley's designs and the sawdust extractor systems were made and installed by the Star Ventilating & Engineering Co. Ltd., Manchester. The lumber yard was laid out to suit the Iron Side-Fork Lift Truck operation.

The lumber produced is mainly for the production of boxes at the Burscough works in Platts Lane, where upwards of 7,000 boxes are produced each day. The Abbey Timber & Kiln Drying Co. have about 21 kilns available when they are required, the lumber being left in stick before use, but when required, the drying facilities of the kilns have to be used.

1950-1970

Over the last twenty years many more firms have established themselves in the Burscough area, some carrying on their work in premises of former industries, several of which I have already mentioned. Most of these later firms, unlike many of the former industries, are not dependent and in many ways are not related to agriculture. The size of the firms range from small family concerns involving two or three persons to several medium sized firms which employ two hundred or more persons. For reasons which I have already given at the beginning of this section, information concerning several industries was not available and, therefore, I shall attempt a fuller account of this period some time in the future.

Burscough Printing Works, Mill Lane

Mr. Taylor, the present owner of the works, commenced in business with Mr. Butterfield in premises behind Mr. Ford's sweets and tobacconist shop at 57a Liverpool Road, Burscough, on October 2nd 1951. As business increased it was found that larger premises were required and, therefore, Mr. Taylor began to look for other suitable accommodation, and in 1956 the works were removed to their present site in Mill Lane. In 1959 Mr. Butterfield left the firm. A small staff is employed at this works and they are chiefly engaged on printing literature and the like for many of the local firms.

Brocklebank's Ltd., Victoria Street

This firm was established in 1958 and originally occupied part of the premises belonging to Stove Equipment in Mart Lane. In 1967 they then moved to the premises previously occupied by Southport Cakes Ltd. in Victoria Street, this being their present location. There are two departments, viz: engineering and plastics and their main products are as follows: electrical equipment of various kinds, winding motors, fenders, mooring and marker buoys and plastic balls which are made in a variety of sizes and colour schemes to meet the demand that each new season seems to produce. Their distribution is far and wide and new markets are being sought as production increases. Since moving to their present site the buildings have had to undergo alteration and, in many instances, existing plant and machinery has had to be modified and in a factory of this type it is something which is a continuous process. The firm employs on average 25 persons in the plastics department and 40 in the engineering department.

Raisbank Engineering Company, Mart Lane

This firm was established about June 1968 and they supply bolts, nuts, screws and tools. Previously, the premises were occupied by Fleming Bros., precision engineers and tool makers who did centre lathe turning, milling, grinding and development work. These premises were originally known as the 'Old Smithy' which was built by Thomas Myers and subsequently taken over by James Martland Ltd., who still used the premises as a smithy for many years.

The Larger Firms

During the 1960s several medium-sized industries have been established in Burscough such as the following: Triangle Controls (belongs to the Dewrance Triangle Group) adjacent to James Martland's Ltd., Mart Lane. This firm was occupied by the firm known at Tate Jones which was established in Burscough in October 1965. The firm is mainly concerned with the making of valves.

Universal Bulk Handling Equipment Ltd.

Two more firms which have established themselves in Burscough during this period are Universal Bulk Handling Equipment Ltd., Orrell Lane and Westbrooks Ltd., Red Cat Lane. Both of these firms originated outside the Burscough area, but Universal Bulk Handling Equipment Ltd., which was founded in 1959 by the present Managing Director, Mr. W. J. Quirk in Burnley, established their main premises and head office at Burscough in 1961. In 1965 the premises which had been used by Stove Equipment were absorbed by the firm and in 1967 the firm extended its premises and at the present time the factory employs over 200 people.

Westbrooks Ltd.

This firm was founded in 1898 as J. C. Westbrook & Co. and subsequently as Westbrooks (Liverpool) Ltd. It was in 1944 that their business began to grow and they moved to new premises in Liverpool but in 1956, due to continued expansion brought about by increased demand, they moved to their new premises in Wigan Road, Ormskirk.

The present firm now specialises in the making of packaging materials which are used extensively in the manufacture of glassware, wines and spirits, foodstuffs and the like which need extra care and protection during transit. Over the years the demand increased to such a degree that further accommodation was sought and fortunately a site was acquired at Burscough (formerly the premises of T. H. Lavery & Co. Ltd.) and this branch of the factory was opened in 1964. At the time of writing about 100 people were employed at the Burscough factory.

Pilkington Bros., Lathom, (Research Centre)

Finally, in connection with industry and employment in the Burscough area, the development of the above firm is important. In 1961 Pilkington Bros., moved to Lathom where they built their Research Centre on a 160 acre site, the present building being in close proximity to the area once occupied by Lathom House, the seat of the Earl of Lathom which was demolished in 1925. The present site was purchased from the Ministry of Health.

Banking

Introduction

With the growth of agriculture and industry which were initially stimulated by the construction of the Leeds and Liverpool Canal in the 18th century and later by the development of the railways in the 1840s and 1850s, Burscough began to develop. Trade in agricultural produce with the Ormskirk, Liverpool and Preston markets grew in the 1840s and, as a result, a number of banks were established in this area in an attempt to facilitate exchange and provide funds or loans to help with the development of agriculture.

By the early part of the 19th century, several different types of bank had developed in this country, such as private banks, joint stock banks and savings banks. The latter type was the first to be introduced into Ormskirk, in June 1822. This type of bank (also known as Trustee Savings Banks) was established for a special reason to encourage thrift among small savers, and therefore would accept small sums of money as deposits. By 1825 a fund of £7,000 to £8,000 had accumulated, mainly from the poorer classes throughout the Ormskirk, Burscough, Lathom and other districts. Initially, the Savings Bank at Ormskirk only opened once a week, but by 1861 the bank was open every Saturday from six to eight o'clock p.m., and every Wednesday from two to four o'clock p.m., and these hours of opening remained unchanged until the early part of the 20th century.

Savings Bank, Burscough

This branch of the Ormskirk Trustee Savings Bank was opened on October 15th 1946 at 49 Liverpool Road North. The hours of business then were as follows: Tuesdays 2.30 p.m. till 4.30 p.m. and Fridays 10 a.m. till 12 noon. The bank was developed mainly because of the policy which was adopted by the then Trustees and Managers to provide every facility for the public to participate and help forward the National Savings effort. Since then the hours of opening have increased and the bank premises have recently undergone a complete change, especially the facade which has been faced with stone and a barrel shaped window put in, which is reminiscent of the more spacious and leisured days of the Georgian era.

Burscough Penny Bank

Savings banks were also called penny banks, but in this case it was something distinct and was associated with the Church of England Temperance Society and the Band of Hope. This bank was established in Burscough on 12th December 1859 and was therefore the first bank in Burscough. The Rev. W. Wannop was the founder of the Burscough Bridge Penny Bank and was largely responsible for its subsequent development. During the greater part of the bank's existence, Mr. Wannop remained the Chairman. The founder members, apart from Mr. Wannop, were Mr. William Peet who was the Treasurer and Mr. Saywell (Master of St. John's C. of E. School) who was the Secretary.

The Penny Bank was opened on Monday 2nd January 1860, and was situated in the infant school-room at St. John's C. of E. School. This bank was open on Mondays only, between the hours of 6 p.m. and 7 p.m. during the winter and the hours of 7 p.m. to 8 p.m. during the summer months. It was started to encourage thrift among the poor, and a very large amount of business was transacted during its existence. (In the first year there were 83 depositors).The main reason for the establishment of this Bank, however, was the payment of the school pence in connection with the day schools. This Penny Bank was a great help to the people of Burscough and it remained in use until the end of December 1895. When the Government gave the free grant, the children's school pence were saved.

Commercial Banks in Burscough

All the commercial banks in Burscough were established as sub-branches of branch banks which were initially established at Ormskirk.

Midland Bank

The Preston Banking Company was established in Ormskirk in 1857 and continued until 1894 when the Bank became known as the 'London and Midland Bank Ltd' (Preston Bank Branch). It was situated in what is today the offices of the U.D.C. in Burscough Street. Subsequently, about the late 1920s, it moved to its present location in Moor Street and in February 1908 a sub-branch of this bank was established at Burscough. The name of the bank was subsequently changed to London Joint City and Midland Bank Ltd., and in recent times the name Midland Bank has been adopted.

The Manchester and Salford Bank Ltd. (sub-branch at Burscough)

This bank was the first commercial bank to be established in Burscough and it was instituted in 1888. The first customer was Mr. John Hankin, chemist, Mill Lane, Lathom. The bank bears the date 1836, the date when the Manchester and Salford Bank Ltd. was established and is not the date the bank was erected.

In 1894 the Manchester and Salford Bank amalgamated with the old private bank of William Deacon and Co., London, which had been established since 1771 and had since become one of the principal banks of the Metropolis. From 1894 therefore, the Bank was known as William Deacon and Manchester and Salford Bank Ltd., and by 1904 was styled William Deacon's Bank Ltd. Today the bank is known as the William Glyns' Bank and is a member of the National and Commercial Bank Group.

Manchester and Liverpool District Banking Co. Ltd.

The head office of this bank was founded in 1829. A branch of this bank was established at Ormskirk on 26th July 1866 and the first Manager was Mr. W. H. Smith who had formerly been Manager of the Preston Bank. At first the bank was situated down Burscough Street, but in September 1874 the erection of the present bank near the railway bridge in Moor Street was begun and was opened on October 6th 1875. About 1920 a sub-branch office was opened at Burscough Bridge next to the present Trustee Savings Bank, but in 1967 the bank moved to its present location on the opposite side of the road; the former premises are now used as a ladies' fashion shop called 'Andred'. In 1969 the Westminster Bank and the National Provincial Bank (which already owned the District Bank and Coutts) merged and has since become known as the National Westminster Bank Ltd.

Westminster Bank Ltd.

This bank was founded in 1834 as the London and Westminster Bank and was established in Ormskirk in the late 1890s, but it was then known as Parr's Bank and was situated in its present location at the Market Cross. Subsequently, by the 1920s, the name of Parr's Bank was dropped and the name Westminster Bank was adopted. In 1922 a sub-branch was established at the Church Buildings, Burscough Bridge, but in 1969 when they merged with the District Bank they transferred to the same building as that of the District Bank and their former office is now occupied by Edward Jackson, auctioneer, estate agents, surveyors and valuers. Mr. Jackson is also the local agent for the Halifax Building Society.

The last commercial bank to be established in Burscough was Barclay's Bank, which was opened in 1956.

Skelmersdale Co-operative Society

This movement was founded in Skelmersdale in 1890 and, as the business grew, branches were established at St. Helens Road, Ormskirk, in 1897 and at Burscough in 1898. The Burscough branch was initially situated in Mart Lane on the corner facing the Burscough Football Ground but, as business grew, newer, larger premises were sought and these were found only a short distance away in Orrell Lane, where it remained until it closed in the 1960s.

After the Second World War, little improvement was made to the appearance of the Burscough branch until the late 1950s when the shop was modernised. However, with the development of the supermarkets and competition from other quarters, the Burscough branch eventually closed. Until August 1962 the Skelmersdale Co-operative Society continued under its own name but from then onwards their interests were absorbed by the St. Helens Society.

The development of banking in Burscough reflects to some degree the increase in trade and wealth and the extension of the sub-branches from Ormskirk and their date of establishment helps to mark the rate of progress in this direction. From the establishment of the first commercial bank in 1888 at Burscough up to the 1920s, banks remained open for less than 2 hours per day for only two and in some cases three days per week: for example in 1924 William Deacon's Bank opened on Monday and Wednesday from 10 a.m. till 12.30 p.m. and on Saturday from 10 a.m. till 11.30 a.m., but in the 1890s only opened on Wednesdays from 9.30 a.m. till 12.15 p.m. and on Saturdays from 9.30 a.m. till 11.30 a.m. Today most of the banks are open every weekday except Saturday, but extended hours of opening have been introduced on different days of the week to offset the inconvenience to customers. The frequency of opening of the banks also helps us to gauge the increase in trade and the establishment of Barclay's Bank in 1956 suggests that the process of growth is still continuing. All of the commercial banks, post office and the Trustee Savings Bank are situated along the main Liverpool-Preston road in the centre of Burscough Bridge and, to a degree, this area represents, in miniature, a retail structure which is characteristic of a central business district of a town.

Amusements and Entertainments

AMUSEMENTS, sports, recreations and entertainments of varying kinds have developed in this area in the past, some have survived and many have now disappeared. Many of the sports and pastimes which developed in the 17th, 18th and 19th centuries in this area were either seasonal or annual and were mainly associated with the land or hunting, and later in the 19th century were connected with agriculture. Some of the diversions which developed in the 19th century, such as agricultural and horticultural shows, I have already mentioned.

In an article written by the late Mr. James Bromley of the 'Homestead', Junction Lane, Burscough, well-known local antiquary in the early part of this century, it is stated:

'An example set by the Court of Charles II (1660) soon permeated all classes of society, including the clergy, amongst whom was the Vicar of Ormskirk they frequented the drinking bouts, cock fights and bowling matches of the period.'

One of the earliest sports appears to be that of horse racing which developed in this area of Lancashire during the latter part of the 17th century, mainly introduced by members of the Stanley family and their friends, who hunted in this area of Lancashire.

The earliest mention of racing at Ormskirk is recorded by the diarist Nicolas Blundell on October 15th 1703:

'I went to Ormsk: Race, five horses run and Mr Edw. Trafford woone'.

This would, therefore, make the Ormskirk race one of the first to be run in Lancashire.

It has been stated in some of the old accounts of these races that there were over 1,000 people attending, mostly on horse back, and there were many wealthier followers of the race who attended in carriages. In the latter half of the 19th century and probably a little earlier people from the Burscough and Lathom districts went at least once a year to watch the Grand National at Aintree by canal barge. By the beginning of the 20th century, however, there was a special boat which left from Moss's Yard, Lathom, which took people to the races at Aintree. From its deck the race could be observed and several important jumps such as the Canal Turn and Valentine's could be easily seen. It is highly probable, therefore, that people from this area attended Ormskirk Races on occasions during the 18th and early part of the 19th century.

Cock fighting is also mentioned in several contemporary accounts and was regarded in this neighbourhood as an important pastime or diversion (especially with regard to gambling). This was indulged in with great zeal by the inhabitants during the 17th, 18th and early part of the 19th centuries, and instances might be given of the lengths to which some lovers of the 'sport' would go rather than miss any chance of success in the cock fighting circles.

The Burscough coursing meetings

During the 1880s and 1890s coursing meetings were held at Burscough, and they took place on the land belonging to Mr. J. P. Berry, who was himself a keen sportsman. By the 1890s the coursing at Burscough had reached its peak and in October 1893 one of the best and most successful meetings took place. There was a 'Burscough Cup' associated with this event and three stakes, the Abbey Stakes, Farmers Stakes and Berry Stakes. At the conclusion of the coursing it was customary for all those connected with the meeting to sit down to a 'real coursing dinner', as it was called, at the Bull and Dog Inn. Mr. and Mrs. Edge were the proprietors at that time. Farming and the day's events were usually the topics of the evening's conversation and after all had been said they indulged in the singing of several songs, notably Nelson's 'Moss Lane', which apparently was sung at the close of every meeting which would not, therefore, have been complete without it.

The Burscough Coursing Club has now gone and the only coursing meeting of any significance that takes place today is at Altcar for the Waterloo Cup. It is of incidental interest to note that coursing affected the attendance of the children at school and the following was recorded in the St. John's C. of E. School log-book:

'1889 Nov. 1st — Coursing in village, hunting with greyhounds'.

The Lodge and dog kennels at Bath Farm

In former times Bath Wood occupied an area of just over 20 acres, but with the introduction of the Liverpool-Ormskirk-Preston Railway in 1849, part of the wood was destroyed. It was customary to build a small lodge on such land as indeed is the case at Bath Wood. At the present moment the Lodge belongs to Bath Wood Farm, but until the break up of the Cross Hall estate in July 1908, the Lodge, kennels and Bath House Farm and Bath Wood formed part of the estate.

The Cross Hall estate consisted of the area of the new park, Bath Wood, the Ruff and a large area of land surrounding Cross Hall. A junior branch of the Stanley family had held the estate on lease from the Earl of Derby since 1562. Unfortunately the Stanley documents connected with this area, which might have thrown some light on the activities in this area, have been lost. From numerous sources, however, I have been able to ascertain the use of the lodge and kennels.

The Lodge was probably built during the early part of the 18th century, and in the 1780s was occupied by a Mr. William Jones who leased the property from the Stanleys of Cross Hall. At that time there was no indication that the 'dog kennels' had been built and there was no reference to them in a survey of 1787. However, at some time between 1787 and the 1840s, the dog kennels as such were built. The Ordnance Survey map of 1845 names both the Lodge and the kennel, but gives no further information. By 1849 the Lodge was occupied by a Mr. William Valentine (lessee) who farmed the land surrounding the Lodge and the premises were described as a house and dog kennel, yard and garden. The field names which derive from this date also indicate that a pack of hounds did exist here and was no doubt used to hunt the fox. It is of interest to note that in Liverpool during the 1770s there was a pack of hounds kept as a subscription pack, called the 'Corporation Harriers' and the field near their kennel was called 'The Dog Kennel Field' or 'Field near the Dog Kennel'. The

The Lodge, photographed in 1958.

The Dog Kennel, photographed in 1969.

fields surrounding the Lodge at Burscough were called 'The Dog Kennel Hey'. Another significant point was the supply of water. Just why this was needed I do not know, but a stream called the 'Brook' flowed through the Liverpool Kennel and, in the early 1940s, the water from the Bath Brook flowed adjacent to the Lodge and around the dog kennel at Burscough. At the rear of the Burscough Kennel the field was called 'Dam Field', no doubt because from time to time the water would overflow. In effect it appears that the water was diverted from the Bath Brook as its natural flow united it with the Mill Dam and eventually with the Ellerbrook. When the railway was constructed, part of the Bath Brook was destroyed and the ditch which had been made to divert the water to the kennel dried up. It is of interest also to note that the small stretch of road which leads from the Lodge and kennel to the junction of the farm road was originally situated further north, near to the old pit and a small field road connected this with Dark Lane. It appears that permission for a road or way was given from Bath Farm to Dark Lane in 1755, part of which remained in use until the early part of the 20th century. About 90 years ago a small unfenced field road was made, which connected Bath Farm with Cross House (near the Priory ruins) and about the same time the present road which connects Bath Farm with Dark Lane was also made.

Today the Lodge and kennel remain in ruins and the former has not been lived in for some time. The last person to occupy the Lodge was an Irishman called Barney during the Second World War who, according to Rachel Knappet in her book 'A Pullet on the Midden', called it the 'cashel' (castle). The turretted roof, its isolated position and the surrounding wall do indeed give one the impression of a castle.

From the evidence available it appears that the Lodge during the greater part of its existence was used as a small farm, and the kennel adjacent was built around the latter part of the 18th century and was used to house fox-hounds, probably up to the 1840s. The hounds would be walked from the kennel to the meet and no doubt the familar cry of 'Tally-ho!', when the fox was sighted, was echoed over these fields in former times.

Bath Farm

It is said locally that the name Bath Farm originated from the fact that there was a Roman Bath here and on the Ordnance Survey map of 1845 'The Bath' is indicated. I have been shown the supposed site of the bath by the present owner but the area is covered by buildings and it would require expert archaeological inspection to prove this assertion either one way or the other. A spring has existed here since ancient times and is indicative of early settlement. Until the water-works were built in the 19th century, the spring was active and the water was of good quality. In the *Illustrated Handbook to Ormskirk and the Neighbourhood,* by George Lea (pub. 1893), appears a photograph of the bath spring, showing Mrs. Alty obtaining water from the spring. There was a bowling green at Bath Farm in the 18th century but this appears to have been destroyed when the farm road was made to the Lodge during the early part of the 19th century. This was probably the first bowling green in Burscough and would probably have been used by the local gentry. Bowling was a very popular pastime among the gentry and nobility, but it was only in the late 19th century that the labouring classes in Burscough started to indulge in this sport.

Preston Guild

There is very little evidence of what took place in Burscough during the 17th and 18th centuries in connection with the Preston Guild, but during the 19th century it was regarded as a time for recreation and for several days all work seems to have stopped. This appears to have been the case at other places as well, for in Blackburn in 1862 a holiday was declared in consequence of the procession of the trades at the Preston Guild. The following entry, which appeared in the St. John's C. of E. School log-book in 1882, shows what effect the Preston Guild had in this area, even at that late date:

'1882 Sept. 6th — School closed on account of Preston Guild, the works in the village being stopped'.

Pigeon Shooting and Gun Club

This was an annual event which was established as a club at Burscough in 1852. The shoot took place at Mr. John Norris's Red Lion Inn at Burscough. The event usually took place in December and in 1859 the prize was a 'fat bullock', valued at £15. The winner had the choice of the money or the bullock. Each member had to shoot at 5 birds. Single barrelled guns had to shoot 1½oz. of shot at 19 yards rise. The boundary was 80 yards and the gun was to be held in 'a sportsmanlike manner' until the bird was on the wing. The shooting commenced at eleven o'clock in the morning and, the day following the main shoot, a sweepstake of 10 shillings was run for novices who had to shoot at 3 birds each, the weight of shot etc. being the same as the above. This club was promoted by Mr. James Berry for many years and it continued until the 1890s.

Skating

Skating was popular among the local people of Burscough and when, during the 1840s to 1870s, flooding was more frequent than today and the winters were more severe, competitions were arranged. These competitions attracted a large number of spectators and in January 1871 a skating competition took place on the Burscough Mill Dam.

Bowling

As I have already mentioned, bowling was a popular pastime in the 18th century among the gentry and nobility and, in the 19th century, the Earl of Lathom built a bowling alley at Lathom House (about the 1870s). The wood for this came from America, no doubt after his visit there in 1873 when the Earl purchased a celebrated shorthorn for about £7,000 at the New York mill sale at Utica. A score book was kept at Lathom and many famous people including royalty played there.

It was not until the 1890s, however, that the first bowling club was established at Burscough. Founded in April 1893 at the Cambridge Hotel, the Cambridge Bowling Club held its first meeting on 19th April of that year. In 1893 there were 60 members and the following prizes, which were given on 13th July 1893, may be of interest:

1st Prize: a pair of trousers.
2nd Prize: set of carvers.
3rd Prize: a sack of flour presented by Mr. T. Peet.

The second bowling club to be formed was the Lathom Bowling Club at the Junction Hotel, Burscough, in September 1895. In that year, the club had over 40 members.

Subsequent bowling clubs were established at most of the inns and public houses in the Burscough and Lathom area but, unfortunately, most of these have now gone and have been replaced by car parks, which, although necessary, are not as picturesque.

Cricket

Cricket did not develop in this district until the 19th century, the first club being founded at Ormskirk in 1825. The first record of a match being played was in 1853, when Ormskirk easily defeated Southport. In this match, Lord Skelmersdale, who afterwards became the the first Earl of Lathom, made seven runs for Ormskirk.

Burscough first appears to have enjoyed a game of cricket even later, for I can find no record earlier than September 1870 when Burscough played against Ormskirk. The match took place at Ormskirk Dyers Lane (known as Elm Place Factory Field). The early games were probably played adjacent to the vicarage or near to St. John's C. of E. School, School Lane. The area of Victoria Park was not used at that time and the land then belonged to the Earl of Derby and was farmed and occupied by a Mr. William Spencer. Mart Lane was only developed in 1887 when James Martland Ltd. built their new premises there and obtained the area of land now known as Victoria Park. It is interesting to note that during Queen Victoria's Jubilee celebrations in 1887 a treat was given to the old people of the village, and festivities of various kinds were laid on for the children on a field in Moss Lane, which was lent by Mr. James Martland. Subsequently, cricket was played at Victoria Park at the beginning of the 20th century and in 1921 a new cricket pitch was laid on the vicarage field, Liverpool Road, belonging to the St. John's C. of E. Cricket Club, but this has now gone. The cricket pitch at Victoria Park is still there.

Football

Throughout the first half of the 20th century, football was probably the most popular sport in Burscough, and the team has provided football of a high standard.

The first match which the Burscough team played was on December 9th 1880 against Croston. The game was played at Burscough and the result was a 3-0 victory for Burscough. According to the report, the game was very fast and the backs and forwards had plenty to do and the Burscough forwards showed some very fair passing, especially during the latter half of the game.

In the early days before the Burscough Rangers emerged in 1906, the Burscough team belonged to the Liverpool and District Amateur Football League in 1898 and at that time there were four teams: Burscough 1st, Burscough Reserve, Burscough Swifts and Burscough White Star. New Lane also had a team at that time but they belonged to the Southport and District Amateur League. In 1898 the Burscough Swifts were 4th in the League.

These early Burscough teams did not play on Victoria Park, but on various fields in the Burscough area. The first team usually played on a piece of land

Burscough Rangers A.F.C. 1925-26

Back Row *(from left): H. Prescott (Groundsman), W. Lyon, W. Ashurst, G. Porter, W. Bennett, W. Martland, G. Cunningham, W. Johnson (chairman), H. Green, A. Forrest and E. Collins (known as Uncle Ernie to everyone) (hon. treasurer).*

Front row: *T. Gregson (trainer), W. Martindale, W. Green, T. Pye, A. Kemp (captain), N. Rawlins, J. Cookson, E. Chapburn and J. P. Sturgees (hon. sec.).*

Burscough Football Club 1951

Left to right (standing) — Stone, London, McGrail, Sutton, Brennan, Steve Jones, Mr. J. Baldwin (trainer).

Seated — Aspinall, Woods, Lynn, Heath and S. J. Jones.

Leisure in the grand style. The billiard room of Sefton House, Junction Lane, Burscough during Mr. Kellet's time there. Below, the house itself.

belonging to Mr. Walker which was used as a recreation field, which I have mentioned in connection with the Burscough Show of 1898. Travis's field in Higgin's Lane was used by Burscough Reserve up to about 1921, and the area now occupied by Mr. Barker's premises was also used for a short time. The New Lane team played on land adjacent to the canal bridge at New Lane.

Victoria Park was owned for many years by Messrs. James Martland Ltd., but in 1951 the club decided to purchase the ground and stand (which held about 400 persons and was acquired from Everton F.C. in 1926) at Victoria Park.

In 1906 the Burscough Rangers F.C. was formed and the club earned a reputation for producing players who made the grade in English League football. As the club progressed, they won many competitions, cups, medals and other trophies, and in 1927 they decided to go into the Lancashire Combination. They started to lose matches, however, gates declined and in 1933 they were in financial difficulties and the club was eventually wound up.

The Burscough Ordnance Stores also developed a football team in the 1890s which competed with local teams and they also held a military sports meeting at Burscough annually in the 1890s.

St. John's Cricket, Tennis and Croquet Club, Liverpool Road.

This club, which was opened in May 1922, was another of the social activities connected with St. John's Church. On the day of the opening, a large crowd had gathered at the vicarage field, Burscough, to witness the ceremony of opening the new pavilion and ground of the St. John's Cricket and Tennis Club.

About 1919 some of the lands in Burscough belonging to Lord Derby were sold and the vicarage field, part of the Derby estate, was also put up for sale. The trustees of St. John's Church purchased the field with a view to developing it as a recreation ground and work in that direction was proceeded with straight away. Initially two tennis courts were laid at the east corner and in 1932 a new cricket pitch was laid down in the centre of the field. The sods for the courts and cricket pitch were given by Mr. Marsden. The pavilion itself was erected voluntarily by members and friends under the direction of the Hon. Secretary of the Cricket Club, Mr. John Spencer, who was a great cricket enthusiast. The pavilion was originally an army hut which, when transformed, met the requirements of the club. There were two sets of dressing rooms for each club with all other necessary accommodation including a cellar underneath for the storage of tennis and cricket equipment. A verandah running along two sides completed the headquarters for the two clubs.

The Tennis Club was opened by the Hon. Mrs. Hamilton Smith, of Sefton House. Mr. Frank Wells was President and Miss Jacques was the Hon. Secretary.

The cricket portion of the pavilion was opened by Mr. William Wells, who represented the trustees of St. John's Church. Mr. William Wells had been a member of the St. John's Cricket Club for over 20 years.

Additions and alterations were made over the years and in August 1950 the Tennis and Croquet Club laid two hard courts which were officially opened by Major Frank Wells.

Times change, however, and the cricket and tennis pavilion has gone, the vicarage field was sold in the 1960s for building purposes and has since become Peters Avenue and Christine Crescent. The tennis courts and croquet ground are still there, but in a disused and delapidated state, being now no more than waste ground.

Carnival Gala

For a number of years the Burscough Rangers held their Carnival at the Stanley Institute, and in 1923 over 200 attended. It may be of interest to note that the first Burscough Carnival Gala took place in August 1930 in an effort to assist the Rangers Football Club. The effort was launched by a newly formed committee of the Burscough Rangers, who were assisted by a loyal and hard working ladies committee.

The event took place on Saturday 12th August 1930 and the procession left Victoria Park, Mart Lane, at 2 p.m. There were various entries from tradesmen in the form of tableaux etc., and there were jazz bands and morris dancers from all parts of Lancashire and Cheshire. The streets of Burscough were gaily decorated with carnival bunting, especially in Mart Lane, Orrell Lane, Victoria Street, Lord Street, Stanley Street and Red Cat Lane, Council Avenue.

In 1946 the Burscough Football Club (known as the Linnets) was formed, and since that time they have achieved a number of outstanding performances.

During the second season, in 1948, they won the Lancashire Junior Cup, the Liverpool Challenge Cup and the George Mahon Cup, and two years later they won the Lancashire Junior Cup and the League Championship. In 1951 they again won the Liverpool Challenge Cup by defeating St. Helens Town 3-1 at Springfield Park. They also reached the semi-final stages of the Liverpool Non-League Senior Cup and the George Mahon Cup. In November 1959, Burscough reached the 1st Round of the Amateur F.A. Cup against Crewe; the attendance was 4,200, the gate £412 and the result was 3-1 for Crewe. The Burscough Football and Social Club (which cost over £6,000) was opened on June 22nd, 1963, by Councillor S. C. Jones at Victoria Park.

Pigeons

The keeping of racing pigeons in the Burscough area has been popular for many years and the Burscough Homers Club was founded in 1918 with three members. Mr. Ashton was one of the founders of the club and Mr. J. Lewis was the secretary, and one of the early presidents was a Mr. F. J. Ainscough.

In their annual report for 1924 the club represented 18 lofts owned by 27 members and no matter where their members were sent, they were able to hold their own. They topped the Ormskirk Amalgamation on several occasions, whilst out of ten specials for the young bird racers connected with the Amalgamation, no fewer than six found their way to the members of the Burscough Club.

Many more races have since taken place and the sport is still popular today and during the first half of the 20th century the railway played an important part, both in this country and on the Continent. Pigeons were transported to various stations where they were realeased at a certain time and during the continental flights special railway vans for this purpose were provided. Since the 1950s, road transport has gradually absorbed most of this traffic, and there has been a corresponding drop in pigeon traffic handled by the railways.

The racing of pigeons in this area developed during the latter half of the 19th century (c.1890) and during this period the Ormskirk and District Homing Society and the Burscough Flying Club developed. One of the early secretaries of the Burscough Flying Club was Mr. T. Nicholson of Burscough.

Today there are many pigeon enthusiasts in this area and their lofts (of varying sizes) can be seen dotted here and there in the Burscough district. A good example of such a loft can be seen along High Lane at the residence of the late Mr. Bruce Smith.

Inns, public houses and beer houses

Inns and taverns have been meeting places since ancient times and their function is probably best described by the following line from Samuel Johnson:

'. . . there is nothing which has yet been contrived by man by which so much happiness is produced as by a good tavern or inn.'

The names of Inns and Taverns usually give one an indication as to some previous activity and nearly all have a story to tell. However, there are certain difficulties which arise such as change of name, due largely to amalgamation or to some personal whim of the owner in times past. Nicknames are also attributed to many inns throughout the country and very often no light can be thrown on the origin of the nickname.

Throughout their lives, inns have performed a multiplicity of services apart from their normal function of providing beer and the like. They have provided the local area with the following services and facilities: various local clubs and societies have made the inn their meeting place, e.g. gun club, pigeon club, cow club, bowling club, coursing club, darts, dominoes, bridge, whist, snooker etc. They have provided rooms for coroners inquests; served as meeting places of the court leet and the court baron; they have been used for concerts; the annual dinner of a firm or other celebrations have also been undertaken at the local inns and many of the older inns such as the Wheat Sheaf (now demolished) in Ormskirk were used as posting stations, excise offices, and hostelries and they were the centres used for the payment of the various charities and doles and have since been used as centres for Friendly Societies and they were invariably used for auctions.

The inns and public houses of Burscough have largely developed along the transport routes of road, railway and canal, with which they have been intimately connected or associated in some way during their existence.

The oldest inns and public houses in Burscough are situated along the Liverpool to Preston main road (A59) and they are as follows: The Bull and Dog Inn (Burscough Town), The Red Lion Inn (Burscough Town), The Packet House Hotel (now the Admiral Lord Nelson, Burscough Bridge) and the Black Horse (Burscough Town). These inns and public houses were established in the 18th century and they all exist as such today, with the exception of the Black Horse which is now used as a shop belonging to Mr. Green.

The Bull and Dog is the oldest inn and was established over 250 years ago, and in 1753 a Mr. Goore was the victualler there. Up to the 1890s the Bull and Dog was regarded as the centre of Burscough and most of the older pastimes of coursing, pigeon shooting, ploughing matches and the like were associated with the place. There are many public houses and inns which bear the name Bull or Dog in their titles and these refer to the sport of bull baiting which was very popular in this area and elsewhere during the 17th and 18th centuries.

In former times the court leet was held at the Bull and Dog and old records such as the court rolls were kept there, and in 1901 these were discovered in an old oak chest there. The chest had not been opened since the old charity school was re-modelled and the contents of the chest were finally removed to the muniment room at Knowsley.

The Bull and Dog Inn is an old hostelry and, like the other three inns in Burscough during the latter part of the 18th and early part of the 19th century, charities were distributed there. These charities were mainly Houghton's and Sutch's charities and the number of people receiving benefits fluctuated between 50 and 90 and the amounts paid varied from 1/6d to 6/ – per person. The Friendly Societies later developed in this area and in 1842 the 'Oddfellows' established a lodge at the Bull and Dog Inn which was called the John Bull Lodge and is still in existence today.

Auctions were held at the Bull and Dog Inn and the Packet House Hotel, especially during the first half of the 19th century, and they were usually concerned with the selling of land and agricultural premises. In 1801 the Bull and Dog was sold by auction to Richard Reynolds who purchased the inn from Mr. Edward Baldwin who then had possession of the premises. During the 1820s a Mr. Cooper Tyrer was the victualler but by the 1840s the inn was owned by Robert Edge, whose family held the Bull and Dog Inn for nearly a century, and in 1947 the inn was sold for £20,000. Over the years the inn has been altered and modified, but many of the outbuildings remain largely untouched. During the early part of the 20th century a bowling green was established here but this has now gone.

The Black Horse Public House was probably named after one of the horses which raced at the Ormskirk races or, as was common during the 18th century, was named in honour of Dick Turpin's mount Black Bess. It is probable that activities at this pub were similar to those at the Bull and Dog, and during the early part of the 19th century, charities were certainly distributed from here also. In the 1820s a Mr. Richard Martland was the victualler and in the 1840s Edward Smith underlet the Black Horse to Thomas Charnock and by the 1850s it was occupied by William Valentine. By the 1870s, however, Hugh Sherrington, who formerly had a beer shop next to the old Burscough Town School, took over the Black Horse Inn. Since the 1870s it has ceased to be a public house and has subsequently been known as the Pear Tree Cafe and is now known as Green's Confectionery and Greetings Card Shop.

The Red Lion is a common name for many public houses throughout England and as such is not related to any local event or tradition in this area. I have already mentioned its connection with the cow club and there was a small brewery here in the 1870s. Charities were again distributed from here and in 1838 the Oddfellows established their 'Rose of England Lodge' at the Red Lion. However, the Oddfellows later moved to the Royal Hotel and subsequently to their present venue at the Stanley Institute. During the 1820s Thomas Fletcher was the victualler, being followed by Ann Watkinson and subsequently by Mr. John Norris who developed the small brewery and cow club there. Subsequent victuallers have occupied the Red Lion, but they are too numerous to mention here.

The Packet House Hotel was established here in the latter part of the 18th century about 1775 and was associated with the development of the canal. Its original name was 'The Bridge Inn' which was used until about the 1830s when the name Packet House was introduced.

The name Bridge was probably associated with the canal bridge which was built adjacent to the inn during the 1770s (the original bridge has long since gone) and which was also associated with the development of the turnpike road in 1771.

The name Packet House is synonymous with the packet boats which plied along the canal from the 1770s to 1855, and therefore the application of the name is obvious. About 1865, however, when Mr. James Thorougood took over the Packet House Inn, he changed the name to 'The Grapes', which he retained until about 1873, when he re-introduced the name 'The Bridge'. When Mr. Thorougood built the Royal Hotel about 1874-85, the name Packet House was again adopted and remained until recently, when it was renamed the Admiral Lord Nelson and another piece of Burscough history was lost.

There was an hostelry here for many years and in the early part of the 19th century it was looked after by John Parr and Co., chaise owners. Similar activities to the other inns were engaged in here and a revival of the old court leet was developed at the beginning of the 20th century.

Again charities were distributed here at the beginning of the 19th century, but a Friendly Society does not appear to have developed here. Concerts were held in times past, especially when a Mr. Abram was the victualler there during the 1790s and early 19th century. Auctions were also held at this inn on the same lines as at the Bull and Dog.

At most of these older inns, alterations, additions and other modifications have taken place and much of the original structures have either gone or have been masked by other materials.

The New Inn. The house at the junction of Pippin Street and the Liverpool to Preston main road (A59), which is occupied by Mrs. Bruce Smith and now known as the 'Manor House', was formerly called the New Inn. However, just whether this house was ever used as an inn is difficult to establish, for even in 1801 when it was sold, it was not described as a public house but was called 'New Inn Estate' which contained about 9 acres which was in the possession of Richard Reynolds, It is interesting, however, to note that Richard Reynolds bought the Bull and Dog Inn and he sold the New Inn to a Mr. John Jones in the same year. For well over 150 years the house has been used as a farm, and in the 20th century has undergone much alteration.

The Anchor Inn (Subsequently named the 'Timbobbin'). This inn was again situated near to the site of the former Burscough Priory along Dark Lane and has not been used as an inn for over 120 years. It is of interest to note that this name, 'The Anchor', also has a religious significance and although it is associated with the sea, the 'anchor' was mainly a religious emblem. More relevant here, however, is the fact that an *anker* was a measure of ale, and the name of this and many other public houses almost certainly derives from that. Only a short distance from the former Anchor Inn is a little house named Cross House which is adjacent to the road leading to the Priory and at whose corner is the base of the old Burscough Priory Cross. This name no doubt was adopted on account of its proximity to this ancient cross and the Priory.

The 'Red Cat' — A mythical public house

Perhaps the most unusual street name in Burscough is Red Cat Lane; its origins are obscure. This road was not called Red Cat Lane in the 1840s and 1850s, but was classified as a public road and was part of Back Moss Lane. The name Red Cat Lane was adopted in the 1860s and it has been suggested that the beerhouse of Jane Rylance (now demolished) could have been called the Red Cat Inn, but I could not find any evidence to support this in all the ale house returns and other sources either in the 18th, 19th or early 20th century. However, the lack of documented evidence could have arisen from the fact that these beerhouses did not require a magisterial licence. In this area there was a field called Red Cock Heyes, where cock fighting no doubt was practised, and at the Bull and Dog there are fields called the Bull and Dog Heyes where bull baiting would have taken place in the 18th century. It is therefore at least possible that 'Red Cat' is a corruption of 'Red Cock'.

Sometimes nicknames were attributed to many places such as the 'Green Window Shuts' which was on the corner of Martin Lane and Lord's Gate Lane. (The house and part of the lanes were demolished when the aerodrome was built in the 1940s). This name, according to Mr. Richard Riley, who is over 80 and who lived there for some time, said that his uncle Peter put some window shutters up which he painted green, the reason being to prevent children passing by from throwing stones at the window; subsequently, the house has always been referred to as the 'Green Window Shuts'. There is another little stone house down Red Cat Lane which has also been put forward as the supposed Red Cat Inn, which was occupied by the Martindale family for a long time. In the 1830s, 40s and 50s I can say that only one beerhouse or inn existed along Red Cat Lane and that was the one run by Jane Rylance. The name Martindale does not appear in any lists or directories in the 19th century or early part of the 20th century as owning, occupying or carrying on the trade of a victualler and, therefore, at this stage does not appear to be the inn in question.

The Scutcher's Arms (junction of Flax Lane and Blythe Lane). This has been described in the previous chapter, in the section dealing with the Lathom Flax Mill.

Junction Hotel (near Burscough Junction railway station). The site of the Junction Hotel in 1846 was owned by a Mr. Hugh Forshaw, but was occupied by a Mr. John Bridge. At that time the premises were only used as a house, which had outbuildings, garden and fold. However, with the introduction of the railway, the house became a beerhouse about 1850 and John Bridge was the first victualler. The name Junction was not adopted until the 1850s when Mr. Richard Blaco was the victualler, and it appears that the name Junction Lane was also adopted at this time, it being formerly called Green Lane.

The second bowling club in this area was established here in 1895, but the green has now gone, having been converted into a car park.

This photograph shows the front of the Scutcher's Arms, with Mr. and Mrs. Garner and their children together with Mr. Fletcher, in about 1905.

A photograph of the Stanley Institute taken about 1919.

The distribution of charities did not take place here, but on January 16th 1883, 'The Royal Lathom and Burscough Tontine Friendly Society' was established at Mr. Pilkington's Junction Hotel. On that day upwards of 50 members were enrolled, and the secretary was Mr. Francis Thierens of Square Lane, Lathom.

Various other activities similar to those already mentioned at other public houses took place, and in recent times Chrysanthemum Shows were held here. The Junction Hotel, therefore, began life as a house, later became a beerhouse and subsequently an hotel, and during that time has undergone much alteration and additions to meet the requirements of today's customers.

Royal Hotel. This hotel was built by Mr. James Thorougood about 1874-1875 who was also the first victualler there for over 14 years. The name Royal is not associated with any local activity and appears to have been chosen by Mr. Thorougood himself. Originally, and for many years afterwards, Mr. Thorougood brewed his own beer on premises adjacent to the Packet House and he supplied most of the inns in this area with beer. Subsequently in 1896 he floated the concern known as Thorougood's Breweries, but this has now gone.

Again charities were not distributed from this inn, but the 'Royal' Tontine Friendly Society was established there on 10th January 1883. It was also announced on that occasion that persons from the age of 16 to 45 years would be admitted free until 31st March, 1883. The secretary was Mr. Peter Hulme of Mill Lane Lathom. The Oddfellows 'Rose of England' Lodge also met there for some time before moving to their present location at the Stanley Institute.

The Cambridge Hotel. Before the Cambridge Hotel was built in the 1860s, the land had been occupied partly by what was then Red Cat Lane and a small beerhouse run by Jane Rylance and some outbuildings belonging to a Mr. Richard Blacks. Subsequently the route of the road was changed on the introduction of the railway in 1855 and a new entrance to Red Cat Lane was made over the railway bridge, which is its present position.

The name of the Cambridge Hotel was not used until after 1872 and I attribute this to the visit of Princess Mary of Cambridge and her husband, Prince Teck, who arrived at Ormskirk in October 1872 and were guests of Lord and Lady Skelmersdale at Lathom House. The following day they visited Southport, where the Princess Mary laid the foundation stone of the Cambridge Hall. In this connection it is quite probable that Mr. Thorougood named his hotel the 'Royal' in opposition to the Cambridge, a practice which was not uncommon with inns during the 18th and 19th centuries.

It was at the Cambridge Hotel that the first bowling club was established in this area in 1892. Charities were not paid out there, but the 'Loyal Order of Ancient Shepherds' was established at the Cambridge Hotel in 1870.

Beerhouses

In 1830 when the duty on beer was repealed, the trade was thrown open, and the sale of beer was permitted in a new class of houses, under licences obtained from the Excise. Each licence cost £2-2s.-0d. and permitted the sale by retail of beer, ale, porter, cider, perry and, in this area, ginger beer. It was not necessary for the licensee to have a magisterial licence, but he was required to enter into bond with sureties for the payment of any penalty incurred by him for any breach of the provisions of the Act and the regulations of the police. In 1869, however, the policy of the Beerhouse Acts was reversed, and licences to retail beer under those Acts were limited to persons authorised by the Justices of the Peace to receive such licences. After 1869 many of these beerhouses closed.

During the period 1830-1836 six beerhouses were established in the township of Burscough and some of these would be given nicknames by the local inhabitants. I cannot at this stage give detailed descriptions or exact locations because time and space does not permit. I have already mentioned three of these beerhouses: Sherrington's Beerhouse near the Burscough Town School, Jane Rylance's Beerhouse near the present Cambridge Hotel and the Beerhouse of John Bridge which subsequently became the Junction Hotel. Other beerhouses were situated as follows: Stock's Beerhouse, Moss Lane, Reynold's Beerhouse, Crabtree Bridge, James Forshaw's, approximately where the disused washing machine shop stands today at Burscough Bridge.

These beerhouses or beer shops just mushroomed up during the 1830s and 1840s in this area, especially along the canal; for example at New Lane no fewer than four beerhouses existed, two of which were situated in close proximity to the New Lane canal bridge and several existed at the Top Locks. It is of interest to note that the Ship Inn which is situated along Wheat Lane (originally Wet Lane) in close proximity to the Top Locks was originally a beerhouse. In the 1840s the site of the Ship Inn was owned by a Mr. George Radcliffe and was occupied by a Mr. John Walmsley, but at that date it appears to have only been used as a house. In the 1850s it became a beerhouse, but only took the name of the Ship Inn about the 1880s. The name Ship Inn is, of course, one of the commonest and oldest names for a public house in England and the name was probably chosen because of its proximity to the canal and the association of boat-building in this area. However, the local people refer to the inn by the nickname of 'Blood Tub' but just how this was arrived at is not known. It might have been given to the inn when it was a beerhouse and could be associated either with a particular outstanding incident, for instance a fight in which someone was killed or the sport of cock fighting which may have taken place there during the last century.

The average number of people convicted of drunkenness per annum in Burscough during this period was 35, over 95% of whom were men, and there was much concern about the amount of drinking on and off the premises of licensed houses. During the 1880s the local branch of the Church of England Temperance Society gave much encouragement and help in developing coffee and cocoa houses and in January 1883 the Burscough Cocoa Rooms were established.

The Burscough Cocoa Rooms

The first suggestion of the establishment of a cocoa room in Burscough was put forward by Mr. Williamson of Burscough Junction in 1879.

The rooms were opened by the Hon. Miss Bootle-Wilbraham on 23rd January 1883 and the premises were situated near to the Burscough Bridge railway station on the main road from Liverpool to Preston. What had formerly been used as a shop by a Mrs. Stock was converted into a general bar and, leading from this room, was another room which was furnished as a 'bar parlour'. In this room were four tables with marble tops and several chairs, and newspapers were also provided so that anyone wishing to spend an evening in the public house (without the drink) would find there all they required.

Mrs. Bootle-Wilbraham paid the entire cost of establishing the Cocoa Rooms and placed a sum in the bank for future contingencies as well as paying the rent for two years. The Cocoa Rooms were run by a Mrs. Maud Swift until 1888 when it appears to have closed down.

The next refreshment room to be established in Burscough was by Mrs. Hugh Culshaw about 1908 in the premises now occupied by the Trustee Savings Bank. In September 1890 a Mr. Roger Culshaw opened the first potato chip shop at Burscough Bridge, the second being opened about 1902 by Mr. John Houldings (known locally as 'Chippy John'). The latter shop was situated partly where Moss's Electrical and Eastwood's shops are off Lord Street today. Several persons occupied the shop after Mr. Houldings, and it was finally occupied by Mr. Eastwood, a brother of the present Mr. Eastwood, who now has the shoe shop.

The Stanley Institute and its associations

By 1901 the population of Burscough had risen to 2,752 and, with the reduction in the hours of work, the improved educational facilities available and the gradually improving social conditions of housing and especially sanitation, it was felt that there was a need for a village or public hall where the people of Burscough could meet.

During the greater part of the 19th century, the inns, public houses, taverns and beerhouses of Burscough were the main meeting places, and as we have seen, they performed a multiplicity of services apart from their function of selling beer and the like. Concerts, dances, bazaars, meetings and a variety of other activities during this period were also catered for by all the schools in this area, and on many occasions one of the assembly rooms at either the Bull and Dog or the Packet House Hotel were used for concerts.

During the early 1860s an annual concert was held at a Mr. Holmes's large Assembly Room Burscough Bridge, and it was known as 'Mr. Watt's Annual Concert'.

At this date I have so far been unable to locate where this assembly room was, but the evidence seems to point to the Packet House Hotel.

The forerunner of the Stanley Institute, the Burscough Reading Room

During the 1870s and before, several attempts had been made to establish working men's clubs in Burscough, but the basis on which it was proposed to start them was such as did not commend itself to the working men themselves.

The residents at Burscough, and particularly the working men employed at Burscough Bridge by the year 1880, expressed their desire and long-felt need for a place where they could meet after the labours of the day for the purpose of reading and instruction. Their need was at last supplied on October 21st 1881 when the Burscough Reading Room was opened by Mr. James Bromley. The plans for establishing a reading room were put forward in June 1881, but one of their main problems was the finding of a suitable meeting place apart from a public house. Ultimately a room adjoining the canal bridge at Burscough was offered to them by Mr. James Thorougood, at a nominal rent, and although the room adjoined the hotel it had no connection with the house and access could be obtained to the room without going into the inn. Similarly to the development of previous institutions in this area, the funds needed to decorate and prepare the room were raised by subscription and the sum of £58-15s.-9d. was raised. Upwards of 60 persons initially enrolled themselves as members and, after meeting all the necessary commitments, the treasurer was left with a balance of £11. In addition to contributing subscriptions, several gentlemen promised to supply the rooms with papers and periodicals, to which the committee added others so that about 39 newspapers and magazines were regularly supplied to the room. There were also various games such as darts, draughts, chess etc., and in 1883 a full-sized billiard table was purchased out the funds.

As time went on membership grew but owing to the size of the room the membership was limited to 100 and, therefore, newer premises were sought. In 1899 enquiries were made about the present site of the Stanley Institute and on 25th March of that year the land was leased by the Earl of Derby to the Stanley Institute Society.

By 1899 the Burscough Reading Rocms had saved £450, but this soon rose to £500: of the latter amount, £450 was contributed towards the erection of the new building and £50 was retained for contingencies. The old Burscough Reading Room was worked on the broadest basis, no man being asked about his religion or politics, but simply required to behave himself.

The present building, which is situated along the main Liverpool to Preston road (A59) and occupying part of Trevor Road, was commenced in 1899 and completed in 1902. The sole contractors were Messrs. A. K. Irving & Sons of Southport, the architect being Mr. H. E. Peach, also of Southport. It was erected at a cost of £3,903-12s.-4d., of which the sum of £2,000 was donated by the Earl of Derby and various other donations amounted to over £1,065; the remaining £838 was collected by public subscription. The furnishing and the completion of the bowling green in 1903 cost a further £700, thus bringing the total cost of the building, furnishing, bowling green and other fixtures to just over £4,600. On the day of the opening the main hall had seating accommodation for over 400 people and there were a number of other rooms suitable for social gatherings, lectures etc., and a large and small billiard room, refreshment bar etc. Adjacent to the building a house was built for the caretaker, in addition to a two stalled stable, cycle shed, and at the rear of the building the bowling green was laid out, being completed in 1903.

This institution was established for the purpose of providing instruction and mental improvement for all classes with no regard to sect or party politics and with no intoxicating drinks — a place where they could meet for reading, conversation, amusement and general social intercourse.

At the right of the principal entrance is a memorial tablet which was unveiled by Lord Derby and bears the following inscription:

> 'Stanley Institute. This building, erected for the instruction and recreation of the inhabitants of the district, was opened on Oct. 1st., 1902 by the Right Honourable Frederick, Earl of Derby K.G.'

The First Ball

This event took place on November 14th 1902 and was held in the 'Constance Derby' Hall from 8 p.m. till 2 a.m. the following morning. Duckworth's (late Ormisher's) Band was engaged, and the tickets (which were limited) were sold for 2/6d. single and 4/6d. double.

Subsequently, after the cinema was established in 1913, these Balls became known as the 'Cinema Balls' and they were held annually on New Year's Eve. One or two days prior to New Year's Eve, the Children's Ball was given. The arrangements were undertaken by Mr. Jack Horrocks, the proprietor of the cinema. On these occasions the main hall was gaily decorated and brilliantly illuminated. A fancy-dress dance was usually the order of the day and all the leading film companies sent prizes for the competition. On some occasions the staff of the cinema also presented prizes. Dancing commenced at 6.30 p.m. and went on until 11 p.m. and on average about 300 children always attended. The Burtonians Band played on many occasions and light refreshments were served free to all. The last of these Children's Balls was held in 1938 and nothing quite like them has been held since. It was the custom from 10 p.m. to five minutes to twelve on New Year's Eve for the Hall to be lit up by gas lights. At this point: 'For Old Times Sake' was played, the lights were gradually lowered until they faded out with the old year and, promptly at 12, the New Year was welcomed and the electric dimmers were turned on, which suddenly flooded the hall with all shapes and sizes and colours of electric light.

Annual dances by several firms and societies, for example The Skelmersdale Co-operative Society, were held here; carnivals, concerts, public meetings, local shows and the like also took place and some of the Rechabite and Box Opening parties for Dr. Baranado's homes will no doubt be remembered by many. The three churches in Burscough also held their annual concerts at the Institute.

The Institute was also used for Technical Instruction Classes for a while and, in connection with the schools of Burscough, cookery classes were established here and some of the schools' choirs practised in the main hall.

The Derby Cinema, Burscough

Burscough was not far behind Ormskirk in developing a cinema and as early as 1907 the first showing of 'animated pictures' took place at the Stanley Institute. The Cinema was not established at this date, but from time to time various film companies gave displays. On the 11th, 12th and 13th April 1907 'The Biograph Animated Pictures' first visited the Stanley Institute from the 'Empire' and 'Palace' Theatres, London. The doors were open at 7.30 p.m. and the programme commenced at 8 p.m. The prices of admission were as follows: 1/6d., 1/ – d., 6d., and 3d.; children were admitted at half-price with the exception of the 3d. seats. There was also a special matinee for the children on Saturday 13th April at 3 p.m., admission being 2d. and 1d.

The Stanley Institute Cinema was first opened on December 11th 1913 and the first programme was as follows:

'The Battle of Paardeburg', 'The Band of Music', 'Quick the Plumber', 'Delayed Letter' and 'Pooluck's Picnic'.

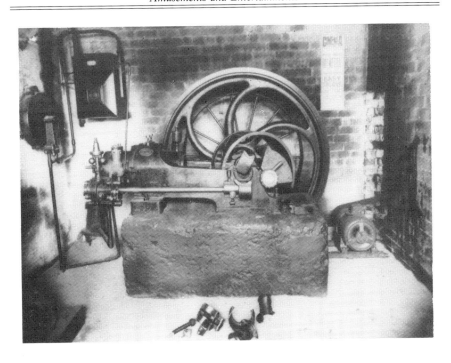

The photograph shows the Electric Motor (right of the photo) which was installed to drive the D.C. generator which fed the projector arc for the Derby Cinema. This photograph was taken previous to the Gas Engine being broken up and carted away. The crankshaft of the Gas Engine broke without warning and hurled a weighty piece of metal against the roof when it was being dismantled. The Electric Motor was installed by the L.E.P. and was in actual operation for the following evening's performance. (The photograph was taken in 1933).

A photograph of the Children's Cinema Ball which was held in the Stanley Institute in 1938.

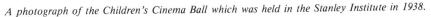

The cinema was open each weekday at 7 o'clock and the performance started at 7.45 p.m. There was also a grand children's matinee every Saturday at 3 p.m.

The cinema was established by the late Mr. John R. Horrocks who rented the 'Constance Derby Hall' from the Stanley Institute. In 1915 it became known as the 'Cinema, Burscough Bridge' and subsequently the title 'Derby Cinema' was adopted. Initially the films were shown from the balcony but, because of the danger of fire, an operating box had to be built. This operating box was built about 1916 by Mr. Ben Turner and was subsequently enlarged about 1918 to house two machines and during the 1940s was enlarged still further to accommodate a re-winding machine for the films, and the box was also strengthened.

One of the first, if not the first, projectionists was Mr. Jack (Scatter) Dutton, who was followed by Frank Berry who was, for want of a better word, a local inventor. I have heard many people say that he would have been famous if only he had patented some of his inventions but, unfortunately, he did not and the credit went to others. Whilst he was at the cinema he improved the apparatus so that the projectionist could use one arc for two machines. In 1921, Mr. Thomas Rosbottom took over as projectionist and remained there until 1940.

It was in 1915 that the serial became popular and the first to be shown at the Derby Cinema was 'The Trey O' Hearts' in April 1915 which was a drama in 15 parts. By 1920 there was still two changes of programme per week, but on Saturdays an extra house was added, the first house being 5.55 p.m. and second house at 8.15 p.m. At that time and until 1940, films were seldom shown on Friday because the hall was invariably used for dancing, concerts, whist drives etc., and on these occasions all the seats were removed from the hall and replaced the following day. By 1940 three changes of programme were introduced per week and the Friday dances and concerts came to an end. During the 1940s the Derby Cinema was patronised by nearly all the local military and Fleet Airarm personnel and on many occasions the notice 'Full Up' was exhibited in the foyer. The seating capacity was 404, but in the 1940s this was found inadequate and very often chairs were placed in the aisle to accommodate as many people as possible.

However, by the early 1960s the cinema attendances had begun to drop and dancing (Fridays) and Bingo (Wednesdays) was introduced in February of that year. In 1965, the lease expired and, as it was not renewed by the Stanley Institute, the cinema closed on Saturday May 15th of that year. The last picture to be shown was *Topaki* starring Melina Mercouri and Peter Ustinov. The Friday night dance which was also introduced in 1961 was discontinued on 14th May 1965; the last performance being by 'The Tudors'.

After the closure of the cinema, it was suggested by the Secretary of the Stanley Institute, Mr. Graham Fairclough, that they should turn the cinema into a social club. Preparations were undertaken and in 1966 the former cinema opened as a social club. Numerous alterations have taken place during the last 5 years and are still continuing, the 'Toffs' room which contained one billiard table has now been converted into a lounge with colour T.V. and furnished in the modern style. The bar has also been extended into the main hall, which would have been unthinkable in the past and would have met with strong opposition.

A vestige of the old 'Reading Room' library continued on at the Stanley

Institute until recent times and, before libraries were developed as they are today, if formed an integral part in the community. Books could be borrowed for 7, 14 or 21 days and were either renewed or changed on Saturday evenings from 8 p.m. to 10 p.m. A penny per week was charged for the loan of each book and, if not returned within 21 days, a fine of 6d. per week was imposed. If any member lost or defaced a book, he had to pay for another one or replace it with a new copy.

Over the last 15 years there has been a great deal of material improvement in the living standards of the majority of the British people and, as a result, a great number of people have purchased their own motor car. This has resulted in a change in the pattern of transport but, above all, has meant that many people in the Burscough area and elsewhere have become more mobile. In this connection the sphere of influence of the Stanley Institute has widened beyond the Burscough area and the people that now use the institute are drawn from far and wide, whilst in former times it was largely used by the community of Burscough as their village or public hall. This improvement in living standards has also brought about change, and former premises have either to be enlarged, modified or rebuilt in some cases to meet new demands and older institutions sometimes have to suffer.

Over the years several clubs have opened up in Burscough, notably the Football Club in Mart Lane, which was opened in 1963 and British Legion in Lord Street, which was established there in 1955 and has recently been enlarged, modernised and rebuilt.

Finally, the Stanley Institute still maintains the tradition of producing good snooker players and, whilst the game has declined in many areas, it is as strong as ever in Burscough.

Amateur boxing has also been introduced in recent years and its influence is growing and the hall is now also used for badminton several nights a week.

Burscough British Legion

This branch was formed in 1927 and two of the founder members were the late Major Frank Wells (Chairman) and Mr. J. Fitzsimmons (Hon. Secretary). The organising secretary of the North Western area at that time was a Mr. C. H. Grant who did much work in forming the branch in 1927. Mr. T. Hampson was elected to the management committee and Dr. Blair was appointed first Honorary Medical Adviser to the branch.

At that time the great work of the British Legion was in connection with pensions. They were a non-sectarian, non-political organisation and, irrespective of which party was in power, if they had a grievance in connection with the Pensions Warrant, they intended to fight it out. The benevolent work was done by Mrs. Martland and other members of the committee, and in 1930 it was intended that a women's section might be formed.

Burscough Services Canteen

In connection with the British Legion, the Burscough Services Canteen was opened in 1940 to provide canteen and recreational facilities for troops stationed in the area. It was in June of that year that the canteen was established in the former Council Offices, Mill Lane, Lathom, but it became overcrowded and it was decided by the committee to build a new canteen. For many months the committee tried to find further accommodation without result and they then applied to the Ministry of Works and Buildings and were fortunate to get a licence granted for the building of a new canteen. A site was obtained in Lord Street, Burscough, and in December 1943 the canteen was opened.

By 1946 it was thought that the building should be converted into a community centre for the people of Burscough and it was also suggested that it could be used as a youth club as well.

In 1947 the British Legion still held monthly meetings in the Legion Rooms, Mill Lane, but in June of that year it was put forward that another site should be found and it was suggested that a hut be built alongside the canteen in Lord Street. By 1948 the membership had reached 340.

The canteen subsequently became known as the 'village hall' but, owing to very little interest being shown in the hall, it was decided after a long discussion that the Association meet the trustees of the branch of the British Legion with a view to the village hall being handed over as a Legion Headquarters.

Therefore, in 1949, the British Legion became established in Lord Street and the premises were then known as the 'National Services Club'.

About September 1955, however, a new Burscough British Legion Club was opened by Sir Douglas Glover M.P., which was built at a cost of £1,500.

Subsequently, during 1969-70, the Club has been rebuilt and is now equipped with dance hall, bar, recreation room containing a billiard table etc., and other amenities.

The British Legion also contributed to the work on the War Memorial at the bottom of Junction Lane in 1948.

Index